Understanding Occupy from Wall Street to Portland

Understanding Occupy from Wall Street to Portland

Applied Studies in Communication Theory

Renee Guarriello Heath,
Courtney Vail Fletcher, and Ricardo Munoz

LEXINGTON BOOKS
Lanham • Boulder • New York • Toronto • Plymouth, UK

Published by Lexington Books
A wholly owned subsidiary of The Rowman & Littlefield Publishing Group, Inc.
4501 Forbes Boulevard, Suite 200, Lanham, Maryland 20706
www.rowman.com

10 Thornbury Road, Plymouth PL6 7PP, United Kingdom

Copyright © 2013 by Lexington Books

All rights reserved. No part of this book may be reproduced in any form or by any electronic or mechanical means, including information storage and retrieval systems, without written permission from the publisher, except by a reviewer who may quote passages in a review.

British Library Cataloguing in Publication Information Available

Library of Congress Cataloging-in-Publication Data

Heath, Renee Guarriello
Fletcher, Courtney Vail
Munoz, Ricardo
Understanding Occupy from Wall Street to Portland : applied studies in communication theory / edited by Renee Guarriello Heath, Courtney Vail Fletcher and Ricardo Munoz ; foreword by David Osborne.
pages cm
ISBN 978-0-7391-8321-2 (cloth) -- ISBN 978-0-7391-8322-9 (electronic)
1. Occupy movement--United States. 2. Protest movements--United States. 3. Communication in social action--United States. 4. Protest movements in mass media. 5. Information theory. I. Heath, Renee Guarriello, 1967- II. Fletcher, Courtney Vail, 1979-
HN59.2.U49 2013
303.60973--dc23

2013022647

∞™ The paper used in this publication meets the minimum requirements of American National Standard for Information Sciences Permanence of Paper for Printed Library Materials, ANSI/NISO Z39.48-1992.

Printed in the United States of America

Contents

Acknowledgments vii

Foreword ix
David Osborn

Introduction: Engaging Occupy: An Introduction to Romantic,
    Functional, and Critical Perspectives xv
Renee Guarriello Heath and C. Vail Fletcher

I: Situating Occupy Globally: The Cultural and Economic Context   1

1 A Genealogy of Occupy within Transnational Contexts, and
    Communication Research 3
    Priya Kapoor

2 "We Are the 99 Percent": Occupy and the Economics of Discontent   17
    William Barnes

3 Neofeudalism and the Financial Crisis: Implications for Occupy
    Wall Street 35
    Majia Holmer Nadesan

II: Local Interpretations of Occupy Portland   53

4 Confessional Tales from the Field: Owning Researcher Methods
    and Positionality 55
    Renee Guarriello Heath, Ricardo Munoz, and C. Vail Fletcher

5 Finding the Space Between: Participative Democracy,
    Consensus Decision-Making, and a Leaderful/less Movement 75
    Renee Guarriello Heath

6	Globalization from Below: Discourses of Horizontalism, Direct Action, and Violence *Ricardo V. Munoz*	99
7	(De) Colonization and Collective Identity: Intersections and Negotiations of Gender, Race, and Class in Occupy *C. Vail Fletcher*	121

III: Re(presentations) and Revelations: Occupy Mediated — 145

8	Violence, Bias, or Fair Journalism?: Understanding Portland Media Coverage of an Episodic Protest *Jennette Lovejoy and Keeler Brynteson*	147
9	An "Official" Account: Delivering Occupy Portland's Eviction Notice *erin daina mcclellan*	167
10	Interconnected Discontent: Social Media and Social Capital in the Occupy Movement *Doug Tewksbury*	189

References	209
Index	225
About the Editors	235
About the Contributors	237

Acknowledgments

A book is always the result of tremendous professional and personal collaborative effort. And so our first thanks are paid to the participants of Occupy Portland. We are in awe of your transparency and openness, and your courage for living and acting authentically. Thank you for sharing your insights; this book is yours in many ways. In particular we want to acknowledge David Osborn, author of our foreword, for reading and contributing to versions of this book. David, you model the values of participation to which your efforts aspire. Other supporting actors in this project include Sarah Dempsey, "cheerleader," and Alison Northridge, our acquisition editor—two who first believed in this project. We also want to acknowledge the significant intellectual contribution to this text by the late communication scholar Nick Trujillo.

Renee: I am indebted to the University of Portland for a generous sabbatical that facilitated the writing and editing of this book. Thank you also to my amazing former students Megan Brown, Carolyn Sutter, and Olga Mosiychuk for contributions to these studies and for providing the impetus for which this journey began. Additionally Elisa Majors, my outstanding research assistant, provided tremendous support by transcribing a seemingly endless flow of interviews and meetings. Of course my partners in this endeavor; Fletch and Ricky, you never failed to lift my spirits in the weediest of editing moments. Most importantly—you know it—my family. Cullen, Kennedy, and Madeline, your names deserve to be in this book because you definitely have some skin in this project. Thank you and please forgive me my crazy moments. Mom, thank you for packing my house—what an awful idea to sell my home and move across the country and write a book all at the same time! And Chris, my partner, thank you. I love you.

Vail: I would like to start by acknowledging my co-editors, Renee and Ricardo. You have both been excellent teammates on this journey. Your level of rigor, intellect, thoughtfulness, and care made working with each of you joyful and memorable! Thank you for sharing this adventure with me—it bookmarks an important place for me in my life and I will always be thankful to have shared it with you. Thank you to my colleagues at the University of Portland who helped me stay sane along the way as I juggled this scholarly activity with my other professional responsibilities. I feel lucky to be working in such a supportive department and university community. Thank you to my family, who never quite remember what it is I am working on, but are beyond excited nonetheless. To Rachel Stohr, the funniest, smartest, most wonderful friend I could have ever imagined. My life is so much better with you in it. And to you, Alice Gates, one of the most empathic, supportive friends I will ever know. Thank you for your unending support during this process. Also, thank you to my partner, Gregory, for simply being here. I am so glad I found you; my life would never have been the same without you. You are my truest North and I love you. Finally, thanks to my animal friends, who loyally sat at my feet and circled my keyboard for hours on end while I worked on this project. You bring me so much calm and happiness.

Ricky: Thanks to Leah Sprain, assistant professor, University of Colorado, Boulder, for her reading and excellent comments on chapter 6 while it was being written. A big thanks to the owners and staff of Anna Bannanas Cafe, St. Johns, Portland, Oregon, for their hospitality and hosting of numerous Occupy St. Johns meetings. And finally, thanks to Occupy St. Johns for letting me practice consensus-process facilitation.

Foreword

David Osborn

The emergence of Occupy Wall Street in the fall of 2011 and the spread of the movement nationally and internationally during the months that followed were an extraordinary time. The work included in this edited volume is part of what will be an important body of academic inquiry into this dynamic and ongoing social movement. This type of inquiry and analysis is essential for understanding these movements and for participants to be able to refine and evolve their work to more effectively impact the social and ecological crises confronting the world in which we live. I was deeply involved with Occupy Portland in the Pacific Northwest and acted as a participant in the ethnography that informs a significant portion of the work in this volume. As a result of this participation and my engagement with the movement I was asked by the editors to write the foreword for this volume.

My involvement in Occupy Portland was a singular and transformational experience. I became deeply involved in the lead up to the occupation of Chapman and Lownsdale Squares that, in Portland, Oregon, began on October 6, 2011. Initially I was involved in collaborating to create the participatory, direct democracy process and structure for Occupy Portland, and then later to organize some of the major direct actions. These included the nationally coordinated actions on November 17, 2011, targeting large, corporate banks and February 29, 2012, targeting corporations part of the American Legislative Exchange Council, both of which are discussed in the chapters that follow. I understand this movement as being fundamentally about agency, in the sense of recognizing and actualizing our power to shape the world in which we live. The juxtaposition of the large, public assemblies making decisions—in which decentralized power is held in the hands of the many several blocks from Wall Street where concentrated power is held in the hands of the few—tells us volumes about this movement. The orientation of the movement to illegality and direct action in which we claim our ability to act to address injustices without appealing to others to act for us, is explored later, acting as if we are already free, further exemplifies the presence of this dynamic at the core of the movement. The rhetoric that came out of Occupy Wall Street that "the demand is a process" also speaks far beyond the brevity of its composition. The notion of demanding a process contradicts the notion of a demand as something that can be given by someone or something. It is in fact stating we demand something that we will do ourselves. The demand, in other words, is to create a form of participatory decision-making that ceases the need for demands and the ability to make demands by fundamentally reshaping social relations with regards to how and by whom decisions are made. The idea that we, as people together in our communities, should be in control of our lives and our futures is essential to understanding this movement and its central meaning. While seemingly obvious and in keeping with democracy it is also something that is far, far removed from the lived experiences of most people in the United States. That so many responded so quickly and so explosively is a testament to the despair and lack of control that is tangibly experienced in American society and the extent to which, contrary to the dominant discourse, it is viscerally felt that the United States is not a democracy.

It is useful to review the events of that period before exploring how we should understand the important inquiries into this movement that are included in this volume. Occupy Wall Street (OWS) emerged on September 17, 2011, with a march against financial capital and the occupation of Zuccotti Park, also referred to as Liberty Plaza, which occurred after participants in the day's action were unable to access the intended location for the general assembly, a plaza outside of Citibank in downtown Manhattan. This small park became the epicenter for something extraordinary that would unfold over the next months. By early October the Occupy movement had spread to at least seventy cities across the United States, including Portland, which began its occupation on October 6, 2011. On October 15, only seventy-four days after the original OWS meeting (August 2, 2011), hundreds of thousands of people gathered in some nine hundred cities in over eighty countries around the world to rally and take action "against the corruption and greed of the 1 percent." This escalation of global social movement activity had been building over the previous eighteen months including the re-ignited May 2010 Greek protests against the austerity measures being enforced by the International Monetary Fund and the European Union. In November of that year massive student demonstrations and occupations in the United Kingdom, including most notably the Tory party headquarters, exploded as students fought a tripling of tuition rates. And at the end of December Mohammed Bouazizi self-immolated (set himself on fire) in an action of desperate protest against economic injustice and in so doing set off movements and revolutions first in Tunisia and then in Bahrain, Libya, Syria, Yemen, and most notably in Egypt.

In February 2011 in the United States thousands occupied the capitol in Madison, Wisconsin, in response to harsh anti-union legislation. In March hundreds of thousands of people returned to the streets in the United Kingdom to protest government austerity measures. Beginning in May participants of the Spanish "15 de Mayo" movement of the *indiganados* (the indignant ones) began occupying Spanish squares throughout the country to reject the political system and institute a directly democratic system of participatory general assemblies. In July the Chilean student movement escalated with students battling in the streets. And again, halfway around the world, at nearly the same time, Israelis came out in the tens of thousands to pitch tents and occupy their cities to take action against the lack of economic opportunity, though notably without addressing the occupation of Palestine or condemning it.

All of this took place in the lead up to the events in Liberty Plaza in New York City on September 17, 2011. All of this also exists in relation to the growth of nonhierarchical, decentralized, horizontal social movements and institutions over the past several decades. Notable examples include indigenous movements in Mexico such as the Zapatistas, the World Social Forum process, the so-called antiglobalization movement, the global climate justice movement, and the social movements in Argentina that emerged in 2001 during the financial crisis. Keeping this context in mind grounds our understanding of the Occupy movement in relation to transnational social movements that are part of growing and escalating global responses to shifts in the world economy. The historical understanding also allows us to see the continuity and alignment of this horizontal movement with recent and decades-old social movement activity rather than as something aberrant or without precedent. It is important to keep in mind this global and historical context and the way in which it fundamentally shifts our understanding of this movement generally, its specific development in Portland, and in considering the content of this volume.

The local manifestation of this movement that I participated in, and which is the focus of many of the contributions of this volume, was in Portland, Oregon. On October 6, in this city at the confluence of the Willamette and Columbia rivers, after less than two weeks of planning, some ten thousand people gathered at Waterfront Park on the bank of the Willamette, surprising both organizers and long-time activists. The illegal and unpermitted march that followed ended in the occupation of Chapman and Lownsdale Squares in downtown Portland. Over the next two months a series of actions saw well over a hundred people arrested and included the expulsion of the police during their first attempted eviction on November twelfth; the shutdown of the corporate banks in downtown Portland on November seventeenth; the shutdown of the Port of Portland on the twelfth of December, as part of a coordinated West Coast port action; and some eighty national actions initiated by Occupy Portland against the American Legislative Exchange Council on February 29, 2012.

That I, as a movement participant, was asked to write the foreword to this book is reflective of the approach taken by the editors and many of the contributors. The opportunity for those in the movement to speak in this academic work is further embodied in the ethnography conducted for this volume. Through this research method, voice has been given to those individuals who made up the movement and together created the extraordinary social change that occurred in the fall and winter of 2011. While at the same time a participant in social movements, I am also part of the academy as a faculty member at Portland State University where I teach and do research on culture and social movements as part of the interdisciplinary general education program. In approaching my work, which is relevant in thinking about this volume, I bring the same values that informed my involvement with the Occupy Portland Facilitation Team and direct action organizing groups to my research and teaching at the university. In many ways I understand myself to be doing the same work in a different context. This includes my orientation towards direct democracy, nonhierarchical social relations, decentralization, and mutual aid that seeks to empower individuals to challenge those systems of power and domination that so constrain and threaten life in early twenty-first century global capitalism. In my research I strive to create a type of engaged social movement scholarship, which aims to be relevant to the movements that are the subject of study. This requires some form of participation and engagement, which for me is a very deep and embedded one. It also requires that we embrace critical understandings of social theory and the notion that knowledge is not simply produced for the sake of creating knowledge; rather it is always connected to and in support of existing power structures and social relations. Thus, this type of engaged and relevant social movement scholarship is *for* particular values and aims to bring into being particular visions of new worlds and new forms of social relations. I believe this approach to be essential in grounding scholarship that is too often irrelevant for the participants of those social movements who will be essential to addressing the serious and escalating social and ecological crises that confront us.

In this volume and in the conversations I have had with the editors, I have been excited by my discovery of significant aspects of this spirit in the work included in the pages that follow. The work included here is demonstrative of academics pushing their comfort zones and areas of "expertise" to participate in engaged, interdisciplinary inquiry of contemporary social movements. Among other places, you can find this in the methodology of ethnography utilized in the volume. You can find it in the passive and active participation of some of the researchers in the movement. You can see it in the focus on power and ideology and the articulated desire to write to "activist-scholars" by one of the contributors. And you can also see it transparently discussed in the confessionals several of the researchers offer in describing the ethnographic methodology, their social position, their engagement with the movement, and the tensions inherent in all of these things. In these elements we find an alignment with the participatory aspects of this movement as well the spirit and approach important to advance the engaged and relevant form of scholarship I describe above. We also find a mirror to the experience many movement participants had in engaging in social movements for the first time as well as pushing their own comfort zones and areas of "expertise" to engage in types of social change work that were unfamiliar to them. The times we live in require this type of engagement by all of us, in the academy and as agents in the creation of the social relations that constitute our society. We do not know what to do to address the crises confronting each of our communities in different and equally terrifying ways. One of the essential lessons of the Occupy movement is that though we do not know *what* we need to do, we do know *how*. Participating together in community we will find the way and in so doing create new worlds in which we control our lives and our futures.

I do not agree with all of the conclusions presented in this volume and I would be troubled if I did given the need for diversity of thought and analysis. I also think that my own engagement in Occupy Portland and the Occupy movement were rife with problems and contradictions. All of this makes the content of this volume even more valuable to inform the work that lies ahead of us through critical inquiry and reflection. Indeed, the editors structure the volume to hold a multiplicity of truths through the utilization of three different frameworks provided by the scholar Nick Trujillo throughout the contributions. This orientation towards the multiplicity of truths is reflective of the horizontal social movements they study, in that the desire of these movements is not to create a singular new world, but rather hundreds of new worlds each reflective of and appropriate to the communities from which they are generated.

This volume is also an example of the type of engaged academic inquiry of social movements that is increasingly needed and which we as academics desperately need to continue developing. Some of the important work included in this volume explores the starkness of the economic inequalities present in this form of early twenty-first-century capitalism, the use of participatory methodologies, reflections on process and structure, power and ideology, the utilization of social media to develop communities of practice, and important analyses of media coverage of the movement. We have much to learn from the explosion of movement energy that occurred in response to the actions of Occupy Wall Street. Learning about rapidly emergent, mass movements is particularly important as this may be the form of social change that we will see in the United States given its relatively weak social movements, failed political institutions, and extraordinary levels of injustice and oppression. I will close with my own, very brief, confessional similar to that which the researchers provide in their chapter on methodology. Many of us who were engaged organizers before Occupy did not believe what occurred in the fall of 2011 was possible. Our minds and imaginations were closed to it, though we tirelessly worked for social change, we also were cynical about the possibilities for the emergence of broad-based popular movements. Let our continued engagement of this movement also continue to remind us of the unbridled possibilities that exist. Let it continue to inspire explorations of deep, community-based agency and the expansive opportunities that exist for social change within the crisis-ridden world we live in. I hope that the content provided here keeps the important reflections about this movement alive and is useful in each of our work, individually and collectively, to bring into being our visions of a just, free, and sustainable future in which our communities have control of their resources and their lives.

David Osborn
March 21, 2013
Portland, OR

DISCUSSION QUESTIONS

1. What is the role of the academy and the individuals employed by these institutions in regards to social change?
2. How can participation enrich academic inquiry into social change and social movements?
3. What does it mean to produce engaged and relevant scholarship for social movements? In what ways does this require participation or the inclusion of a multiplicity of voices drawn from the movements which are the subjects of study?
4. What are the forms of social change that are likely in the contemporary social and political context of the United States? To what extent should we understand the Occupy movement as a prefigurative (foreshadowing the future in the present) vision of those forms? How does this impact our scholarship, research, and studies?
5. What is the relationship between methodology and the type of engaged and relevant social movement scholarship described above? Are there particular research methodologies better suited to this form of scholarship?

Introduction

Engaging Occupy: An Introduction to Romantic, Functional, and Critical Perspectives

Renee Guarriello Heath and C. Vail Fletcher

> I can't find a place to pitch my tent. Every inch of what used to be the north lawn of Chapman Square is covered with tents and tarps and pallets. The same goes for Lownsdale Square to the north. I'm moving into the Occupy Portland camps so I can find out what happens when a protest turns semi-permanent in America's most dissent-happy city—Aaron Mesh, Willamette Weekly, embedded journalist, Portland, Oregon.

The Occupy movement began in August 2011 when Occupy Wall Street ignited protests throughout the United States, Canada, and other western countries in opposition to the growing economic disparity felt by many. It is arguably the most visible social movement in the United States in four decades. Since the well-known social movements of the twentieth century that advanced civil and women's rights and protested military involvement in Vietnam, several factors that either did not exist or have changed greatly since then affect the way we practice and understand social movement organizing today. First, during the last thirty years the economic conditions in the United States have vastly changed as middle-class Americans have steadily lost their wealth, and incomes have declined. Student loans are no longer payable, living wage jobs are declining, and families cannot support home mortgages on one income. The tools of organizing have changed too. Instant technology and social media have altered individuals' relationships and reliance on traditional media such as television. Smart phones, Livestream, Facebook, and Twitter, to name a few technological advancements, have significantly improved our ability to inform and mobilize large groups of people, not to mention have enhanced our ability to participate in the public sphere in ways we could have never imagined. And philosophies of social movements have evolved as many resistance movements ground themselves in consensus principles if not in contrast to, alongside, other traditional, adversarial resistance techniques (Della Porta 2008). Given the centrality of economics and communication (i.e., social media and consensus) in the Occupy movement, the purpose of this book is to apply contemporary economic insights and theories of communication to better understand this movement at this current juncture in history.

This book has two goals. The first is to examine social movement phenomena from various theoretical lenses. With theory as a lens, each chapter teaches us something different about social movements using Occupy as a case, foregrounding some aspects, while backgrounding others. In particular, this book steps outside of social movement theory to analyze the macro- and microprocesses of the Occupy movement, demonstrating the saliency of communication theory. The core of this edited volume applies theories of semiotics; consensus and participative democracy; discourse and ideology; intersectionality, colonization, and collective identity; media; rhetoric; and social media, ideally supplementing courses on these subjects. Similarly, this book assembles a collection of various epistemological practices as each chapter asks a different type of research question and thus employs varying methods of data collection and analysis (e.g., ethnography, content analysis, rhetorical criticism, critical discourse analysis, etc.). The details of the ethnographic project, featured in part 2 of this book, illuminate the challenges and opportunities of a multiperson, multifaceted interpretive study that may also be relevant to students and scholars of research methods. Thus, the contents of this book demonstrate wide application of relevant theory and methodological practice. Together and separately these studies answer the question what do we learn from Occupy when we approach knowledge from a particular theoretical and epistemological lens?

OCCUPY THROUGH MACRO, MICRO, AND MEDIATED THEORETICAL LENSES

This three-part volume is organized by complementary theoretical and methodological perspectives; broad critical cultural and economic, local interpretive ethnographic, and mediated rhetorical and media studies. Part 1 of this volume, "Situating Occupy Globally: the Cultural and Economic Context," begins by considering the larger social and historical context that birthed the Occupy movement. The goal of this part of the book is to create a shared understanding of the social movements that preceded Occupy as well as the national (and global) economic conditions that created the tipping point that led to the rapid expansion of the Occupy camps and demonstrations—more than 900 in more than 80 countries throughout the world (Tedmanson and Byers 2011, in Tewksbury chapter 10 this volume). In chapter 1, "A Genealogy of Occupy within Transnational Contexts, and Communication Research," communication and cultural studies scholar Priya Kapoor positions Occupy among the major movements and activist forums that have contributed to its practices and ideologies. She considers what themes in this volume add to communication studies of social movements.

The next two chapters in this part provide rich explanations of the complex economic conditions that serve as a precursor to the movement. In chapter 2, macroeconomist William Barnes grounds the subsequent communication-centered studies by contextualizing the ideologies and actions associated with the movement. In, "We are the 99 Percent: Occupy and the Economics of Discontent," Barnes provides a description of economic conditions and events that have been associated as the impetuses to the movement. His analysis fleshes out how and why targets of the movement connect to broader economic issues. Barnes breaks down some of the complicated economic institutional relationships and policies that are often very confusing to understand and have at times left those outside of the Occupy movement wondering how the Occupy participants' acts of resistance are related. This analysis provides an economic vocabulary in which to understand the concerns of Occupy participants. Majia Holmer Nadesan completes part 1 with her weighty analysis of the term, neofeudalism. In the chapter, "Neofeudalism and the Financial Crisis: Implications for Occupy Wall Street," Nadesan complicates interpretations of this powerful signifier. She adroitly moves the reader through a muddle of intricate practices of financial institutions that explicate the rise in both academic and popular press authors' use of the term neofeudalism. Nadesan concludes with the provocation that violence committed against Occupy participants may constitute greater power to the term neofeudalism and ultimately sway mainstream Americans and others to sympathize with Occupy actions.

In part 2 of the book, "Local Interpretations of Occupy Portland," the authors examined one of the largest and most organized Occupy efforts in the country located in Portland, Oregon. This section of the book constitutes an emic, hermeneutic exploration of the lived experiences of participants of Occupy. Juxtaposed to the macroanalyses presented in part 1, part 2 seeks to understand the microprocesses of Occupy with care to the participants' understanding of their own actions (Deetz 2005). A hermeneutic analysis interprets the texts of participant voices sensitive to the context in which they were constituted, but also analyzes these texts within critical theoretical frameworks (Deetz 2005). The goal of part 2 is to create plausible interpretations that represent a truth, not *the* truth of the Occupy experience.

This section begins with chapter 4, by editors Renee Guarriello Heath, Ricardo Munoz, and C. Vail Fletcher, "Confessional Tales from the Field: Owning Researcher Methods and Positionality." We partnered in a year-long ethnographic project and describe the primary methods used in the case studies that span five chapters of this volume. The ethnographic process is made transparent with explicit detail of the site, data collection, and gathering methods. Through confessional tales (Van Maanen 1988) we describe the analytical decisions and researchers' identity and positionality struggles that surfaced in this project including the ethical and personal questions that arose throughout the process. This chapter helps to introduce the Occupy Portland project and the forthcoming chapters.

Chapter 5, "Finding the Space Between: Participatory Democracy and Consensus Decision-Making in a Leaderful/less Movement," is an analysis of the values, structures, and process of the movement written by Heath, a scholar of community collaboration and democratic communication. Heath describes the communication ethic that is grounded in consensus principles and illuminates the paradox of leaderlessness as the movement transitioned from a social service-oriented camp to a more ambiguous network of subcommittees. She dissects participants' understandings of consensus and the skills and outcomes of these organizing processes. This work illuminates the tensions inherent in participatory consensus decision-making and argues for holding these tensions in balance as data suggest that prioritizing particular consensus values over others has detrimental consequences for organizing.

In chapter 6, "Globalization from Below: Discourses of Horizontalism, Direct Action, and Violence," Munoz introduces the reader to three of the more powerful ideological discourses of the movement. Munoz analyzes the romantic, functional, and critical discourses of Occupy using a Foucauldian lens. In particular he identifies that within the larger new activist ideology, discourses of horizontalism, direct action, and nonviolence negotiate the dialectical tension of appropriated and distributed power. As a trained and embedded facilitator in the movement, Munoz unearths the principles that underlie Occupy actions and inactions.

C. Vail Fletcher's chapter, "(De) Colonization and Collective Identity: Intersections and Negotiations of Gender, Race, and Class in Occupy," examines why identity has become such a salient (and contested) part of the movement both locally and globally. In addition, Fletcher, a scholar of identity, conflict, and culture, draws upon theories of colonization and collective identity to elucidate the relevant debates and discussions in the movement that problematize the intersectionality of class, gender, nationalism, and race. Fletcher's analysis of identities held in tension comprises a critical accounting of Occupy's so-called horizontal ideology.

In part 3 of the book, "(Re)presentations and Revelations: Occupy Mediated," authors analyze Occupy attending to the texts created by others. This part of the book asks the important question, what do we learn about a social movement when our understanding is mediated through reporters, newspaper editors, city officials, and bloggers? This section of the book is revealing as it demonstrates how particular understandings of Occupy participants and actions are constituted by an outsider, or the etic perspective. It also investigates the generative role of social media establishing it as something much more than a mediated text.

In chapters 8 and 9, a richer portrait of Occupy Portland is painted by media studies and rhetorical analysis. First, Jennette Lovejoy and Keeler Brynteson conducted a content analysis of the media coverage that followed Occupy Portland during the most visible period of the movement—the encampment. This chapter, "Violence, Bias, or Fair Journalism? Understanding Portland Media Coverage of an Episodic Protest," provides a unique look at how the media in Portland addressed, framed, and reported the events of Occupy when activists were protesting in downtown Portland. By looking at newspaper theme, bias, and sourcing, this research explicates the landscape of news coverage in the two main newspapers of the city, and also points to differences in how each newspaper covered this social movement, especially related to violence and bias. Their analysis facilitates critical reflection regarding how and what receives news coverage. The reader will enjoy comparing the news coverage to the ethnographic and official accounts provided by participants and city officials in other chapters.

In chapter 9, "An 'Official' Account: Delivering Occupy Portland's Eviction Notice," erin daina mcclellan takes a rhetorical perspective of the Occupy Portland movement. mcclellan analyzes the official rhetoric of Mayor Sam Adams as he justifies his management of the occupation of public spaces. The rhetoric of Adams in this chapter stands in juxtaposition to the vernacular voices of participants depicted in part 2 of this volume. mcclellan's chapter illuminates the incompletion and absences of official accounts. While teaching us something about how progressive officials in a liberal city struggled to balance civil liberties, her analysis draws attention to the inadequacies of traditional rhetorical readings.

The last case study presented in this volume expands the theoretical contribution of the text by applying social media theory to Occupy Wall Street. In chapter 10, "Interconnected Discontent: Social Media and Social Capital in the Occupy Movement," Doug Tewksbury explicates the central role of social media in the Occupy movement. Tewksbury helps us understand social media not just as a channel of communication but as constitutive of social movement organizing. His findings point to the generation of communities of practice that no doubt alter how social movement organizing happens in the twenty-first century. Indeed, Tewksbury's analysis gives us reason to believe that the Occupy movement has evolved into specialized, decentralized communities of practice that have the potential to mobilize Occupy interests for years to come.

ROMANTIC, FUNCTIONAL, AND CRITICAL UNDERSTANDINGS

The second goal of this edited volume is to provide in-depth data that problematize universal narratives about Occupy. One of the challenges of studying Occupy is that members of this movement are committed to not allowing any one person (or entity) define it. Because Occupy participants are hesitant to speak for the movement, a research project set out to describe and analyze Occupy must admit some hubris absent in the movement's own participants who were determined to not speak on behalf of each other. One way we acknowledge the power in the researcher/participant relationship (Dempsey 2010) and attempt to honor the individualism and postmodern fragmentation of this movement is to consider our findings in light of the three interpretive lenses of the romantic, functional, and critical. Nick Trujillo (1992) argued that interpretive work should adopt romantic, functional, and critical frameworks when seeking to understand organizing phenomena. While the romantic lens brings forth the "virtues of an idealized past" (351) (and we would argue future), the functionalist perspective focuses on the pragmatic work accomplished by the construct of analysis. For example, Trujillo argued functional perspectives of baseball culture emphasized its role as a "socializing agent" into the world of work reinforcing a Protestant work ethic (351). Finally the critical perspective as described by Trujillo examines power and control and explores the isms, such as consumerism, militarism, sexism, and racism (351). We find these frames useful as they complicate our analyses, and foster the avoidance of resting on simple, universal descriptions and explanations. These frames honor not a specific truth about Occupy, but many truths about the movement brought forth in the pages ahead. Trujillo's interpretive frames respect the dynamism of a movement that has evolved from occupying public squares as a focal point to a sophisticated, dispersed network of now-experienced activists and lay educators able to mobilize coordinated actions in cities and across the country in ways that were not present before the occupation of Wall Street.

Each author adopts the language of Trujillo in their own way to complexify their findings and consider alternative ways of understanding Occupy actions. For example Fletcher and Heath utilize Trujillo's interpretive frames as analytical categories. Their analyses, explained in-depth in chapter four, utilized the romantic, functional, and critical as a method to organize their data around distinct research questions. Other authors weave Trujillo into their interpretations but do not strictly organize their data around the romantic, functional, and critical lenses (e.g., Munoz; Nadesan; Tewksbury). Finally, authors who draw upon different epistemologies (e.g., Lovejoy and Brynteson) and different methods of analysis (mcclellan) adopt Trujillo's language to reread their findings. We believe the themes of the romantic, functional, and critical provide a richer and more interesting accounting of the forthcoming cases. And they honor our desire to not arrive at grand conclusions about a constantly changing movement.[1]

UNORCHESTRATED THEMES: TIME, SPACE, AND STRUCTURE

While the romantic, functional, and critical themes in this book were intentional and orchestrated among the editors and authors, we find other overlapping themes emerged from this collection of studies. In particular these studies are also united in their relevance of time, space, and structure, which help us to make sense of this movement and are thus worth mentioning. To begin, what counts as *this movement* anyway? While it is arguably easy to pinpoint when it started in North America (*Adbusters.org*), it is equally difficult to determine when and if it has ended. As we complete this book in the early spring of 2013, we have trouble answering this question definitively.

Time matters as we try and understand the movement. In part 1, Kapoor, Barnes, and Nadesan largely focus on the conditions and events that led to the movement. They center on that which precedes Occupy, feeding theories of antecedent causes to a social movement. Historical accounts are essential for not only understanding the past, but predicting the future. A less definitive timeline is drawn in the ethnographic studies depicted in part 2 of the book. Participants moved in and out of the movement throughout the interviewing period making it difficult to determine what counted as "the movement." Outside of the definitive encampment period, significant events such as rallies, protests, and sit-ins happened episodically and continue to happen at this writing. But has the movement ended? The camp in Portland, Oregon, lasted six weeks from October 6 to November 12, 2011, which is why Lovejoy and Brynteson focused on that time period as one that drew the most significant media coverage. Yet, Occupy participants continued to camp individually outside of Portland's City Hall as recently as January 2013. Time is an essential element to interpreting the actions and the news coverage of Occupy Portland.

Mcclellan's study of the mayor's speeches and interviews around the eviction of participants from the Portland camp is also relevant for its timing. This event was consistently reported as one of the most significant ("highpoint") moments of the occupation experience by campers. The night of the eviction drew ten thousand supporters from neighboring cities such as Seattle, Washington. Local churches, labor groups, and cyclists who formed a tranquil barrier between campers and the police united in support of Occupy in a grand effort to promote peaceful resistance in a joyful and party-like atmosphere. Hence the timing of this event justifies the importance of the texts mcclellan uses to analyze official rhetoric. In her analysis mcclellan also explains how essential sequencing matters in the arguments depicted in the mayor's justification of evicting the campers. Time is also an important factor as we examine social media in Tewskbury's study and consider the outcomes and scaffolding left in the wake of the more visible protests. His analysis leaves us considering what social media structures are now in place for the future of Occupy or other movements that are likely to draw upon the actors and actions from the Occupy movement. These studies cannot escape the significance of time in our understanding of their findings.

Space is also thematic in these accounts. Kapoor positions Occupy within a global geographic perspective. Her description of movement forums explicates how movement ideologies and tactics are shared as one way to overcome spatial challenges in the building of global social movements. Nadesan's study of the signifier neofeudalism and Tewsbury's case study of the discourse created within the context of the Alternative Banking Working Group of the New York General Assembly remind us that conversations on the Internet are influential regardless of geography in the twenty-first century. And in the ethnographic studies in this volume, space was indeed the point—the occupation of public parks and squares and sidewalks forced passersby to engage with the movement in very real and significant ways. Although relatively small numbers of participants officially camped, the encampments themselves functioned to invite outsiders to take notice of their presence (and ideally their motivations and goals). Finally, in the most deliberate study of space, mcclellan's analysis of the mayor's eviction speeches and interviews elucidates how time and space were utilized to justify the disbandment of the camps. mcclellan interrogates the concept of space, asking what are public spaces like parks for if not to offer a gathering place for the public? Her analysis establishes that definitions of what counts as public space are always negotiated.

Space also operated in metaphorical ways in the movement. Many participants in the ethnographic study (part 2) remarked on how Occupy "created space" for them to share their perspectives and/or engage with their discontent about the income, health, and privilege disparities present in their lives. This often-newfound sense of space seemed to act in quite profound and perhaps cathartic ways as it helped participants to air their personal frustrations while simultaneously unveiling the mutual knowledge that they were not alone in their struggle with the current state of affairs in the country. Overall, space operated to significantly heighten the movement's relationship with the public at-large, the media, and city officials, while also providing a platform for personal voice and agency (a completely new experience for some of our interviewed participants).

Structure also functioned predominantly across the studies depicted in this book. Kapoor reminds us that Occupy did not happen without the scaffolding of ideology, practices, and sharing of information born from salient movements and activist conferences in the twentieth and twenty-first centuries. Chapters by Barnes and Nadesan reveal that the basic structure of the economic system in the United States was fatally flawed and thus continually rewarded the 1 percent of the population with a hugely disproportionate amount of the country's wealth. Chapters by Heath, Munoz, and Tewksbury tackle head-on emergent themes related to the structures embedded in the dominant philosophy of horizontalism, and its influence on organizing action. For example, the first task that Occupy participants faced was how to structure their meetings in ways that promoted consensus building, egalitarian values, and collaborative democracy. Hand signals were created for general assembly meetings to meet the immediate need for structure in what many hoped would be a structureless movement. Tewskbury's study of social media further explicates these horizontal decision-making structures that evolved out of the general assemblies and were reified through a strong technological structure of online-offline discussion groups. Fletcher's chapter illuminates grander, insidious structures as she attends to the important and often unfortunate role that systematic oppression and class recreate—structures that enhance marginalization and silencing. Finally, mcclellan's chapter deconstructs how the arguments of city officials were constitutionally structured in order to provide accepted justifications for limiting the free speech rights of evicted Occupy campers.

CONCLUSION: ENGAGING LEARNING

Certainly many other themes connect these chapters including the obvious theoretical findings regarding the dialectical tensions and paradoxes embedded in the values and practices of Occupy participants. In these cases we learn *from Occupy* that our theories of horizontal leadership, violence, and communication are underdeveloped at this current time and perhaps too dogmatic. But when we attend to the second goal of the book—to use various lenses to understand what we learn *about Occupy*—we also see themes of education, in which case almost every chapter refers to an intellectual and/or educational thread that teaches us that Occupy participants in many cases know more than most of us about our political and economic state of affairs. And in almost every chapter we also see a romantic theme of hope and optimism, despite participants' claims to be skeptics. Occupy fueled a growing optimism that citizens can affect their communities.

Hence, the purpose of this text is to expand upon these themes as we invite the reader to engage with the book whether you are reading to learn more about applied theory or whether you are curious about the Occupy movement, or hopefully, both. To that end, every author in this volume has included discussion questions in their analysis, including, as you might have noticed, David Osborn, who wrote our foreword. Each chapter ends with an invitation and provocation to join in the discussion regarding what we learn from and about Occupy with these case studies. In the spirit of the Occupy movement and its clever engagement of social media, this conversation, which commences here in this book, will continue online at our website: www.occupycommunication.org. Before reading any of the chapters in this book, you might begin by considering the assumptions and knowledge you bring regarding the Occupy movement. Do you live in a city that had a prominent Occupy presence? If yes, what did you notice? If not, how does your perception of Occupy differ from your classmates' or friends' who did engage or experience Occupy locally? Whatever the themes relevant to you, the many lenses of Occupy offered in this anthology work to encourage readers to draw their own conclusions and predictions regarding the legacy of the Occupy movement.

DISCUSSION QUESTIONS

1. What do the authors mean by an *emic* versus *etic* perspective?
2. What other phenomena do you believe could be better understood through romantic, functional, and critical interpretive lenses?
3. As you read through this volume, consider what other themes, besides time, space, and structure, emerge in your understanding of Occupy phenomena.

NOTE

1. As a side note, each chapter of the book positions Occupy participants in slightly different and intentional ways. For example, Occupy participants may be referred to as protesters, participants, citizens, etc., based on the assumptions made by the researchers.

I

Situating Occupy Globally: The Cultural and Economic Context

"A world capable of holding many worlds cannot be built out of the imposition of truth upon the lowly masses."—Alex Khasnabish 2008, 244

Chapter One

A Genealogy of Occupy within Transnational Contexts, and Communication Research

Priya Kapoor

"You cannot evict an idea." "Lost my job, found an Occupation."—Protestor Slogans, (Milkman, Luce, and Lewis 2013; 33, 11)

As a communication scholar of cultural studies, I have been asked to position Occupy scholarship within the larger social and historical landscape of movement and cultural studies.[1] In this chapter I also consider the contribution communication scholarship lends to theorizing social movements. Indeed, social movement literature lacks communication theory and scholars have noted this dearth of theorization (Huesca 2001). As a field that is conducive to studying a vast array of patterns of interaction, communication studies possess the requisite tools to scrutinize contemporary social movements. As such, I will begin with a description of significant social movements that have contributed in some way to the experience of Occupy. I situate Occupy within a larger repertoire of transnational social movements that connect us to an alterglobalization problematic of how to forward a project of global social justice within repressive regimes of capital and state. I establish a genealogy between the Occupy movement and other new social movements, namely, Chipko 1973, Zapatista 1994, Battle in Seattle 1999, international forums—especially in Beijing and Tunis (1994–2013), and the Arab Spring 2011.

After situating Occupy historically within this genealogy of social movements, I explore some of the themes in social movement knowledge that present gaps ripe for communication scholarship gleaned from the studies in this volume that are disrupting these theoretical silences. Communication scholars are keen to study movements where collectivities of people are "taking risks and defying authority" (Palmer-Mehta 2012, 326), accordingly, I conclude the chapter introducing a few of the richer contributions communication theory more generally is adding to social movement research.

CONTEMPORARY MOVEMENTS AND EVENTS ESTABLISH PRECEDENCE FOR OCCUPY

A proper starting place for understanding Occupy's location in history is to first consider its relationship to other sites of struggle occurring before, during, and alongside Occupy. This is not a unique movement; nor are the agitating factors that instigated this movement. More specifically, an important critique of the Occupy research and media coverage in the United States is that it is too often positioned as a movement that was born in the "West," and not necessarily attached to a larger pattern of global discontent and/or unrest. Yet a closer examination reveals that Occupy could be viewed more sincerely as intrinsically connected to struggles of power, inequality, and injustice happening at sites on all corners of the globe. A more honest and holistic depiction of Occupy would be to weave its existence and action into the other ongoing battles being waged by others. I will discuss a few specific examples of these preceding and ongoing movements that served as precedents below.

Several movements around the world have chipped away at monolithic governmental practices of nation-states and capitals, which over time have successfully pigeonholed citizens' roles in an active public. I have chosen to focus on four particular movements because these movements, like Occupy, display certain common traits in how they deal with internal organization and governance, and external political action. The above-listed movements have evolved as transnational over time, even though they might have originated in one region. These movements are youth-based, engage with local realities, resist state directives of ownership of natural and monetary resources, and address wealth and income inequality and corrupt regimes of power that hold unconditional control over the masses. Like these movements, Occupy and new social movements make us hopeful of the viability of collective action.

"Battle in Seattle" or the Seattle N30 WTO Protests

The Seattle antiglobalization mobilization has become the touchstone of northern hemisphere protests in recent times. Several scholars consider Seattle and the Zapatistas' movements as a "key foundational moment in what became the global justice movement or global civil society" (Edelman 2009, 111). Serving as an immediate precursor to the 2011 Occupy movement, Seattle World Trade Organization (WTO) has led to the Quebec City, Genoa,

Miami, and the World Social Forum protests. Seattle WTO protests (also labeled N30 to denote their beginning on November 30, 1999) forged, for the first time, strong links between denizens of the global North with those in the global South.

The gathering drew close to fifty thousand protesters whose alliances and links were international and representative of grassroots concerns around the world. Edelman (2009, 110) attempts a list, "French farmers, Korean greens, Canadian wheat growers, Mexican environmentalists, Chinese dissidents, Ecuadorian anti-dam organizers," and the list continues. Edelman also fields the charge of writers—Elizabeth Betita Martinez (2000) of *Colorlines*, as well as Glassman (2002), and Hadden and Tarrow (2007)—that the presence of persons of color and those from the global South was minor. Edelman believes that N30 was an important gathering for small agriculturalists from around the world and their participation, however minor, has had a far reaching impact on several farm-based, seed-save movements outside of the United States. The mobilization in Seattle became a strong people's statement of the unfair trade and business practices under the aegis of General Agreement on Trade and Tariff (GATT) treaties, the Structural Adjustment Programs (SAP) in Africa, Asia, and Latin America by the International Monetary Fund (IMF) and the World Bank. Seattle made other forms of networking possible. Edelman (2009, 124) notes: "movements that are unable to attain their objectives in domestic politics seek out international allies in order to pressure governments to conform to international norms." This strategy of alliance building is a common outcome now of several United Nations-initiated conferences and of many successful social movements (Keck and Sikkink 2007; Moghadam 2012).

With the spotlight on globalization, Seattle became a cosmopolitan moment for the United States. Imre Szeman (2002, 1) hails Seattle a "pedagogical" moment as protestors learned the rules and value of fair trade with poorer nations. Seattle WTO protests marked: (a) the ascendency of the police force as the "first line of defense of a capitalist economic system" (Gillham and Marx 2000, 213), (b) the states' claiming of public space such as parks, street corners, and sidewalks to ostensibly protect other nonprotesting citizens; and (c) the establishing of transnational companies and governments as offenders that institute unfair rules of trade between nations whose military and economic might are unequal.

Edelman (2009, 122) observes that "the anti-WTO protests engendered optimism and gave new energy to diverse movements, some of which were closely allied with or echoed or expressed the demands of peasants and farmers."[2] Because of the increasing crisis in the agricultural sector, farmer protests were already rampant in Western Europe, India, and Latin America. While transnational corporations have tried to curb labor movements and unions, it was actually the unorganized labor, the farmers and peasants who came to the forefront of opposing procorporate and free-trade policies (Edelman 2009, 112). As a small but significant act of resistance on behalf of farmers, José Bové led a demonstration in front of McDonald's Restaurant on November 29, 1999. McDonald's is a symbol of junk food, beef consumption, and unfair trade policies against France by the United States. Bové smuggled 200 kilograms of Roquefort cheese, set up a stall in the melee and distributed it during Seattle N30. Direct resistance, advocacy alliance-building, street protest, nonviolent tactics as well as anarchist tactics became the pedagogic yield of Seattle N30 for the Occupy movement.

From the Zapatista Rebellion in Chiapas, Mexico, to India's Chipko Movement

The Occupy movement inherits the values of direct democratic process and participation from the Zapatista and Chipko movements both of which are hailed as important precedents for new transnational movements around the world. The Zapatista movement of 1994 was organized to oppose and moderate forces of globalization. The Zapatistas succeeded in garnering global support for indigenous rights through organized networking and the Internet. Scholars remind us that the initial Zapatistas' armed rebellion of 1994 that metamorphosed into a broader social movement did not desire to wrest state control but to mobilize civil society.

The *zapatismo* lobbied a global civil society and set up a convention in the Lacando´n Jungle of the Chiapas in August 1994 to discuss democracy and are therefore known as "unorthodox rebels" (Stahler-Sholk 2001, 493). They held subsequent meetings in 1996 and 1999 to discuss governance, neoliberalism, and decision making. These forums invited global civil society and made zapatismo global (Khasnabish 2008). Activists from around the world went home with new ideas and new alliances. The Zapatistas "saw their role as catalysts in a dynamic struggle in which local and global actors influence each other" (Stahler-Sholk 2010, 269). They have made an effort to stave off market rules via government mandates to define their own priorities, without a view to profitability, especially in agri-business and local ecology. The Zapatistas have created a project of autonomy and democratization that remains a challenge in an existing nation-state political system (Stahler-Sholk 2001, 516). Despite the challenges, zapatismo is a vision of hope (Khasnabish 2008) and inspiration with concrete outcomes.

Just as the locus for the Zapatistas was the Locando´n Jungle, the Chipko movement (in the 1970s) made the forests of Northern India, in Uttarakhand, a site of conflict. A movement led primarily by women, enraged to see their forests, the primary livelihood of the farming and village communities, felled systematically for commercial profit. They embraced the trees as the bulldozers came to fell timber for supplying and selling it in the open market. The loss of community-owned forests (Shah 2008),[3] and the even graver loss of ground cover had made a mountainous terrain become dangerously susceptible to erosion, routine monsoon landslides, displacement of farm labor, and loss of income from farming. Chipko, which means "to stick/attach oneself to without leaving" became an important rebellion, watched and monitored globally, as it revived the Gandhian anticolonial protest sensibilities (Haigh 1988) and ideals of self-governance, indigenous rights, and communal control of forest and land resources from state control.

The lessons of Chipko from the 1970s, separated from Occupy by approximately thirty years, are refined further by the Zapatistas, who kept their organizational structures and leadership aboveboard and open to public scrutiny. Zapatistas and Chipko have invoked activists from around the world forming a shared circle of knowledge and experience. Moore (2011) has researched the linkages between Chipko and the Clayoquot Sound peace camp in British Columbia. "Eco-terrorists" of the Earth Liberation Front of the Pacific Northwest have borrowed strategies inspired by Chipko. An encouraging note for Occupy via Chipko is that the participatory citizen politics of the 1970s has not dissipated; rather, it has continued to mobilize future generations of local youth.

International Forums: Allied Networks that Strengthen Social Movements

This section links transnational forums from 1994 onward, as providing inspiration and ideas for the Occupy movement in support of continued political action. Chang's (2012) succinct articulation of a forum reflects deeply on the importance of international meetings and the World Social Forums (WSF) for Occupy. He says: "a forum is also a door (*foris*), a place to an outside, to other places, other forums. A forum is therefore a forum of forums, of meetings to come, of gatherings that continue to gather, of exchanges in womb" (369). Keck and Sikkink (1998, 89) research the "dense exchanges of information and services" between transnational advocacy networks (TANs), associated actors and grassroots stakeholders so activists are able to suffuse transnational economic and development policy with social justice agendas. International forums and conferences provide that important common ground to activists for *dense exchanges* of ideas. Even though most conferences are planned for elite administrators, civil society and break-off summits force diverse perspectives—rather than simply governmental ones—to bear on international policy decisions.

Some successful international conferences that saw the rise of global civil society are: the United Nations International Conference on Population and Development in Cairo (ICPD) (1994), Fourth World Conference on Women in Beijing (1995), the Nongovernmental Organization (NGO) Forum in Beijing (1995), the World Social Forum (2001), and the World Summit on Information Societies (2003, 2005). An emerging historical link between TANs and new social movements confirms Huesca's observation earlier that neoliberal capitalism has eroded the power of labor unions and political parties; therefore, social movements bear the responsibility of citizen politics (see Nadesan chapter 3 in this volume for a discussion of neoliberalism). Therefore the power of activism is channeled into new social movements such as Occupy.

It is simply a conceited notion that activists from two ends of the globe do not talk with each other. The incidence of international meeting grounds and the explosion of user-generated social media have created multiple synergies and information exchange between actors that do not speak the same language but share the same experience of domination and state hegemony. The subversively planned, breakaway NGO Forum in Beijing in 1995 attended by approximately 30,000 women and men helped establish the power of activism and international non-governmental organizations. The NGO Forum became the harbinger of the slogan "women's rights are human rights," introducing the rights discourse into the feminist movement.

Valuable social movement themes apparent in the deliberations in international forums are: (a) imperatives of institutional, governmental reform leading to transparency; (b) nuanced democratic roles of civil society and other stakeholders such as the state, the private sector, and international organizations; and (c) the importance of recognizing collective cultural identity and human rights. The impact of these ideas has influenced most social movements since. Some recent examples of synchronous movements that share principles of socioeconomic justice are: the Anna Hazare anticorruption movement in India (2011) that has called for accountability in public dealings by government officials; the struggle for democracy and governance, given the sobriquet of the Arab Spring (2011) in the Middle East; and the call for major reform in financial markets, as in the Occupy movement (2011) in the United States.

The World Social Forum in Porto Alegre, Brazil,[4] in 2001, a gathering of international civil society organizations, was fueled by Latin American activism and contributed to furthering the agenda for future global social justice movements. The overwhelming success of the forum encouraged organizers to hold a biannual WSF meeting. When the World Social Forum was held in Mumbai in 2004, several other social justice issues became salient including: (a) open-source software, (b) the War on Terror, (c) a global antiwar movement, and (d) Dalit/indigenous rights. World Social Forum has evolved into a key international event to strategize for equitable globalization at the grassroots level around the world. The intrinsic connectedness of grassroots movements and their stake in the global civil society is established at these organized international forums. The venue for the World Social Forum in

2013, Tunisia (March 26-30), is also the epicenter of the Arab Spring. Therefore the WSF becomes an added mobilization for civil society and youth in the country.

World Summit on Information Societies Tunis 2005 as Precursor to the Arab Spring: Synchronicities with Occupy

Scholars note the lock-step timing of the Occupy movement in fall 2011, following the powerful transnational Arab Spring during the previous year. Just as Occupy, the Arab Spring became a powerful testimony for global social justice by disenfranchised youth. Just as Occupy, the Arab Spring revived the exuberance of social media enthusiasts extolling their emancipatory potential. In a "cruelly ironic" (Kapoor 2011, 3) turn, the Arab Spring sparked in Tunisia, a Maghreb Arab nation that did not have a codified national communication and information policy (Said 1998). Despite this glaring lack in 2005, Tunisia was chosen as host of the World Summit on Information Societies (WSIS), six years before the Arab Spring became a household name.

A lineage worthy of exploration is one between the Arab Spring and the WSIS held in Tunis in 2005, as a follow-up stage-two conference of WSIS Geneva in 2003. Multistakeholder partnerships among the state, transnational corporate interests, and civil society were emphasized at this major world conference. The outcome of WSIS 2005 was a prodigious list of commitments that several countries signed collectively. These commitments of information justice have proven difficult to abide by. The recent government prohibitions on WikiLeaks, and other cases of information censorship, attest to the difficulty of powerful governments to release control over information sources and channels (Kapoor 2011).

The calls for freedom of information and free expression proved powerful within Tunisia, as the WSIS host, and the nation of origin for the Arab Spring. The self-immolation of Mohammed Bouazizi in Sidi Bouzid, a small rural town in Tunisia, became a trigger to a larger transnational movement—the Arab Spring. Specifically, Articles 4, 42, and 90, of the WSIS Tunis Commitment (2005) and Article 81 of the working group on the Internet governance report, called for a complete elimination of the tight information censorship by the Tunisian government (or the government of any state). The Tunis Commitment (2005) emphasizes a "respect for human rights and fundamental freedoms" and that "good governance at all levels are independent and mutually reinforcing. [We] further resolve to strengthen respect for the rule of law in international as in national affairs" (World Summit on the Information Society 2005).

These selective messages of the Tunis Commitment ring clear for the Tunisian, Libyan, Egyptian, and Bahrainian revolutionaries who took to the streets in 2011. Centering the lives of people for the purpose of political governance was radical in Tunisia in 2005. That is also the time when an award-winning blog, *Nawaat.org*, and other political blogs were coming into their own in North Africa. Despite the lull in the Western media about WSIS, close attention was paid by Tunisian media activists, feminist groups, and civil society activists. They rallied at processions in downtown Tunis, where the global civil society (already participating in WSIS) eagerly joined them in solidarity. Despite the silence in Western media, regional North-African and African media, Al-Jazeera in particular, were active and consistent in their reportage of protests and daily life since 1996. This story of connections has a place in analyses of social movements because the Arab Spring is most often labeled the Facebook revolution or the Twitter revolution. These happy labels often obfuscate the seething unrest and dissonance of disenfranchised youth at the ground level. While it is popularly believed that Bouazizi was college educated, he did not even pass high school. His may be a more important profile of youth in the rural parts of the Arab world—those amenable to digital use, especially telephones, but not with direct or easy access (Comunello and Anzera 2012).

The Arab Spring has moved rapidly from its revolutionary fervor into a phase of discontent and violence as in the case of Egypt (*New York Times News Service* 2013). Libya and Bahrain, during the initial phases of the Arab Spring, and now Syria have moved into sheer state-initiated violence and repression. Through its tales of struggle and strife, the Arab Spring has provided intellectual and motivational fodder, indeed preparation to resist state violence and control, to several movements around the world. The Occupy movement in the United States, Canada, and Europe is one of those noteworthy movements. Again, properly placing Occupy among the lineage of these movements—Chipko 1973, Zapatista 1994, Battle in Seattle 1999, international forum—especially in Beijing and Tunis (1994–2013), and the Arab Spring 2011—allow the reader to view Occupy as being part of a larger struggle by individuals and citizens across the globe. Ideally this placement of Occupy amidst these preceding movements strengthens the claims of the participants as it readily makes a trend of discontent more salient.

ADVANCING SOCIAL MOVEMENT STUDIES WITH COMMUNICATION SCHOLARSHIP

Having provided a brief introduction of the social movements relevant to the studies in this book, I next assemble fruitful avenues for strengthening movement research, particularly as it relates to communication studies. Though not inclusive of the scope of all the gaps in the social movement literature, I focus below on research openings that are present in the studies included in this edited volume thematically conceptualized as (a) social media, (b) identity, (c) participation, and (d) policing protest, nonviolence, and violence and capitalism.

Social Media and New Social Movements: Activism not Slacktivism

Social media studies provide an important contribution to building contemporary social movement theory. Twitter, Facebook, WikiLeaks, Al-Jazeera, and the blogosphere have all played a significant role in new social movements, the most recent being the Arab Spring and Occupy movements. Scholars remind us it may be naïve to make facile links between social media and the success of citizen protests. For example, Comunello and Anzera (2012) term causal links between social media and social change as technological determinism since citizen access to technology is an issue despite the ubiquity of social media. But because the Internet and social networks make the networked nature of "societies more visible while empowering networked individuals" (465), they warrant careful consideration.

Nanabhay and Farmanfarmaian (2011) employ the Castellian theorization that power is shaped by various networks to remind us that it is the interplay between real-world protests, social and mainstream media (Rainie and Wellman 2012 cited in Comunello and Anzera 2012) that makes a movement successful and noteworthy. Accounts of the Arab Spring and Occupy have primarily acquainted us with the efficacies of social media and the Internet used by virtuous, but rebellious citizens. However, Comunello and Anzera (2012, 465) argue, "we are not dealing with a zero-sum game: social media can be effective tools both for the rebels and for the repressive machine." The Tunisian Government phished Facebook connections during the first wave of protests in 2011 and hacked into the web pages and accounts of established activists and bloggers. Egypt's Mubarak regime also tried to cut off social media connections and phone coverage during Tahrir Square protests in 2011 but did not succeed in quelling the unrest.

Hence many questions remain regarding the role of social media, power and agency, and activism in social movements. Communication scholars and social constructionists will undoubtedly want to challenge earlier studies that displayed scant confidence in organizing through social media stating "a strong and sturdy movement's leadership cannot be easily adapted to the horizontal, rather than hierarchical architecture proposed by social media" (Comunello and Anzera 2012, 465) as Tewksbury does in chapter 10 of this volume. Indeed Tewksbury shows how focused forums such as the Alternate Banking Working Group provide us a rigorous understanding of democratic processes, actualized via social media within the Occupy movement.[5] A burgeoning communication scholarship will add to the claims we can make about social media and its constitutive role in social movements.

Identity in Social Movements

According to cultural theorist Stuart Hall from his essay titled, "Who Needs Identity?" wherever agency and politics are at stake identity becomes a central concern. Identity, Hall reminds us, bears a "pivotal relationship to a politics of location" (Hall 1996, 2). Identity as an analytic category provides depth to studies of social movements. Taylor and Whittier (1992) argued there is a paucity of studies on politicized group identities; specifically, these authors examined how lesbian (read: political) contributions to the feminist movement are erased by the oft-cited term, *cultural feminisms*. The role of collective identities in social movements highlights how ideology maintains collective action (Taylor and Whittier 1992). The notion of political collective identity is salient to Occupy and a trope that can be carried forth to the study of social movements to come.

Along these lines, we know that even grassroots movements reflect the inequities of society. While socioeconomic class was at the core of the concern in Occupy, racial and gendered aspects were left unaddressed or remained open-ended. A recent study by participant researcher Campbell (2011) foregrounds race in Occupy, employing the theoretical constructs of the prison industrial complex. Campbell (2011) argues that the particularities of race in America—the lack of acknowledgement of the historical nexus of prison construction, confinement of the Black population, and their systematic exclusion in other profitable organizational contexts—have not allowed Occupy to be anything other than a movement that is white-led and in the service of white, middle-class youth. Campbell (2011) also indicts independent and progressive media such as *Democracy Now* and *The Real News Network* in their lack of effort to represent people of color despite coverage of Occupy Wall Street (OWS).

Intersectionality is a salient lens to deconstruct identity as it relates to class, race, and gender in social movements. For example, in Milkman, Luce, and Lewis's (2012, 6) study, an Occupy protester holding a sign on student indebtedness at OWS emblazons, "Home of the Fees, Land of the Slaves." (This sign juxtaposes student debt with more extreme structural inequities of racism and underclassism while playing on the word free and fees). There is intertextuality and dialogue between ideas and historical time periods here—antebellum slavery and contemporary student debt. This is a small example of minor discourses being showcased despite the unresolved issues in the movement. Milkman, Luce, and Lewis (2012) suggest that the "open" structure of OWS drew in members of several communities—politicized or not—

to the protest-site happenstance. This was possible despite the exclusion Campbell articulates above. The homeless, the mentally ill, and the disaffected came anyway and were drawn in to the movement when presented with a critique of capitalism and Wall Street practices at demonstrations or a general assembly meeting.

Future research on social movements (such as the case study of Occupy Portland depicted in Fletcher chapter 7 in this volume), must continue to take into account the complexity identity, particularly the intersectionality that race, gender, and class play in mobilizing, motivating, and sustaining activism, as well as the larger impact movements have on bringing these inequities to the forefront of mainstream political thought, or not.

Participative Democracy as Insufficiently Theorized in Social Movements

Participation is a key value in a democracy, yet social and grassroots movements' literature does not sufficiently engage participation (Huesca 2001; Jacobsen and Storey 2004). The Habermasian theories of communicative action and the public sphere in connection with participatory communication have an appeal in the Occupy study. While the rubric of participation is employed widely to understand new social movements, participation itself is understudied (Jacobsen and Storey 2004). Accompanying participation are the processes of cultural and social change, and communication and power differentials in organizational contexts. In his theorization, historically relevant for postindustrial societies, Habermas (1987) does not explicate plurality of human experience and is often charged with universalism (Jacobson and Storey 2004). However, Habermasian theories meaningfully engage ideas that are relevant to democratic processes, the formation and engagement of multiple public spheres, free speech, and accompanying rights of speech (Jacobson and Storey 2004; see also Heath chapter 5 and mcclellan chapter 9 in this volume).

Jacobson and Jang (2001) have invoked Habermasian *discursive democracy* that argues for the protection of *public autonomy*. This form of state-protected autonomy does not just serve the individual alone, "but [it acts] also to advocate effectively for the conditions that sustain selfhood along with others in one's community of value. For this, meaningful access to public communication and political participation are required within a political culture that valorizes cultural pluralism" (437). In other words they are articulating a political philosophy of state that allows for discursively fair governance. The concept of public autonomy has tremendous value for social movements, which get buffeted around by state administrative powers when they are simply looking for a way to articulate their outrage and publicly express the compromised ideals of democracy and state. Occupy would not be vilified by the media and administrative rhetoric if ideals of discursive democracy were in place. By attending to participative democracy, scholars of social movements may penetrate status quo ideas of what counts as fair governance within both movements and democratic governments.

Policing the Protest, Nonviolence as Protest Tactic, and the Relationship between Capitalism and Violence

As a final theme, police action has become a key intervention by the state to keep public spaces from expressions of dissent. This issue is an important one for the Occupy movement and constitutes an important area of investigation in modern social movements. While most Occupy protesters were not brutalized by the police in the same way that the Seattle protesters were, public space became contested ground. Occupy encampments were given notice and cleared under police supervision from Zuccotti Park in New York to Lownsdale Square in Portland. The police tactics used globally and in the United States for the dispersal of protestors does not inspire confidence in citizens about their right to free speech, dissent, and political participation. Activists have rightly feared for their own and fellow citizens' freedoms and civil rights (Herbert 2007). The territorial spatial authority that nation-states and local bureaucratic functionaries exert on public land where protests occur is absolute. Protestors have routinely been presented as disrupters of peaceful everyday life by media outlets, thereby diluting their important political messages (Herbert 2007; Lovejoy and Brynteson chapter 8; and mcclellan chapter 9; this volume).

Occupy protesters and those from transnational movements are trained in nonviolence tactics. Nonviolence in new social movements has myriad interpretations variable from movements of the past. In this book Munoz's (chapter 6) research elaborates that the definitions of violence and anarchy are in continual negotiation yet the will to remain nonviolent is strong. Peace and nonviolence are powerful strategies for sustained freedom and long-term rebellion and used as such by Mahatma Gandhi[6] to overthrow the British Raj and by Nelson Mandela to change the anti-apartheid government in South Africa. The protestors of Battle in Seattle, Occupy, and other grassroots movements have undergone extensive training to maintain their own form of peace and decorum. The protesters' belief in nonviolence even in the face of police action establishes an interesting juxtaposition: Protesters are typically portrayed as unruly and rioting whether in Seattle, New York, or downtown Portland (Rausch et al. 2007; DeLuca, Lawson, and Sun 2012), thus making studies such as Munoz's in this anthology vital to restore a balanced rendering of activist behavior in social movements.

In addition, Munoz's study illuminates the philosophy of seemingly violent protestors such as Black Bloc and problematizes the notion of violence in the context of the brutality created in the wake of capitalism. Future research on social movements must continue to explore the relationships between violence and capitalism, the definitions and justification for nonviolent protest, and as the next two chapters in this volume explore—scholars of social movements, including communication scholars, must take the time to understand the complex social, historical and *economic* conditions that lead to particular protest practices, tactics, and strategies (see Barnes chapter 2 and Nadesan chapter 3 of this volume for economic studies).

CONCLUSION

The Occupy movement is fertile ground for communication theory-building. Occupy steers existing research in a meaningful direction so that the momentum of this genre of study is maintained by the field. The recent surge in communication studies of social movements has to do with the proclivities and political leanings of the scholars engaged in studying social movements as much as it has to do with the interdisciplinary nature of the field. Therefore, the insights on theory development in studying Occupy will expand the scope of existing literature.

The fledgling social movement literature continues to burgeon since global news coverage of new social movements—such as the Arab Spring and the Occupy Wall Street movements—has brought forth the deep significance of youth uprising globally. Despite the incidence and interest in social movements among communication scholars, the area remains undertheorized. Political science and sociology have typically held their sway on study of movements. But this is changing as other work justifies the flourishing contribution of communication theory to social movement scholarship. For example, Mohan Dutta (2011) hews his model for communicative social action from postcolonial theory and the work of the Subaltern Studies Collective. Dutta advocates for a culture-centered theory of communication and social change. A culture-centered theory is one that is committed to dialogue, is cognizant of marginalized discourses of neoliberalism, and has a transformative potential at the grassroots level. The inspiration for Dutta's emergent theory of social change and protest is the scourge of historical territorial colonialism and the more recent neocolonial tendencies of global trade and capital. Postcolonial theory, Dutta reminds us, is not just in opposition to traditional colonial structures but explores the emancipatory potential of peoples' movements. The theorists reviewed above provide an ideological opening for future study of Occupy and other social movements as they evolve.

DISCUSSION QUESTIONS

1. Why is it important to position Occupy in a transnational context? What are the dangers of not doing so?
2. What were the primary contributions to the Occupy movement made by each of the movements/forums identified in the first part of this chapter?
3. Compare and contrast the circumstances of Occupy participants and participants from other movements described in this chapter. What are their commonalities? What are their differences?
4. What other movements and transnational efforts do you think contributed to Occupy that were not mentioned in this chapter? In what ways do they influence the movement?
5. Consider the four themes of communication research that are gleaned from the forthcoming studies in this book and write a research question that addresses one of those theoretical areas.

NOTES

1. Thanks go to graduate student Mariko Thomas for her expert library search skills and eye for detail. I also want to thank former graduate student Sean Rains for his research assistance on the WSIS Tunis conference.

2. Farmers serve as the backbone of agricultural economies. New trade policies have seen the family farm owner squeezed over his or her right to buy seeds and remain viable in the world trade market. The farmer suicides in India are worthy of note as genetically modified sterile seeds and indebtedness have driven the agricultural head of the household to take their own lives—200,000 farmers have lost their lives in this manner since 2007 (Shiva 2009). An extreme bodily sacrifice resulting from modernization, following world trade strictures and resultant agricultural debt, is a befitting ode to the interrogation and collapse of WTO ministerial in Seattle (Shiva 2004).

3. First during the British Raj from 1815 onward and then during post-colonial India.

4. Battle in Seattle, 1999, set the tone for the success of the WSF in Porto Alegre in 2001.

5. Tewksbury uses the term slacktivism citing Hardt and Negri (2011). In his work he demonstrates that social media activism is not *slacktivism* (slacking off plus activism).

6. Mahatma Gandhi effectively strategized nonviolence (1930s–1940s) to craft several noncooperation movements such as the legendary Salt March and ultimately the Quit India movement during the British Raj. The Salt March was a protest undertaken as a *padyatra* or journey-by-foot by freedom fighters who collectively rebelled as the British colonists imposed tax on salt—a basic necessity of life. In contemporary times Nelson Mandela has employed strategic nonviolence to oppose the apartheid regime of South Africa.

Chapter Two

"We Are the 99 Percent"

Occupy and the Economics of Discontent

William Barnes

> And why are four hundred to five hundred people disrupting the other 99 percent of this city . . . The reason why is because the top four hundred people in this country are disrupting the rest of us. And they're disrupting the rest of us in such a radical . . . pillaging, messed up way that four hundred to five hundred of us have to get out in the streets to show that inequity.—Rochelle, Occupy Portland participant, December 2011

> Something has happened to our sense of values, when the end of making money justifies the means . . . when the norms of society change in a way that so many have lost their moral compass, it says something significant about society.—Joseph Stiglitz, The Price of Inequality, xvii

"We are the 99 percent." In our history, it is rare that a phrase so quickly and intensely focuses the national mind—in this case on the long simmering issue of growing inequality in the United States. This is one of the legacies of the US Occupy movement, starting with Occupy Wall Street in Zuccotti Park in New York and spilling out into cities large and small across the country, including Portland, Oregon. Politicians, teachers, the press, citizens, and activists are all now increasingly engaging the issue of inequality and the concept of fairness. The "99 percent" immediately begs questions like: Who are the 99 percent? Am *I* in the 99 percent? Who are in the 1 percent? Why? As we explore the answers to these questions, the current degree of US inequality relative to our past history and to other countries—in income, wealth, power, education, access to health care, and opportunity—is coming into clearer focus. Many of us do not like what we are learning. Something is happening. A line has been crossed, and the critical issue of whether our current economic and political system is functioning adequately and fairly for its citizens is now squarely in the mainstream debate. The Occupy movement, daring to point out that something isn't right, and cleverly drawing from the work of economists to highlight the 99 percent, has certainly been a big part of the reason this is so.

Conditions were ripe when the Occupy protests began in September of 2011. The perceived absence of fundamental financial reform and the lack of accountability in the face of widespread suffering following the global financial crisis was a major catalyst. When *Adbusters* proposed a peaceful occupation of Wall Street on September 17, 2011, to protest the corrupting effect of corporate influence on democracy and the rising and persistent levels of inequality in the United States, the timing was right. *Adbusters*, an anticonsumerist website, magazine, and foundation out of Vancouver, British Columbia, has a long history of pioneering new forms of social activism by creatively using the power of the mass media. The campaign, which according to insiders was initially advertised through Adbusters's Media Foundation e-mail list, sparked a spontaneous reaction that took on a life of its own (Fleming 2011). Students, union workers, activists, artists, the young and old, job holders and the jobless—all gathered in Zucotti Park, and soon enough, in communities across the country. *Adbuster*s's initial poster, with a ballerina dancing on the charging Wall Street bull, riot police in the background, set the mood: irreverent, creative, but dead serious about challenging the status quo.

As the Occupy movement evolves and the nation continues to grapple with the aftermath of the financial crisis, a group of influential academics, policy makers, and well-known US citizens have emerged arguing that many of the concerns of those in the movement are on target, and that it is very much in the long-term national interest to work for political and economic reform. Joseph Stiglitz, former chief economist for the World Bank and a Nobel Prize winner, has noted that the slogan, "We are the 99 percent," may mark an important turning point in the debate about inequality and class in the United States. Stiglitz's work draws on the groundbreaking work of Piketty and Saez (2003) and has been popularized in a series of articles in *Vanity Fair*, starting with the article "Of the 1 percent, by the 1 percent, for the 1 percent" and culminating in a book, *The Price of Inequality* (Stiglitz 2011, 2012b). He is unabashed in his portrayal of the contrast between the lives of the 1 percent and the 99 percent. In Stiglitz's words, "the vast majority is suffering together, and the very top—the 1 percent—is living a different life" (Stiglitz 2012, xvi). Warren Buffet, one of the world's wealthiest people and certainly one of the 1 percent, is similar in his critique of the current state of inequality and the need for change. He has consistently invoked the unfairness of current US tax policy, and in the process has bolstered the present drive to increase income tax progressivity (Buffet 2011). In response to a question on "class warfare" against the rich, Buffet recently put it succinctly to Business Wire CEO Cathy Baron Tamraz, "Through the tax code, there *has* been class warfare waged, and my class has won . . . It's been a rout" (Becktold 2011, par. 2).

Occupy participants have sought to argue that major institutions, policies, and legal structures are all part of a political economic system that unfairly, and with little transparency, preserves the advantage of the top 1 percent. Underlying the protests and the groundswell of support from the public, two themes are apparent that resonate with current warnings sounded by economists like Stiglitz, Paul Krugman, and others. With the financial crisis and the terrible aftermath still fresh, one theme is that the current market capitalist system is fragile, prone to undesirable outcomes that jeopardize the long-term health of the economy and society. These outcomes include the recent rise in extreme income and wealth inequality, the dramatic instability revealed by the financial crisis, the related rise in long-lasting unemployment, underemployment, and job insecurity, and ongoing environmental degradation and pollution. Another theme is that the US government—the actor responsible for regulating market capitalism, is not doing enough to mitigate these problems. By reinforcing these themes through a huge variety of ongoing activities in communities across the country, the Occupy participants have raised consciousness and have tapped into a great deal of frustration and insecurity among a large pool of the US population.

When studying the numbers on middle-class income stagnation in the past three decades, it is not hard to understand this frustration and insecurity. The next sections of this chapter further set the scene for this book by highlighting recent research related to the roots, and the evolving goals, of the Occupy movement. The final section of the chapter briefly highlights several key areas of focus for Occupy activity: the financial sector, the recent Supreme Court *Citizens United* decision, and the American Legislative Exchange Council. As others in this volume will explore in greater depth, Occupy participants have many ideas about policy reform and alternatives to the status quo and how to achieve these alternatives. One area of agreement is the conviction that the current degree of inequality in income and wealth in the United States is extreme, and unhealthy.

INCOME AND WEALTH INEQUALITY IN THE UNITED STATES

The public is well aware that inequality exists in the United States in income, wealth, and in many other outcome measures, including access to education and health care. However, citizens typically underestimate the current degree of inequality in these outcomes. In wealth—a variable measuring individual or household net worth at any given time rather than flows of annual income—there is evidence that the underestimation is extreme. From a representative sample of US citizens, Michael Norton and Dan Ariely (2011) found that when over 5,000 people were asked to guess the relative shares of the five wealth quintiles in the United States, the respondents estimated that the richest 20 percent and the poorest 20 percent had about 59 percent and 3 percent of the wealth pie, respectively (in multiples, this is about 20 to 1). Norton and Ariely draw on the well-known work of Edward Wolff (2010) on wealth inequality and document that the real numbers for the United States are closer to 84 percent and 0.1 percent. This translates to multiples in the high 100s to 1.

Interestingly, Norton and Ariely's survey also showed that the distribution *preferred* by US citizens was far less skewed than either of these distributions above. In the survey, 92 percent of Americans preferred a distribution similar to the distribution of a disguised Sweden, where the top quintile has 36 percent of the pie and the bottom fifth has about 11 percent (in multiples, this is a bit over 3 to 1). This preference was common across party, race, and class lines. This should tell us something about the instincts of the Occupy participants as they highlight the concentration of income and wealth at the top and the relative insecurity and lower standards of living at the bottom—they are channeling what most Americans already feel. Americans are fine with a 3 to 1 ratio of wealth inequality, preferring Sweden's income ratios (though the ratios were presented blind) by a very large majority. However, they are not fine with the reality of today's incredible levels of inequality in the United States (which they gravely underestimate).

Indeed, "We are the 99 percent" is an appropriate phrase. In the past three decades, much of the income and wealth growth has gone to the top 1 percent and above. Thomas Piketty and Emmanuel Saez (2003, 2010) have completed path-breaking archival work using Internal Revenue Service data to document pretax income shares for the top 1 percent for the past one hundred years in the United States. They show that the top 1 percent of US tax filers received well over 20 percent of the total pretax income share in the United States in the Gilded Age of the 1920s. Through the 1930s and up to the 1970s the share dropped dramatically to less than 10 percent for much of this period. Since 1980, there has been a dramatic rise back up to pre-Great Depression era levels—above 20 percent.

In a report released just after the Wall Street Occupy protests, Lawrence Mishel and Josh Bivens of the Economic Policy Institute drew on the Piketty and Saez research and starkly illustrated the gains to top income earners since 1979 relative to the bottom 90 percent, represented below (Mishel and Bivens 2011).

In their report, Mishel, and Bivens also include the finding that almost 60 percent of the total income gains between 1979 and 2007 went to the top 1 percent. This is a very sharp contrast to the postwar years prior to this period,

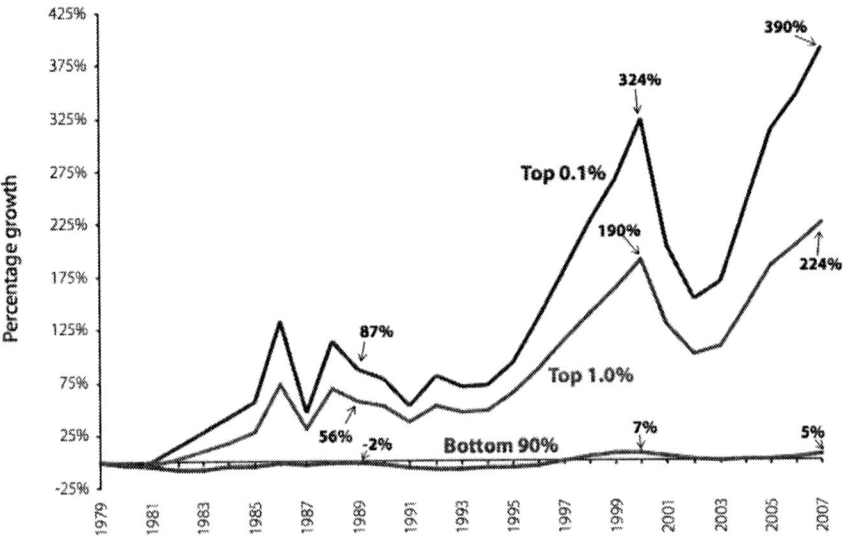

Figure 2.1. Incomes Rise Fastest at the Top Percentage Growth in Household Income by Rank on Income Scale, 1979–2007 *Source*: Mishel, Lawrence and Josh Bivens. 2011. "Occupy Wall Streeters are right about skewed economic rewards in the United States." *EPI Briefing Paper #31*, October 26. www.epi.org/publication/bp331-occupy-wall-street/ Economic Policy Institute, data derived from Piketty and Saez (2010). Reprinted with Permission.

when the economic spoils were broadly shared across all income quintiles. Stated another way, in the past 30 years the top 1 percent took a larger share of the total income gains than the bottom 99 percent combined. Within the top 1 percent, the top 0.1 percent took 36 percent of the total income gains in that same period.

For the top 0.1 percent, the almost 400 percent growth in income over this period translates to a roughly 12 percent share of the total income pie, or roughly the same as the share that the bottom 50 percent receive (Logan 2011). In other words, by 2007 the richest person in a room of one thousand people made as much income as the bottom five hundred people added up. Given the concentration in the top 0.1 percent, Paul Krugman, Nobel Laureate in Economics and a prolific op-ed columnist for the *New York Times*, has pointed out that "We are the 99.9 percent" would actually better capture what has happened (Krugman 2012).

For reference, in 2011 the average income in the 1 percent bracket was about $1.5 million, with the top 0.1 percent averaging $6.7 million (Tax Policy Center 2011). Just looking at CEO incomes, the median CEO in the top one hundred publicly listed firms took home $14.4 million in 2011 (Singer 2012, par. 10). But this pales in comparison to the incomes of hedge fund managers. In 2011, many hedge fund managers made $100 million, or far more. At the top of the pile in 2011 was Ray Dalio, the founder of Bridgewater Associates, who took home $3.9 *billion* (Creswell and Ahmed 2012, par. 7).

Wealth inequality is even more concentrated than income inequality in the United States, and the increase in wealth inequality in the past three decades has been dramatic as well. Wolf (2010) has shown that the top 1 percent had about 30 percent of total wealth holdings thirty years ago—and that now the corresponding figure is roughly 40 percent. Mishel and Bivens (2011) report that median wealth in real terms actually fell from 1979 to 2007, while wealth for the top 1 percent accelerated, going from 131 times the net worth of the typical citizen in the early 1980s to 220 times by 2007. Looking more closely at who received the total wealth gains, those in the top 1 percent and the 4 percent below them did very well, receiving a large share of the total gains.

Finally if we look at the top 0.1 percent or even narrower than this, wealth concentration is stunning. For example, an often-cited statistic is that the six

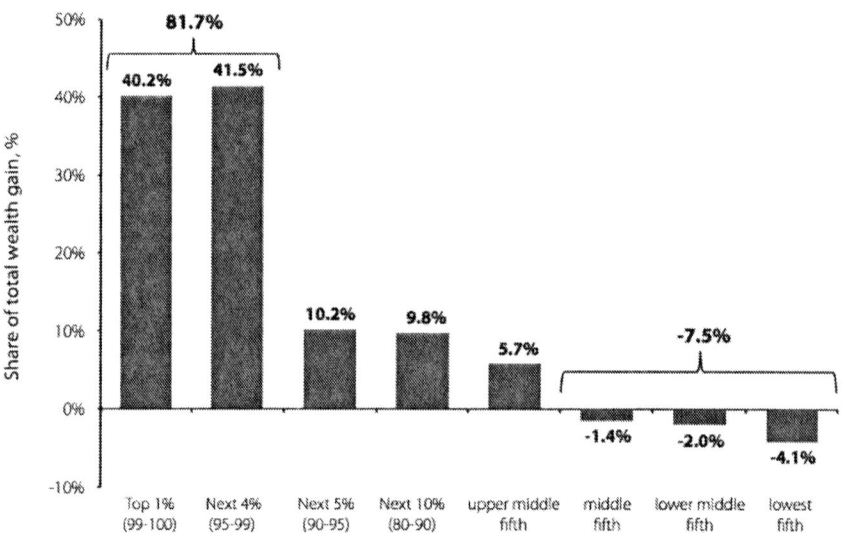

Figure 2.2. The Rich Gain Most of the Growth in Wealth Share of Total Wealth Gain, by Percentile Rank in Wealth, 1983–2009 *Source*: Mishel, Lawrence and Josh Bivens. 2011. "Occupy Wall Streeters are right about skewed economic rewards in the United States." *EPI Briefing Paper #31*, October 26. www.epi.org/publication/bp331-occupy-wall-street/. Economic Policy Institute analysis of Wolf in Allegretto (2010a). Reprinted with Permission.

Walmart heirs now have as much wealth as the bottom 30 percent of the population added up—69.7 billion dollars. A revision to this statistic after the recovery has now estimated that with a net worth of 93 billion dollars, the six heirs have as much wealth as the bottom 41.5 percent of the population, or fifty million United States households (Allegretto 2011b).

In the recovery period since the 2008 global financial crisis, many within the 99 percent have been hurt badly because of stagnant wages, high unemployment and underemployment, while the rich have done relatively better as investments have recovered. According to a recent study by Saez (2012) widely cited in the media, average real family income grew by 2.3 percent in the first year of the recovery, but it was very uneven—with the top 1 percent growing their income 11.6 percent in one year and the bottom 99 percent growing their income by 0.2 percent. This translates to the top 1 percent garnering 93 percent of the income gains. Saez cites this uneven growth as being one of the explanatory factors for the rise of Occupy demonstrations, and notes that the gains for the 1 percent are due in part to the stock market recovery, which boosted capital gains and dividend income for the wealthy.

It is important to note that the overall trend toward much more concentration of income and wealth holds even after taxes and transfers have taken place. For example, the Congressional Budget Office finds that the trends in the distribution of household income after taxes and transfers from 1979 to 2007 indicate accelerating gains for the top 1 percent similar to the pretax figures cited above by Piketty and Saez. Real incomes for the top 1 percent went up by about 275 percent, while real incomes for the rest of US households went up much more slowly, with the lowest quintile getting the least, less than a 20 percent increase (Congressional Budget Office 2011). In other words, redistribution through taxes and transfers did not do much to stem the rise in inequality of the past three decades. Echoing Warren Buffet above—the top 1 percent and the top 0.1 percent are doing very well relative to the lower brackets even after they pay their taxes, thank you.

ROOT CAUSES OF INEQUALITY, THE CONSEQUENCES, AND THE PATH FORWARD

The groundbreaking academic research of Piketty and Saez on income and Wolff on wealth was beginning to break into mainstream outlets just before the Occupy protests. Bernie Sanders, the independent Senator from Vermont, famously went on the floor of the Senate on October 10, 2010, in a marathon protest of Obama's decision to extend the Bush tax cuts for two more years. In his speech, he argued that the richest 1 percent have disproportionately benefited from economic growth in the past thirty years. In Sander's words, "The fact is 80 percent of all new income earned from 1980 to 2005 has gone to the top 1 percent. People should be mindful of this fact: The last time that type of income disparity took place was in 1928. I think we all know what happened in 1929" (Sanders 2010).

Economists and other researchers attribute many causes to the recent acceleration of the rise of inequality and have varying recommendations on how it should be addressed, but it is worth noting some of the more prominent recent arguments that have been made. Many of these authors generally reinforce the concerns and goals of the Occupy participants. They include Joseph Stiglitz and Paul Krugman cited above, Robert Reich, the former labor secretary under Bill Clinton, a number of the Economic Policy Institute researchers, Dean Baker of the Center for Economic and Policy Research, and Jacob Hacker and Paul Pierson, authors of *Winner-Take-All Politics*. All make similar points; three are highlighted below.

First, the US lower and middle classes do not deserve the stagnant incomes of the past thirty years. Despite a doubling of US labor productivity during this period, a large percentage of the fruits of those productivity gains have gone to the top 1 percent, as discussed above. This contrasts sharply with much of the postwar-period record up to 1980, when the economic gains associated with doubled productivity gains in that period led roughly to a doubling of incomes in all quintiles (Reich 2011). To the extent that this is because the 1 percent pursued behavior and political representation that assures undeserved "trickle up" of these gains from the bottom 99 percent, this is essentially rigging the game. In other words, these authors point out that the real story during the past thirty years is not "trickle down" from the ownership class to the working class as the economy grows; the real story is trickle up due to redistribution from the poor and middle class to the rich. This amounts to what economists, rather blandly, call "rent seeking" when an organization or an individual seeks economic gain from others without returning benefits back to society through wealth creation.

Dean Baker of the Center for American Progress puts it bluntly in his recent book, *The End of Loser Liberalism*, arguing that rent seeking is the point for many of those in the United States who are rich or representing the rich:

> In reality, the vast majority of the right does not give a damn about free markets; it just wants to redistribute income upward. Progressives have been useful to the right in helping it to conceal this agenda. Progressives help to ratify the actions of conservatives by accusing them of allegiance to a free market ideology instead of attacking them for pushing the agenda of the rich. (Baker 2012, 2).

While some economists choose to highlight misplaced tax policy as being a primary cause of upward redistribution, Baker highlights the rapid rise in pretax incomes including through factors such as: (1) the bailout of the banking class while millions of homeowners lose their homes, (2) the enriching effects of patent monopolies (particularly drugs in health care), (3) weak corporate governance that has led to management writing its own salary checks, and (4) the weakening of labor laws and the labor movement. At least two of these—the bank bailouts and the weakening of the labor movement—are factors that Occupy participants have highlighted in many of their events. By directly confronting channels of upward distribution and questioning them on their face, Occupy is doing what Baker argues should be done.

Second, Stiglitz (2012a, 2012b), Hacker and Pierson (2010), and others argue that working to mitigate these trends through government policy and institutional change will not slow growth down or hurt the economy; rather, it could very well *improve* growth and economic stability.[1] This flies in the face of the general argument that inequality must be tolerated for the sake of growth; the key point is that the degree of inequality is so high that it is now restraining the economy. Stiglitz has been particularly forceful in making the point that the current state of affairs will hurt us all sooner or later. For example, he starts his more recent *Vanity Fair* article asking this: "Why won't America's 1 percent—such as the six Walmart heirs, whose wealth equals that of the entire bottom 30 percent—be a bit more...selfish? As the widening financial divide cripples the US economy, even those at the top will pay a steep price" (Stiglitz 2012a, par. 1).

One motive for this reasoning has roots in Keynesian theory: if income and wealth concentrate too much at the top, aggregate spending will fall because the rich tend to save a large portion of their income. As demand falls, income falls further, and a vicious cycle can ensue that leads to reduced growth, profits, wages, and pain for all. Another point is that rent seeking largely functions as a way for the ownership class to redistribute more income and wealth up, which by definition does not create value and growth for the economy. Stiglitz cites the disproportionately large financial sector in the United States as an example where this is rife, functioning largely as "a market in speculation rather than a tool for promoting true economic productivity," and is thus the "rent-seeking sector par excellence" (Stiglitz 2012a, par. 11). Examples include the predatory lending practices of the past decade and the exorbitant credit card fees and charges that both merchants and consumers endure.

As citizens become increasingly jaded about rent seeking and other behavior that is unfairly rewarded, it demotivates them. Stiglitz broadens the concept of fairness and makes this point:

> In a society in which inequality is widening, fairness is not just about wages and income, or wealth. It's a far more generalized perception. Do I seem to have a stake in the direction society is going, or not? Do I share in the benefits

of collective action, or not? If the answer is a loud "no," then brace for a decline in motivation whose repercussions will be felt economically and in all aspects of civic life. (Stiglitz 2012a, par. 16).

Fairness also includes having access to opportunity. Stiglitz and other researchers have documented the fragility of the American dream and the relative lack of economic and social mobility that US citizens now face compared to other countries, including most of Europe and all of Scandinavia (Noah 2012a, 2012b; Stiglitz 2013).[2] Stiglitz argues that as citizens realize that opportunities are no longer present and hard work and striving may not pay, trust evaporates. As trust evaporates, gridlock can ensue—economic transactions don't happen or are less frequent, citizens don't vote, and everyone looks over their shoulder as cheating proliferates. All of these factors can translate to outcomes that hinder social progress and healthy growth, which inevitably impact the 1 percent, too.

A third point that many of these researchers make is that pursuing social change through policy reform and a broad-scale re-examination of our current social norms and institutions is imperative, particularly if we wish to maintain a recognizable democracy that represents the best interests of the middle class, and ultimately all classes. What is happening to our society is eroding the base upon which sustainable success is built in the long run. As Stiglitz (2011, 2012a, 2012b), Krugman (2012), Hacker and Pierson (2010), and others argue in various ways, the current level of inequality and instability in society, brought on in part through the rise of undue corporate influence in politics and the failure of the political economy, must be confronted and mitigated.

The Occupy movement has certainly heightened awareness and opened some space for policy reform that might not have otherwise been possible. The recent fiscal cliff fight is an example of this newfound discourse. For example, without the increased national attention on extreme inequality since 2011, would marginal tax rates for the highest income earners have gone up as readily—from 35 percent to 39.6 percent? This next section briefly explores focal points of the Occupy movement and reform efforts at the national and local level, discussing the financial sector, the Supreme Court Citizens United decision and corporate personhood, and the American Legislative Exchange Council. It is intended to provide initial context for later chapters investigating the tactics and goals of Occupy participants in more depth.

Occupy the Banks

There is no doubt that Occupy "Wall Street" and its regional variants are motivated by the rising relative size of financial institutions in the United States, and the implications of this rising power. Mirroring the meteoric rise of inequality in the past thirty years, the growth of the financial sector has been similarly dramatic, doubling in size (Mishel and Bivens 2011).

This growth did not come from increased and more efficient lending for plant and capital equipment for other sectors of the economy. Instead, much of it derives from the invention of complex financial products like derivatives and other debt-based investment products.

Prior to the financial crisis of 2008, some argued that the rise of esoteric debt-based investment products would increase financial fragility in the economy and warned of the risks. Those warnings were not heeded. In a prescient 2002 annual letter to Berkshire Hathaway shareholders, Warren Buffet famously said, "We view [derivatives] as time bombs both for the parties that deal in them and the economic system . . . In our view . . . derivatives are financial instruments of mass destruction carrying dangers that, while now latent, are potentially lethal" (Buffet 2003). Not long after this was written, credit default swaps, a form of derivative that insures against default in a bond or a security, played a pivotal role in the financial meltdown in 2008. Chapter 3 of this volume will cover the financial instruments that contributed to the financial crisis and the implications for the

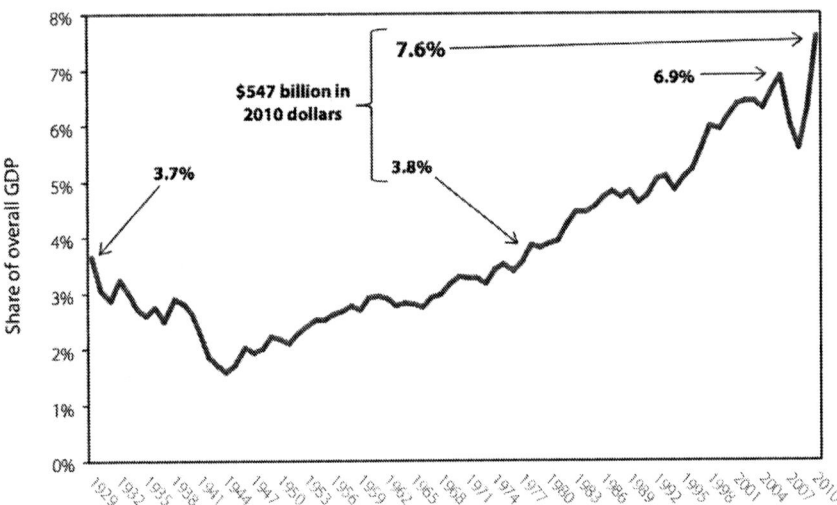

Figure 2.3. The Rich Gain Most of the Growth in Wealth Share of Total Wealth Gain, by Percentile Rank in Wealth, 1983-2009 *Source*: Mishel, Lawrence and Josh Bivens. 2011. "Occupy Wall Streeters are right about skewed economic rewards in the United States." *EPI Briefing Paper #31*, October 26. www.epi.org/publication/bp331-occupy-wall-street/. Economic Policy Institute analysis of Wolf in Allegretto (2010a). Reprinted with Permission.

Occupy movement in greater detai—including the role of credit default swaps.

In the face of these developments it is understandable why Occupy started with Wall Street financial institutions. Occupy participants have engaged in activity highlighting the unparalleled rise of power in the financial industry, the lack of transparency and accountability, and the exposure of citizens to excessive financial instability and systemic risk. Occupy participants protested Wall Street power beginning in Zuccotti Park, with a now infamous Tumbler page appearing at the same time featuring personal statistics and stories of struggle and hardship, much of it due to excessive indebtedness to the banks. Occupy participants later held a huge national day of protest on November 17, 2011, protesting the power of the banks, including in Portland. They "Occupied the Board Room" by sending 6,000 letters to Bank of America, Goldman Sachs, Morgan Stanley, Wells Fargo, Citigroup, and JP Morgan Chase to illustrate common struggles of Americans facing default and debt. An Occupy the Board Room (2013) web page lives on. From the home page:

> Life gets awfully lonely for those at the top. What can we do to let them know someone's thinking of them? Maybe they need some new friends!
>
> Make your voice heard by the Wall Street elites who wrecked the economy and made the rest of us pay. Click on someone below and tell them a story that you think they should listen to. Just got a college degree and nothing to show for it? Just got evicted while your banker gets bonuses? Share your special story with someone who ought to know. (Occupytheboardroom.org 2013).

The web page features the CEOs of the top six banks in the United States—and when you click on a name, a message window appears saying "Congratulations! You have a pal in the top 1 percent." The web page not only sends an e-mail to the appropriate address, but it also makes the e-mail public.

Since 2011, there have been many avenues for banking reform discussion and hints of impact at local levels. Through 2011 and 2012 Occupy participants created bank-centered working groups–including the Alternative Banking Group of Occupy Wall Street (featured in Tewksbury chapter 10 of this volume) and the Occupy Bank Working Group—to explore alternative banking systems characterized by wider ownership, greater transparency, and less risk (Adler 2012). Participants have pushed city councils to pass resolutions to encourage depositing money in smaller local regional banks and credit unions. For example, Portland, Oregon, Occupy participants were consistent in their calls for curtailing abuses by major banks, including fraud in mortgages. Due in part to pressure from Occupy and related groups, by May of 2012, Portland, Oregon, city commissioners passed a "responsible banking" resolution that calls for depositing money in local banks and credit unions and re-evaluating how it contracts out for banking services (Jung 2012).

Occupy the Courts and *Citizens United*

> *"I'll believe corporations are people when Texas executes one of them."*—A popular poster at Occupy events (Diamond 2012, par. 1)

Another consistent concern of Occupy participants is corporate personhood and the recent Supreme Court case *Citizens United* versus Federal Elections Commission. The *Citizens United* decision on January 21, 2010, overturned parts of the McCain-Feingold campaign finance reform act on the grounds that it violated the First Amendment and the corporate right to free speech. This effectively dismantled limits to political expenditures by corporations and unions, and the result has been a torrent of money in campaigns. *Citizens United* has been widely criticized for the finding that corporations are entitled to the same free speech rights as individuals—part of a long stream of decisions drawing on the precedent of corporate personhood.

The Occupy movement has successfully staged many events and activities since 2011 on *Citizens United* and corporate personhood, building offshoots such as Occupy the Courts and teaming up with organizations like Move to Amend, Public Citizen, and Common Cause. In January of 2012, around the second anniversary of the *Citizens United* decision, hundreds of events were staged. Flying under Occupy the Corporations, #J20, #J21, and Occupy the Courts banners, the participants tapped into a broad movement to roll back *Citizens United* and corporate money in US politics (Kroll 2012). Specific aims ranged from a constitutional amendment to end corporate personhood to empowering Congress to regulate money in politics.

Cities across the country have begun passing resolutions calling for a constitutional amendment to end corporate personhood in the interest of meaningful campaign finance reform. On January 12, 2012, Portland, Oregon Occupy participants worked with Move to Amend and Common Cause to press city commissioners to pass a resolution "that corporations should not receive the same legal rights as natural persons do, that money is not speech and that independent expenditures should be regulated" in political campaigns (Jung 2012). On January 20, 2012, the day before the *Citizens United* anniversary, hundreds of demonstrators gathered in Portland's Pioneer Courthouse Square calling for a constitutional amendment to establish that corporations are not people and that money through campaign donations is not speech.

American Legislative Exchange Council

The last point of focus in this section is Occupy's effort to expose the American Legislative Exchange Council (ALEC) to more scrutiny and to point out the influence of corporations in tipping the legislative process in their favor. ALEC is a 501c3 organization that includes legislators, businesses, and foundations in its membership. It produces "model legislation" for state legislatures, and it explicitly says it promotes free-market and conservative ideas on its webpage. As the ALEC website itself puts it:

> More than 30 years ago, a small group of state legislators and conservative policy advocates met in Chicago to implement a vision: A nonpartisan membership association for conservative state lawmakers who shared a common belief in limited government, free markets, federalism, and individual liberty. Their vision and initiative resulted in the creation of a voluntary membership association for people who believed that government closest to the people was fundamentally more effective, more just, and a better guarantor of freedom than the distant, bloated federal government in Washington, D.C. (American Legislative Exchange Council 2013).

Occupy has undoubtedly helped to raise awareness of ALEC since 2011 in the media and the public, and the press and attention has been less than flattering for the nonprofit. A recent *Mother Jones* article titled, "Occupy Rallies Against Powerful Right-Wing Group You've Never Heard Of," reflected the lack of knowledge in the public sphere about what ALEC does (Harkinson 2012). *Businessweek* recently wrote that part of ALEC's mission is in presenting industry-backed legislation as grassroots work (Greeley 2012). In "Conservative Non-profit Acts as Stealth Business Lobbyist," the *New York Times* recently wrote that "special interests effectively turn ALEC's lawmaker members into stealth lobbyists, providing them with talking points, signaling how they should vote, and collaborating on bills affecting hundreds of issues like school vouchers and tobacco taxes" (McIntire 2012, A1). This same article notes a recent Common Cause IRS complaint that ALEC is abusing its tax-exempt status through cunning lobbying and noted that despite claims of bipartisanship, 103 out of 104 leadership positions within the group were filled by Republicans.

Portland, Oregon, Occupy participants have taken a leading role in calling attention to the activities of the American Legislative Exchange Council. On February 29, 2012, Portland Occupy participants held a "F29" event that drew more than one thousand people downtown to march against corporate influence in politics. Nicholas Caleb, speaking for Occupy Portland, was quoted by the local news, KGW, stating: "We took action today to challenge ALEC, a group made up of the world's largest corporations, as well as many state and federal politicians. ALEC writes legislation focused on amassing more profit for the wealthiest 1 percent at the expense of our communities" (KGW.com staff 2012). Participants marched through the city, stopping at businesses belonging to ALEC, including Wells Fargo. Three Occupy participants chained themselves to the Wells Fargo Tower with bike locks.

Amidst Occupy activity on ALEC and with media exposure on ALEC increasing in the past year, announced corporate withdrawals from the group have increased significantly. Companies withdrawing from ALEC include Coca Cola, Pepsi, Walmart, Johnson and Johnson, Bank of America, and yes, Wells Fargo (Sourcewatch 2013). Would media interest in ALEC have occurred independent of Occupy focus on the group? Would Wells Fargo have dropped its membership without the Occupy movement's activities in the past year? Occupy's focus on ALEC, a seemingly obscure nonprofit, is arguably sophisticated and strategic. It is a sign that the movement is reading the fine print and asking hard questions about the role of corporate power in our lives.

CONCLUSION

> I think we just really lost our way. And so the Occupy movement is, how do we get people to recognize that they're part of this bigger thing, and share ethics and values and morals that really help to bring everyone up, instead of push some down while some people get away with more?—Elayne, Occupy Portland participant, Nov. 2, 2011

The Occupy movement is not an historical outlier; it is already part of the long arc of the American experience of pushing for middle-class democracy and values. One overriding goal of Occupy is clear, implied in the slogan "We are the 99 percent" and certainly in the quote above: a more inclusive society that reflects and advances the interests of the many—not just the few. Pushback is an ongoing part of the process. As Occupy and indeed all concerned citizens pursue political and economic reform that lessens rent seeking and other forms of corruption, some of the primary beneficiaries of the status quo, including within the political and corporate classes, will inevitably resist. Hacker and Pierson (2010) argue that fixing the playing field of American politics "remains the essential task. . . . It is a task that will require the heroism of sustained renewal" (305). In this, many Occupy participants seem resolved to build on the first year and a half of the movement. They are in it for the long run.

There are strands of hope threaded through this evolving story. Through collaboration and more informed citizen participation there may be opportunities for reform that reflect long-standing American values—values that honor democracy, access to opportunity, fair play, and a robust and sustainable standard of living for all. To realize these opportunities, all US citizens need a better understanding of the characteristics of the status quo, why it came about, what the disadvantages are, what alternatives can be achieved, and how to achieve them. The Occupy movement certainly will be remembered as part of this process of discovery and renewal in the early part of the twenty-first century—groundwork laid that just might lead to a reform movement that grows, community by community, working for a future that honors and respects the needs of present and future generations.

DISCUSSION QUESTIONS

1. The Occupy slogan "We are the 99 Percent" is rooted in the growing disparity over the past thirty years between the top 1 percent and the bottom 99 percent in terms of income, wealth, and other social outcomes such as health care and access to education. Review the details discussed in the chapter. You may wish to supplement the chapter details by reading the very short paper cited in the chapter by Norton and Ariely (2011) or watching this excellent infographic video based partly on their study: www.youtube.com/watch?feature=player_embedded&v=QPKKQnijnsM. Is the degree of inequality in the United States a surprise to you? How would you have answered the Norton and Ariely survey? What did you think the level of wealth inequality in the United States was, and what would be your ideal distribution for the United States? Is your ideal degree of inequality the same degree that you would associate with a healthy economy? Do you agree with the argument that the current level of inequality in the United States is unhealthy for the economy, and for society? Why or why not? Why do we tolerate inequality in the first place? How do we determine when inequality has become too extreme—what are the signs?
2. This chapter discusses the idea that at least some of the gains to the 1 percent over the past three decades may be due to "rent seeking" at the expense of the bottom 99 percent. Discuss this. Do you think this is the case? What are some concrete examples of rent seeking in the economy? What distinguishes this period in time from the period before the early 1980s, when income and wealth gains were more broadly distributed?
3. The chapter cites three areas where Occupy has focused since the September 2011: the financial sector, *Citizens United* and corporate personhood, and ALEC. Do you agree that these should be areas of concern? What efforts on the part of the Occupy participants stand out as noteworthy and/or effective to you? What do you think Occupy participants should focus on, and why?

4. What are the broad implications of this chapter, including policy implications? What would you propose going forward? Are you in favor of policy reform within the existing political economic framework? If so, what kind of reform? If you think more fundamental reform is required, what should be done? Are there any "model" countries that you would point to?
5. What do you think will happen going forward? What will be the legacy of the Occupy movement? Discuss how the history books will write up "We are the 99 percent." Do you agree with Joseph Stiglitz and the chapter author that this might mark a turning point?

NOTES

1. An influential recent International Monetary Fund working paper argues that there is strong empirical evidence that too much inequality can reduce the duration of growth periods in particular countries. See Berg, Andrew G. and Jonathan D. Ostry. 2011. "Inequality and Unsustainable Growth: Two Sides of the Same Coin?" *IMF Research Department*, April 8. www.imf.org/external/pubs/ft/sdn/2011/sdn1108.pdf.

2. Stiglitz has recently argued that upward mobility in the United States is becoming a statistical oddity, drawing from the economic mobility literature. Just 6 percent of those born into the bottom income quintile move into the top quintile, which is low relative to most other industrialized countries. Among other causes, Stiglitz pinpoints the increasing difficulty that the lower income quintiles have in obtaining affordable access to quality education, including college and graduate school. As this continues, Americans are beginning to realize that their cherished notion of the American dream is in great danger. See Stiglitz (2013).

Chapter Three

Neofeudalism and the Financial Crisis

Implications for Occupy Wall Street

Majia Holmer Nadesan

> I don't think Occupy is about camping in a park. It's Occupy Wall Street and I would like to get it back to that. I think the real struggle is income inequality . . . that's the greatest strength is that we want our country back. We do not want a country run by corporations.—Teresa, Occupy Portland Activist, Respiratory Therapist, Mother, Occu-rider, August 2012

Discontent with the political governance of the economy has risen significantly in the United States in the wake of the largest financial crisis to hit the nation since the 1930s. The financial crisis that began in 2007 still impacts wage levels, unemployment figures, and economic opportunities six years after it began. Many observers of American society remain dissatisfied with the government's handling of the major players responsible for the crisis, including the nation's largest banks and insurance companies. Popular discontent can be seen expressed in op-ed pieces, books, and blog posts in print and electronic media. One powerful signifier has been used by a range of critics to critique the origins of the crisis, the handling of the crisis, and the aftermath of the crisis: "neofeudalism."

The signifier neofeudalism can be found on blog posts, online editorials, and in published academic criticisms. What is particularly interesting about neofeudalism is that critics representing a range of political and economic perspectives have employed it. Some who employ the term neofeudalism seek to reform capitalism by restoring "free market" operations, while others deplore capitalism in its entirety. These disparate critics envision divergent paths toward achievement of "universal opulence," a long-term goal of economic thought. Yet, considerable agreement can be found across their analyses of the failures of the current political and economic order. For both anticapitalists and those romantics who yearn for a reinvigorated, entrepreneurial market economy, neofeudalism is used to describe an entrenched, oligarchic society with totalitarian tendencies and a general disregard for enforcement of rules and regulations when elite interests are concerned.

This chapter explicates two different worldviews informing uses of the term neofeudalism and looks at whether these worldviews can be found in discourses that identify with Occupy Wall Street (OWS). The first worldview referred to here as romantic can be found in online blog posts and articles using neofeudalism to describe a debased capitalism requiring reforms aimed at reinstating morality, market disciplines, and entrepreneurialism. This worldview is often nostalgic, presuming that America once represented a more democratic "producers republic," characterized by small and medium sized enterprise in the context of a disciplining market. This is a Jacksonian, aspirational ideal for contemporary capitalists unhappy with the reign of large, transnational corporations without national allegiances. This nostalgic yearning for a producers' republic doesn't simply inform economic criticism, but also has shaped critiques of a wide range of American social institutions, including baseball. Nick Trujillo's (1992) description of romantic critiques of baseball revealed nostalgic yearnings for a purer and more communal America. In a similar fashion, some who use neofeudalism do so to delineate out a degraded market space that is implicitly compared with a purer, more communal and entrepreneurial producers' republic governed by a disciplining market.

A second and more radical worldview—a critical orientation—implicit in discourse employing the term neofeudalism presumes that capitalism is always characterized at a fundamental level by conflicts of interest. More radical critics of capitalism argue that capitalist accumulation strategies will recognize no limits, ultimately destabilizing human societies and natural ecosystems. For this group of critics, neofeudalism signifies the devolution of advanced capitalism and a deep disillusionment with the promise of socialism because of the failure of government to represent the public good. Those who use neofeudalism in this rhetorical context are generally suspicious of "Keynesian" reforms aimed at stabilizing markets through government reforms (Keynes 1936).

This type of radical critique of social institutions circulates widely in American academic and cultural criticism. In his analysis of baseball culture, Trujillo (1992) observed that critics of the sport deplored its commercialization, militarism, and tendency to be used as a technology of control by business and the state. Critics argue that the effect of the instrumentalization of baseball as a tool of exploitation and control is social alienation. This kind of radical critique persists today and informs the worldview of many critics who use the term neofeudalism. However, this more radical critical orientation tends to be found in the margins of political discourse, including OWS discourse.

After examining these worldviews found across uses of the signifier neofeudalism, the chapter then moves to explore relevancies for OWS. The Occupy Wall Street movement is diverse in membership and viewpoints. Research reveals that Internet search results for the combined signifiers OWS and neofeudalism tend to be slightly more radical in their critiques of the economy and government's reformist capabilities when compared to proposed OWS reforms found in seminal OWS texts, such as *This Changes Everything: Occupy Wall Street and the 99% Movement* (Van Gelder 2011). Put another way, those identifying with OWS while using neofeudalism as a trope tend to be slightly more radical than the Keynesian center found in some of the OWS movement's more formal discourses. Loosely described, Keynesians and neo-Keynesians believe the state can successfully regulate and stabilize capitalism. As this chapter will demonstrate, many—although, certainly not all—OWS discourses presuppose the state's capabilities for reform.

Thus, the chapter concludes tentatively that those who believe the United States is devolving towards something different—something neofeudal—are less likely to hold hope for the possibility of reform and, consequently, are for the present more likely to be found at the political margins of OWS discourse. Capitalist romantics and critics are both found at the margins of OWS discourse. However, federally organized police force used against past and future OWS demonstrations may radicalize the OWS movement specifically, and the broader society more generally. Should that happen, neofeudalism may feature more prominently, signaling growing social pessimism about reform.

This chapter begins by exploring how the term neofeudalism has been articulated by a range of romantic and critical observers and then moves to examine empirically the conditions of advanced western capitalism that are agreed upon indicators of neofeudalism. Neofeudalism emerges in theoretical and empirical accounts in relation to growing financialization of the economy, elite control of resources, cooptation of government regulation, and lack of criminal enforcement of financial crimes. The chapter illustrates these trends using the case example of Abacus, a collateralized debt obligation (CDO) created by Goldman Sachs. Abacus illustrates the lack of criminal accountability perceived as endemic to neofeudal advanced capitalism. After establishing how neofeudalism signifies for both romantics and critics, the chapter turns to address the role of neofeudalism in OWS discourses.

NEOFEUDALISM: THE SIGNIFIER

Neofeudalism is an evocative signifier. It is a semiotic "sign" that connotes a worldview constructed in populist political discourses, found primarily, albeit not exclusively, on the Internet. It's appropriate to examine Wikipedia's definition of the neofeudalism given that its discourse is primarily electronic:

> Neofeudalism literally means "new feudalism" and implies a contemporary rebirth of policies of governance and economy reminiscent of those present in many pre-industrial feudal societies. The concept is one in which government policies are instituted with the effect (deliberate or otherwise) of systematically increasing the wealth gap between the rich and the poor while increasing the power of the rich and decreasing the power of the poor (also see wealth condensation). This effect is considered to be similar to the effects of traditional feudalism. (Wikipedia 2012).

Wikipedia's definition emphasizes economic policies and practices that shift wealth from the majority of the population to elite groups. Neofeudalism is not intended literally to signify a new kind of feudalism (see Troubador 2010). Instead, the signifier operates as a powerful rhetorical trope for a diverse group of observers critical of contemporary global capitalism. In the most general sense, the term neofeudalism is used most frequently by Internet activists when describing the worldwide growing wealth gap and the lack of legal accountability by corporations and financial actors responsible for the financial crisis in both the United States and Europe.

Neofeudalism is used extensively by romantics who yearn for a purer more entrepreneurial capitalism. For example, activists Max Keiser and Stacy Herbert have played an important role in publicizing the idea of neofeudalism through their *RT (Russia Today)* broadcasts and blogging at Maxkeiser.com. Keiser and Herbert see neofeudalism as arising from corrupted markets and seek to restore entrepreneurial "free market" operations. Keiser often describes the US economy as a "Neo-feudalistic, Gulag Casino Economy" (see video Keiser 2011). Keiser and Herbert have particularly critiqued elite financial executives, such as Goldman Sachs's Lloyd Blankfein, for eroding the rule of law, describing him as "an enemy of the state" (see video Keiser 2010). Blankfein is infamously known as describing himself as "doing God's work" when challenged about Goldman's role in the financial crisis (Phillips 2009). Keiser and Herbert can be regarded as romantic in that they yearn for entrepreneurial free enterprise and disciplining markets.

Likewise, the heavily trafficked and decidedly procapitalist website ZeroHedge.com often features articles by critics declaiming American neofeudalism, as illustrated in the titles of these guest posts: "The E.U., Neofeudalism and the Neocolonial-Financialization Model," by Charles H. Smith (2012), and "Krugman, Diocletian and Neofeudalism," by Arizonomics (2012). Neofeudalism is a rather nostalgic construct when articulated by those who employ it to deride what they see as the corruption of capitalism. Neofeudalism is rhetorically pitted against a purer, romanticized form of capitalism characterized by small and medium-sized enterprise operating in a "free," but disciplining market.

Neofeudalism is also used by activists critical of capitalism itself. For example, Mark Mirabello's 2009 *Handbook for Rebels and Outlaws* briefly describes neofeudalism as "a system in which an elite of technocrats, strategists, and corporate barons control the country, with the rest of the population effectively denied any meaningful decision-making role" (188). Journalist and writer Chris Hedges (2010) describes neofeudalism in his *Death of the Liberal Class*, arguing that unfettered capitalism is "plunging" society into a state of "neofeudalism" (156). Hedge's uses the term twice in his recent book, but doesn't elaborate in detail upon what is meant by neofeudalism. Garrett Johnson's 2011 essay, "Slouching toward Neofeudalism," probably offers one of the most detailed explanations of the concept:

> Neofeudalism is a concept in which government policies are designed to systematically increase the wealth gap between rich and poor while increasing the power of the rich over the poor. It's a party-neutral idea. There is no cabal pushing the plan, merely the sum effect of pressure from the wealthy elite. . . . Another manifestation of neofeudalism is the growing power of corporations, that leave the poor dependent on private interests more powerful than the government, a situation resembling traditional feudal society. Currently the *top 1 percent* of society own 40 percent of the nation's wealth. The lower 50 percent of the nation have the mean assets worth less than $28,000. The richest 10 percent are worth, on average, 143 times that, or $3.976 million. (emphasis in original)

Neofeudalism emerges across these critics' accounts as an evolving form of social organization dominated by corporations and elites capable of subordinating both individuals and the state to their ends.

Academic use of the term neofeudalism has been relatively limited to left-leaning critics. Harold J. Perkins's 1999 book, *The Third Revolution: Professional Elites in the Modern World*, described neofeudalism as the concentration of the production of goods and services in large corporations (164). Economist Michael Hudson has probably been most vocal with the use of the concept in his extensive economic critiques of the financial crisis and austerity measures in both the United States and Europe. Hudson's work is interesting because it reaches vast nonacademic audiences as his interviews and editorials are posted across a diverse array of Internet sites, including procapitalist sites such as ZeroHedge and Max Keiser. For instance, a 2011 *RT* interview clip with Michael Hudson can be found posted at ZeroHedge under the title "Neofeudalism and the stealing of assets via fire sales—IMF the

Hangman" (Hudson 2011). Noam Chomsky also used the term in his 2003 book *Hegemony or Survival* when he describes the gradual reduction and planned privatization of social-welfare programs (such as Social Security) and education as "reminiscent of feudalism" (120).

Neofeudalism emerges across these diverse accounts as a broad, somewhat ambiguous, signifier that encapsulates for social critics across the political spectrum perceived failures of western democratic capitalism. For some critics, the idea of neofeudalism is a rallying call for reforming capitalism by enforcing ethical, free market operations and unleashing market disciplines. For other critics, neofeudalism is the inevitable outcome of capitalist modes of economic ownership and production. This chapter looks at the idea of neofeudalism as it has been constructed from both romanticized and critical perspectives and turns now to examine areas of agreement across orientations and strategic points of disagreement in the solution frames advocated for neofeudal developments.

NEOFEUDAL TRENDS: MONOPOLY CAPITALISM

Surprisingly there is considerable agreement among those who use the phrase neofeudalism to describe empirical trends in capitalism despite differences in paradigmatic orientation. Those romanticizing capitalism and those critics eschewing it agree that today's market is highly consolidated and, often, monopolistic. There is also agreement that capitalism has evolved into a system with highly polarized access to wealth and opportunity. There is even agreement that elite interests (the "feudal" lords) located in powerful institutions—particularly financial corporations—have special privileges and special legal immunities (Greenwald 2013). Disagreement resides in the solution to neofeudal developments. The romantic procapitalists argue for enforcing antitrust legislation, while unleashing market and legal disciplines to end the "moral hazard" seen as allowing untrammeled wealth and power. In contrast, the critics of capitalism argue that capitalist excess is inevitable without massive and revolutionary reforms.

Left or right, critical or romantic, those who use neofeudalism rhetorically see advanced capitalism as monopolistic. Although the language used to describe the extant system varies—for example, advanced capitalism, corporate capitalism, market fundamentalism, the Washington Consensus—considerable agreement exists on the nature of the problem itself. Ownership of the world's resources, including stock in the powerful industries of banking and energy, tends to be increasingly consolidated. As Barnes's chapter explains, inequality grows, yet government seems ineffectual in preventing financial crises that erode living standards.

Even the most elite capitalists concur that wealth has become consolidated globally and that trend is particularly pervasive in the United States, as illustrated by a Citigroup document dated October 16, 2005, titled, "Equity Strategy: Plutonomy: Buying Luxury, Explaining Global Imbalances." The document describes a world "dividing into two blocs—the plutonomies, where economic growth is powered by and largely consumed by the wealthy few, and the rest" (1). The United States is a "key" plutonomy characterized by "disruptive technology-driven productivity gains, creative financial innovation, capitalist-friendly cooperative governments, an international dimension of immigrants and overseas conquests invigorating wealth creation, the rule of law, and patenting inventions" (1–2). Technology that replaces workers, financial "innovations" capable of accumulating wealth outside of production (e.g., through securities transactions), and through overseas colonial exploitation of resources and labor are the mechanisms whereby wealth is accumulated by the evolving order. Governance by plutonomy is a characteristic feature of the evolving neofeudal order. The data support Citigroup's conclusions.

Globally, in 2006, prior to the Great Recession, 1 percent of the world's population was believed to control 40 percent of the world's wealth (CBCNews 2006; Randerson 2006). One analysis of 43,000 global corporations revealed a core group of 1,318 corporations with interlocking ownerships. The study, conducted by Stefania Vitali, James B. Glattfelder, and Stefano Battiston (2011), used network analysis to explicate the degree of consolidation of corporate control. Their findings revealed unprecedented global consolidation of corporate ownership and control. Each of the core 1,318 corporations had ownership links to two or more other companies, although most were linked to twenty other corporations. The 1,318 corporations owned, through their shares, the majority of blue chip and manufacturing companies, controlling 60 percent of global revenues. Further analysis revealed a tightly linked "super entity" of 147 corporations, mainly in finance, with interconnected ownership. Consequently, less than 1 percent of corporations essentially controlled 40 percent of the entire network. Furthermore, the study found that 734 "top holders of stock accumulate 80 percent of the control over the value of all TNCs." The authors conclude: "this means that network control is much more unequally distributed than wealth. In particular, the top ranked actors hold a control ten times bigger than what could be expected based on their wealth" (36).

Household ownership of wealth in the United States echoes the consolidation found in the network study. The top 20 percent of US households owns 89 percent of all equities (Byron and Talley 2011). The top 0.1 percent of the US population, about 315,000 individuals, receives half of all capital gains on the sale of shares or property and these gains constitute 60 percent of the total income made by the Forbes 400 (Lenzner 2011). US wealth consolidation grew during the Great Recession as most households lost, on average, 40 percent of their wealth from 2007 to 2010, according to the US Federal Reserve (Mui 2012). Yet the assets of the wealthiest Americans were less affected and even grew for the wealthiest individuals. In the "recovery" of 2009–2010, the top 1 percent of US income earners captured 93 percent of the income growth.

Elite groups controlling these resources are often described within the United States as the "1 percent" but this group is clearly global. Janine R. Wedel (2009) argues in *Shadow Elite: How the World's New Power Brokers Undermine Democracy, Government, and the Free Market* that elite groups are deliberately "upending rules and authority" in order "to wield high-level power and influence" (ix). In other words, Wedel sees monopolization of wealth and power as a deliberate strategy pursued by elite groups. Surprisingly, even some procapitalist romantics, like Max Keiser and Stacy Herbert, agree that elite groups have particularly benefited from "austerity" and "structural adjustment" programs as they have served as efficacious macroeconomic policies for shifting wealth upwards since the late 1980s. Structural adjustment programs, not unlike those that were imposed upon the developing world in the 1980s, are now being imposed upon advanced western economies, such as the United States, Ireland, Greece, Spain, and countries within Eastern Europe, as politicians call for austerity in the wake of spiking government deficits caused by bailouts to the financial sector. Structural adjustment programs—including privatization, cuts in social spending, and deregulation—effectively consolidate assets as wealthy interests are able to purchase assets at fire sales as a result of privatization and foreclosures.

The financial crisis and its aftermath have illustrated for both critics and romantics the empirical realities of an evolving system that offers few economic opportunities for living wages for the majority of the population, particularly in the US context, which will be examined here. First, romantics and critics agree that deregulation of financial markets was responsible for the crisis and for enabling unprecedented growth of financial power, primarily consolidated in a few very large corporations. Both critics and romantics agree that deregulation was a deliberate strategy pursued by elite interests in the United States. Finally, both critics and romantics agree that the policies used to manage the crisis and its aftermath benefit elite interests and have further consolidated capitalism in the hands of a few. It's helpful to examine these arguments in the context of the conditions of possibility for the financial crisis.

Deregulation was indeed deliberately pursued by financial interests and was promoted by both US Democrats and Republicans. The repeal of Glass Steagall by the Graham-Bleach-Bliley Act of 1996 under President Clinton broke down barriers between investment and retail banking while the Commodities Futures Modernization Act of 2000 deregulated derivatives trading.

These policies were designed by and significantly benefited the financial industry. In contrast, these policies hurt many US manufacturers by driving up the US dollar, making manufactured products less competitive on price.

Kevin Phillips (2006) claims that growing economic inequality coincided with the rise of finance as the dominant economic sector, beginning in 1974. This is the same time period cited by other observers as ushering in a series of neoliberal reforms that deregulated trade and labor, while failing to enforce antitrust laws (Nadesan 2008). Global finance grew in power during this period relative to other industries, especially within the United States. Within the United States, financial-sector profits exceeded those of manufacturing by the mid-1990s; by 2004, financial firms commanded nearly 40 percent of all US profits, primarily by managing, packaging, and trading debt and credit instruments and managing debt-related corporate restructuring (Phillips 2006, 266). US banks grew to dominate their domestic economies: by 2010, six US banks, held assets in excess of 63 percent of the US Gross Domestic Profit (Moyers 2010). Bryan, Martin, and Rafferty (2009) claim there is no direct historical equivalent for this new form of financialization, not simply because of the size of financial institutions, but also because securitization and financial derivatives "*are transforming capital accumulation*" in ways unimaginable by Marx and the classical economists (my italics, 459). Contemporary financialization requires little labor to produce value (Nadesan 2011).

US economic growth became dependent upon the extension of credit (i.e., debt) as wages alone were insufficient for producing aggregate demand sufficient to ensure growth. As manufacturing faded in the 1990s, housing and commercial real estate development became more important forces of economic growth. Cheap and readily available credit was critical for the expansion of the construction industry. Debt contributed to short-term aggregate demand and produced revenue for financial services through fees, interest, and the creation of debt-based investment products. Consequently, the US economy became dependent upon the endless production and circulation of credit and credit backed financial instruments. Debt creation became a main engine of growth. Lenders were incentivized to extend credit because they quickly packaged and then sold the debt, primarily to institutional investors, such as pension funds. Accordingly, the *New York Times* explains how banks make money through "securitization," a process of bundling debt, focusing on mortgage-backed debt:

> Banks make their money from taking the mortgages and bundling them into bonds that they then sell to investors, like pensions and mutual funds. The higher the mortgage rate paid by homeowners and the lower the interest paid on the bonds, the bigger the profit for the bank. . . . The mortgage industry has a yardstick for measuring the size of those profits. It compares the mortgage

rates paid by borrowers and the interest rate on the mortgage bond—a difference known in the industry as the spread. (Eavis 2012, A1)

By packaging mortgages into bonds, banks created financial products whose sales exceeded the interest that the banks would have received on the loans had they been held. This model also reduced the banks risk of default.

The wealth created through the fees, sales, and interest accumulation tied to securitization of debt—and the derivatives derived from securitized debt—outstripped most all forms of value creation in the economy. Derivatives are types of securities that derive their value from the "value of another asset that varies in price" (Gelderblom and Jonker 2005, 191). Innovative new derivative forms emerged from new computing technologies and from novel mathematical algorithms for measuring and predicting risk in the early twenty-first century. Therefore, although derivatives such as futures have been around for centuries, the reification and quantification of risk enabled by computerization expanded global derivatives products and trading and also enabled creation of ever more abstract derivatives based in bundled securities, such as collateralized debt obligations (CDOs). CDOs are essentially risk-based products derived from the calculations of defaults for mortgage-backed securities (Tavakoli n.d.). The Commodities Futures Modernization Act of 2001 deregulated derivatives, guaranteeing growth. By 2006, the CDO market was valued at $4.7 trillion (Prins 2011, 55; Prins and Ugrin 2010). Indeed, in 2006 alone, "there were $US550 billion of 'collateralised debt obligations' issued" (Uren 2008).

Informed and often elite speculators bet on the likelihood of CDO default using credit default swaps. Credit default swaps (CDS) were invented in 1997 by JP Morgan Chase's Blythe Masters. CDSs were (and continue to be) sold by insurance companies to investment and commercial banks, if equipped with enough cash, as documented by Michael Lewis (2011) in *The Big Short* (104–136). They "insure" risky investments, often in excess of the value of the underlying insured investment. Before the crisis, CDSs were unregulated and companies that issued them typically failed to hold adequate reserves (collateral) against outstanding contracts (Levisohn 2008). American Insurance General (AIG) sold credit default swaps to the large investment and commercial banks, among other buyers, on securities (particularly CDOs) derived from mortgages. For the most sophisticated players, the risk of default on the debts underlying the securities was hedged by purchasing these credit default swaps from insurers, such as AIG. Indeed, betting on debt default using a credit default swap could be more profitable than holding and trading intact debt-based securities. Credit default swaps are a derivative that succeeds with financial volatility. By 2008, the market for credit default swaps was valued at $45.5 trillion (Prins 2011, 60).

Perhaps the most glaring example of deliberate financial fraud by an informed elite group can be found in the example of Abacus, created by Goldman Sachs employee Fabrice Tourre and the hedge fund Paulson and Co. in 2007 (Clark 2010a, 2010b). Abacus consisted of synthetic collateralized debt obligations selected and packaged by Tourre and Paulson that Goldman sold to its clients, while assuring them that the underlying mortgages were unlikely to default. Meanwhile, Paulson and Co. shorted (i.e., bet against) Abacus by purchasing credit default swaps from the Royal Bank of Scotland, which incurred a $840 million liability from backstopping the hedge funds deal (Goldfarb and Tse 2010, A1). The credit default swaps would pay out to Paulson and Co. when defaults occurred in Abacus's underlying securities.

Goldman told clients Paulson and Co. was involved in Abacus, but failed to mention that Paulson was *betting against* the Abacus CDOs Goldman was pushing. ACA Financial Guarantee Corp filed suit against Goldman in 2011 for deliberately misleading the company about the Paulson's investment in Abacus. Goldman allegedly told ACA that Paulson and Co. (one of Goldman's clients) "was betting on a deal, when in fact Paulson was betting against it" (Chung 2013, C3). Goldman claims it didn't mislead ACA and other investors, despite incriminating evidence that surfaced in the form of Fabrice Tourre's e-mails to his girlfriend. In these e-mails, Tourre referred to himself as "fabulous Fab" and described creating "Frankenstein" products that were nothing more than "pure intellectual masturbation" sold to naive widows and orphans (Clark 2010b).

Despite blatant evidence of intent to deceive, the US Securities and Exchange Commission failed to seek criminal charges against Goldman (Albergotti and Rappaport 2012). Instead, Goldman settled a civil fraud suit by paying $550 million. Journalist gadfly and would-be reformer Matt Taibbi (2013) recently penned an indignant letter about the government's failure to right the wrongs of Wall Street's many transgressions, titled, "The federal rescue of Wall Street didn't fix the economy—it created a permanent bailout state based on a Ponzi-like confidence scheme. And the worst may be yet to come." Taibbi also expresses outrage shared by both romantics and critics over the consolidation of wealth that has resulted from the financial crisis.

Emerging in the aftermath of the global financial crisis that began in late 2007 is a world order dominated by a few governments and corporations that have unprecedented control over global resources. Government prioritization of corporate interests over public welfare during the financial crisis was reflected in the lopsided allocation of funds to banks, including the bailout of investment banks that should not have been eligible for relief, and the unlimited backstopping of AIG's credit default swaps while average Americans, who saw work hours and income collapse, received little to no support. During the height of the great financial crisis, secret Federal Reserve loans to the biggest banks totaling $7.7 trillion enabled them to reap $13 billion in profits (Ivry, Keoun, and Kuntz 2011). US homeowners, who faced around $6.5 million in delinquent and foreclosed mortgages, saw little-to-no relief (Keoun and Kuntz 2011).

In 2009, Graham Bowley reported in the *New York Times* that the federal financial "bailout helps fuel a new era of Wall Street wealth" enabling "hefty bonuses" to corporate Wall Street executives (Bowley 2009). Goldman Sachs alone received $70 billion in combined funds from Troubled Asset Relief Program (TARP), the Federal Reserve, AIG, and the Federal Deposit Insurance Corporation (FDIC), although it was not FDIC insured (Ratigan 2009). The bailouts helped the banks grow bigger by allowing them to acquire distressed assets during the turmoil of the recession. As of 2010, six US banks, held assets in excess of 63 percent of the US Gross Domestic Profit (Moyers, Johnson, and Kwak 2010). Perhaps most telling, the US government largely declined to prosecute those financial agents responsible for the crisis within these monopolists, many of which profited from rampant foreclosure fraud in the wake of the crisis. Reflecting on these data, Economist Simon Johnson observed: "The US increasingly displays characteristics that we have seen many times in middle-income 'emerging markets'—new dimensions of vast inequality, forms of financial instability that benefit the best connected, and consistently easy credit for the privileged" (Johnson 2009).

Although federal stimulus helped states plug education and health care spending in 2008 and 2009, US states began massive public sector cuts to education, social-welfare and health spending, and infrastructure maintenance in 2010 (Krugman 2010; Miller and Feld 2010). Growing inequality stifled post-recession recovery. While US corporate profits reached unprecedented levels by 2012, both in absolute dollars and as a share of the economy, unemployment reached the highest level since the Great Depression (Blodget 2011). Over one half (55 percent) of Americans' wages were affected in the forms of job layoffs, wage and hour cut backs, and unpaid furloughs during the recession years of 2007 to 2009. Thirty-two percent of Americans reported unemployment during that period. On average, US citizens lost 20 percent of their household wealth from 2007 to 2009 (Pew Research Center 2010). Data published in 2011 indicate that 14 percent, or one in six Americans, lives below the official poverty threshold (Fox Piven 2011). The losses of household wealth, wages, and benefits are ongoing and point to the growing impoverishment of the nation at the same time that the federal government is proposing widespread cuts in social spending, particularly in the area of health (but not military spending or financial bailouts) (McKinnon 2010). In contrast to the eroding status of the liberal economic subject of "Main Street," the economic subject of might—the modern transnational corporation—grew in power and influence during the great economic contraction.

Neofeudalism is used as a powerful rhetorical trope by those outraged by these financial crimes and the failure of government to redress them. For example in the case of Goldman Sachs, the romantic blogger emptywheel (2012) writes in the post, "The Goldman Sachs Department of Justice Would Like to Apologize to Mr. Blankfein for the Inconvenience" that the Department of Justice has become a powerless entity within the "neofeudal land." emptywheel declares, the "DOJ Has Become Just another Cog in the Machine Slowly Turning Our Great Democracy into a NeoFeudal Land."

Romantics and critics see neofeudal control as a global phenomenon. For example, the romantic-leaning well-trafficked site, *Naked Capitalism*, uses the term to criticize Eurozone efforts to deal with Eurozone bank liquidity problems caused by exposure to derivatives in this blog post: "Eurobanks' Latest Scheme to Escape the Pain of Recapitalization" (2012):

> . . . officialdom is completely unwilling to stand up to continued banking industry looting and will allow schemes almost certain to create the need for even bigger bailouts to be foisted on ordinary citizens. This is neofeudalism wrapped in the mantle of modern financial technology.

Naked Capitalism sees the move by regulators to fix insolvency caused by derivatives exposure with banking consolidation as further entrenching the neofeudal economic order of reigning too-big-to-fail oligarchs.

As illustrated by these examples, those who use the term neofeudalism have little faith in government reforms because of the institutional power of elite groups and because of the regulatory capture of key government agencies. For example, a blogger named masaccio (2012) at the left-leaning site Firedoglake illustrates critics' cynicism toward those "progressives" who still hold out the possibility for government reform by citing Chris Hedges' description of neofeudalism. masaccio begins by critiquing "liberals": "Liberals have been neutered by capitalism. Once upon a time, they spoke of Malefactors of Great Wealth. They said that these morally bankrupt jackals were ruining people's lives. Nowadays, liberals just don't talk like that." masaccio then quotes Hedges' explanation of how purges against more radical elements enabled slippage toward "corporate neofeudalism."

In sum, neofeudalism is a signifier used by romantics and critics who examine the "deep politics" of a world order seen as dominated by entrenched elite interests impervious to the law. Their critiques are primarily, albeit not exclusively, aimed at the financial order of "too big to fail" banks able to extract wealth through deceptive and often fraudulent financial products such as derivatives. Proof of their imperviousness to law and order is illustrated by lack of criminal prosecution for clear fraud as illustrated by Abacus, the Libor Scandal, MF Global, and other financial crimes.

OWS AND NEOFEUDALISM

The Occupy Wall Street movement has operated as a loosely unified coalition of individuals reflecting a variety of viewpoints, united primarily by their opposition to a perceived degradation of the American political and economic systems. The participatory nature of the movement enables heterogeneity in worldviews among its membership. Examples can be found of both romantic and critical worldviews. Interestingly, those who hold more revolutionary views within OWS are more likely to use the term neofeudalism.

Many within OWS aim to reform capitalism using government. These individuals believe that capitalism is reformable and that government has the capacity to act in the public interest. Within this group there are divergences in worldviews: Some are Keynesian and some yearn for a reinvigorated producers' republic, otherwise romantically known as "Main Street." Across subtleties in vision, these groups aim for regulatory reforms. For example, the preliminary comments, in "What Needs to Change" at the beginning of Part II in *This Changes Everything: Occupy Wall Street and the 99 Percent Movement* (Van Gelder and the staff of *YES!* magazine 2011), focus on redesigning the banking system toward public banking, progressive tax shifts, and living-wage jobs. These are Keynesian measures designed to engineer demand by reducing inequality through regulation, taxation, and government infrastructure (the latter of which now extended to include banking). David Korten's chapter in the book titled, *Six Ways to Liberate Main Street from Wall Street* (2011), signifies a romanticized mythos of a main street "market" populated by bustling small and midsized entrepreneurs. The use of Main Street conveys yearning for a simpler and purportedly more moral capitalism. These two examples show traces of romantic yearnings as well as more pragmatic Keynesian program proposals. These discourses are not likely to linger on signifiers such as neofeudalism.

Where neofeudalism does show up in the OWS movement is among more radical critics of capitalism. For example, Occupy Denver held a March against Neo Feudalism in July 2012:

> Occupy Denver's "march against neo feudalism" was a smashing success. Despite torrential rainfall occupiers slowly gathered in La Alma Park as the rain gave way. La Alma's radical history in the 60s found itself in good company with Occupiers, Anons, anti-capitalists, disenfranchised democrats and everyone else who wanted to thumb their nose at the empire. (*OccupyDenver.org* 2012)

Colorado Indymedia (2012) covers Occupy Denver's March against Neo Feudalism with the subtitle "Revenge of the Wage Slave" in a piece that begins with Karl Marx and ends with a rhetorically compelling call to action:

> We don't want to end up like communist China or communist Russia, we want to learn from the lessons of history so as to not repeat them. We say down with feudalism. Down with exploitation. Another world is possible. Other worlds ARE possible. With all the means of technology at our disposal, is this really all we are capable of?

The critical left still has voice and activist presence and has found in OWS a way to reach a broader audience.

The critical left within OWS is using the term neofeudalism, but it's unlikely they believe public banking, progressive taxation, and greater wage controls will alone resolve slippage towards neofeudalism. The critical left is also less certain about the state's capacities for implementing and enforcing reforms given its historical role in sanctioning the economic exploitation of workers, while relying on them for cannon fodder for imperialistic undertakings. The hard left is cynical about the state's willingness to operate cooperatively and transparently and so it may be this component of OWS most likely to confront state repression. It is clear from search results that neofeudalism has informed at least some critiques of repressive policing used against OWS demonstrators.

Among the most circulated images of police brutality were those of pepper-spraying police at the University of California, Davis. Images of peaceful and prone students being assaulted by police with weapons-grade pepper spray certainly demonstrated fascistic impulses. Although college students demonstrating on campus got the limelight, many other OWS demonstrations were also subject to police brutality. Neofeudalism seems an apt signifier for expressing OWS outrage against this treatment. In May of 2012, OWS in New York filed a lawsuit against the city of New York and JPMorgan Chase and Co. for violating demonstrators' civil liberties, as explained by David Pederson (2012) in his "Home of the Bewildered Serf and Land of the Feudal Lords" published in the *Huffington Post*:

> First, Occupy Wall Street (OWS) filed a *lawsuit* against the City of New York and JPMorgan Chase and Co. Brookfield Office Properties and Mayor Michael Bloomberg are also defendants in the suit. The complaints of the suit are simple and well documented: the New York Police Department made false arrests, used excessive force and violated free speech rights of protesters and journalists. OWS is firing a salvo for America's bewildered serfs against their feudal lords.

A definite kind of neo-"feudalism" can be found in this article. This evocative imagery may serve rhetorically to establish OWS as a bastion of democracy in the context of societal degradation. Still, as illustrated by this lawsuit, OWS is operating within a reformist frame by virtue of its very reliance on legal litigation.

Unfortunately, OWS belief in procedural justice within the extant system may slow its capacity to respond to unanticipated, unilateral state repression. The reasons for decline in OWS visibility and demonstrations is subject to much dispute, but one important explanation circulating meme-like across the Internet concerns the use of repressive force by local and national authorities to suppress dissent. Naomi Wolf (2011) described the excessive use of force against the demonstrators in the *Guardian*:

> US citizens of all political persuasions are still reeling from images of unparalleled police brutality in a *coordinated crackdown against peaceful OWS protesters in cities across the nation this past week*. An elderly woman was pepper-sprayed in the face; the scene of unresisting, supine students at UC Davis being pepper-sprayed by phalanxes of riot police went viral online; images proliferated of young women—targeted seemingly for their gender—screaming, dragged by the hair by police in riot gear; and the pictures of a young man, stunned and bleeding profusely from the head, emerged in the record of the middle-of-the-night clearing of Zuccotti Park. (emphasis mine)

Documents revealed through a Freedom of Information Act (FOIA) request reveal that the FBI had been helping organize nationwide crackdowns. The Partnership for Civil Justice (2012) published their investigation of the federally organized crackdown in December of 2012 by the FBI, which targeted OWS:

> FBI documents just obtained by the Partnership for Civil Justice Fund (PCJF) pursuant to the PCJF's Freedom of Information Act demands reveal that from its inception, the FBI treated the Occupy movement as a potential criminal and terrorist threat even though the agency acknowledges in documents that organizers explicitly called for peaceful protest and did "not condone the use of violence" at occupy protests.
>
> The PCJF has obtained heavily redacted documents showing that FBI offices and agents around the country were in high gear conducting surveillance against the movement even as early as August 2011, a month prior to the establishment of the OWS encampment in Zuccotti Park and other Occupy actions around the country.

The documents reveal that the FBI deployed "campus liaison" teams to sixteen separate US universities. Were they responsible for the pepper-spraying of peacefully demonstrating students?

The US federal government has been considering how to confront domestic unrest for some years now. In 2009, the American Civil Liberties Union challenged Department of Defense training material given to local police around the country that defined constitutionally guaranteed and lawful demonstrations as low-level terrorism (ACLU 2009). Reformists within OWS, particularly of the Keynesian variety, may have difficulty reconciling their more idealized notions of state operations with the mechanics of the expansion of the surveillance-security state.

The paranoid state has been studied quite extensively by civil libertarians, many of whom continue to hold faith in the capabilities of free markets. Max Keiser and the popular center-right figure, Alex Jones, offer highbrow and lowbrow examples of civil libertarians who, as mentioned previously have played important roles in promoting the online circulation of the neofeudal signifier. These individuals have sympathetically covered OWS, but have not identified themselves with the movement. No doubt civil and economic libertarians distrust the Keynesian elements within OWS, while sympathetic to its concerns.

OWS, NEOFEUDALISM, AND THE FUTURE

The financial crisis crystalized for many the problems of early twenty-first century capitalism. When the engine of continuous debt-creation was stopped for a brief historical period the entire economy collapsed radically. Inequality and declining living standards were revealed when access to credit for the growing underclasses halted. Stories of home foreclosures, homelessness, and rising poverty and hunger then circulated. The resulting level of structural adjustment as states, counties, and cities around the nation shed services and employees exacerbated the impact of the financial crisis, deepening its social impact.

The result was that many in America who had been dismayed by economic developments associated with advanced, neoliberal capitalism found their voice in a variety of venues and across the political spectrum. This chapter has looked at those who use the term neofeudalism to describe growing inequality as a result of oligarchic global capitalism. Those most likely to use the term are at the margins of political discourse in that they are less likely to believe the state is capable of reforming monopoly capitalism. What is particularly interesting is that those who use the term neofeudalism are situated on margins both left and right. For the libertarian right, neofeudalism signifies romanticized longings for an entrepreneurial Main Street market. For the hard left, neofeudalism signifies the inevitable degradation of capitalism itself as a system beyond reform. For these reasons, neofeudalism circulates through, but does not permeate, OWS discourses. The (Keynesian) reformists within the OWS are less likely to rely on an evocative signifier like neofeudalism than those within the movement who link directly to the hard left, for whom progressive taxation and regulatory reform are insufficient for resolving the contradictions of late capitalism.

However, OWS has confronted brutal crackdowns and discovered that these were organized with the assistance of federal authorities, as mentioned above. Demonstrations have become framed by the DOD as low-level terrorism. The pepper-spraying of peaceful, sitting college students demonstrated to the nation that dissent was regarded by US "security" institutions as dangerousness. Some within the OWS may become increasingly impatient with reforms given they are occurring very slowly and have not redressed the institutional power structure of the banking industry, which is now more monolithically consolidated than prior to the crisis. Neofeudalism is a powerful signifier for those who see the political and economic systems as mutually reinforcing oligarchic control of resources and power. The evocative imagery of a neofeudal society populated by dispossessed serfs is rhetorically compelling for diverse audiences with divergent aspirational ideals. Those who use the term neofeudalism express the worldviews and ideals of individuals on both margins of the political spectrum. It will be interesting to watch how trends toward growing impoverishment within the United States, particularly for individuals under age thirty, shape political discourse (e.g., see Pear 2011). It may be that discourses like neofeudalism, now found at the margins, may move into the center.

DISCUSSION QUESTIONS

1. What is meant by "neofeudalism"?
2. Those who use the term neofeudalism have lost faith in both the market and the state. Why?
3. If the libertarian right and the hard left agree on neofeudalism, what don't they agree on?
4. Why is it that we don't see much use of the term neofeudalism by Keynesian OWS members?
5. What political developments might "radicalize" OWS?

II

Local Interpretations of Occupy Portland

It's one thing to live in the camp and have a real experience of what's happening and the networking and the communion and the selflessness. And being up at eight in the morning and seeing the guy in the wheelchair who can't even walk but he's got the dustbin, and the one guy's sweeping and he's moving the dustbin and moving his chair around. I mean, just heart-rendering moment after heart-rendering moment of, like, people being, acting selfless, who wouldn't normally otherwise do that. And then you open the paper and everybody thinks every other camper is Molotov man.—Mac, Occupy Portland Participant, November 2011

Chapter Four

Confessional Tales from the Field

Owning Researcher Methods and Positionality

Renee Guarriello Heath,
Ricardo Munoz, and C. Vail Fletcher

The next three chapters compose case studies that followed Occupy Portland, Oregon, from its first weeks as a camp to its eventual organization as an office and affinity-group structure that continues to exist at the writing of this chapter in the winter of 2013. Van Maanen (1988) wrote that, "Ethnographic writings can and do inform human conduct and judgment in innumerable ways by pointing to the choices and restrictions that reside at the very heart of social life" (1). Indeed the case study of Portland, and the three analyses generated from it, constitute in-depth study of one of the most active Occupy protests in the country outside of Occupy Wall Street (OWS). According to Yin (2009) case studies are valuable for method for understanding complex phenomena. A case study approach allows for in-depth investigation and examination and provides a space for participant voices facilitating the agency of those embedded in the focus of study. Given that one of the goals of this book is to demonstrate how applied communication theory works to teach us something new about social phenomena, these case study analyses are grounded in each contributor's area of expertise. Together they construct a more comprehensive understanding of Occupy Portland specifically, and provoke parallels to the larger Occupy movement generally.

This chapter proceeds with a description of Portland, the camp, and the organizing activities that followed its disbandment. We next describe the participants and the methods used by this team to collect and analyze data. Finally, each of the authors contributing to the Occupy Portland ethnography, and this resulting section of the book, discuss their own experiences and positionality in confessional tales that describe how we approached the study of a social movement instigated by economic inequality (Van Maanen 1988). In these tales we make transparent our own flaws and vulnerabilities in the research process.

THE CAMP AND PARTICIPANTS

Chapters in this part of the book are the result of a collaborative study that began as an ethnographic class project in Renee's qualitative research methods course at the University of Portland when Occupy Portland burst into the public view with the encampment of two downtown spaces, Chapman and Lownsdale parks.[1] Portland, Oregon, a city of nearly 600,000 people, is known for its progressive politics and its commitment to environmentally friendly bicycling. The city hosts a thriving nonprofit industry, which accounts for more than thirteen billion dollars in revenue and 13 percent of the state's private-sector jobs compared to manufacturing, which holds 10 percent of the state's private-sector jobs (Curverwell 2012). It also has a vibrant activist community that attracted would-be Occupy participants even before the movement manifested in late summer of 2011 to work on social problems such as food justice, the environment, and nuclear energy. The mild climate absent of extreme weather has also fueled a large homeless population (see Fletcher chapter 7 in this volume for a fuller discussion). The downtown area has several homeless shelters and is extremely walkable from its positioning on the Willamette River waterfront with its ten bridges that connect the west and east sides of the city. All of these factors came into play in the story of Occupy Portland.

The occupied parks in downtown Portland sat adjacent to one another and for thirty-eight days beginning October 6, 2011 (with a march of ten thousand people), were colorfully adorned with tarps and tents. The rainy fall illuminated the paradox of Columbia Sportswear clothing and gear rampant in a movement committed to draw attention to economic disparities. The camp became an eclectic home for the houseless, the anarchists, the unemployed, those "waiting for a movement," and the inspired. An outdoor kitchen served 1,500 meals to nearly six hundred campers daily at the camp's peak operation (Meachum, 2012, October, 6). A medic tent, an information booth, a library, and an art tent, were just a few of the structures that were erected in this pseudo camp city. During the early weeks, general assembly—or GA meetings, as they were often called—described in detail in the next chapter, attracted up to one thousand people, drawing participation from campers and supporters who did not camp but wanted somehow to affiliate with the movement. Occupy Portland, deemed the largest Occupy encampment in the country by visiting filmmaker Michael Moore, maintained an early and positive relationship with the city officials, led by a progressive mayor, Sam Adams.

The camp served as an interesting catalyst in the Occupy movement by providing a tangible space from which to organize. In other words, it was much more than a symbolic act of resistance. Initially participants could participate in general assembly meetings twice a day. They could easily congregate at each other's tents. And discussion, education, and organizing flourished. At the same time that the camp facilitated a centralized organizing space, it manifested in a fragmented do-it-yourself (DIY) culture that was a complex and ever-changing structure of committees, caucus, and affinity groups. Ironically, some of the most visible organizers associated with Occupy during the encampment, although they were local fixtures in the movement, did not actually sleep in the rainy parks of Portland. David, a major influence in the organizing of the facilitative processes used in Portland, did not camp after the first week. "I'm a light sleeper," he confessed.[2] He described the romantic spirit of the camp. "I mean this notion that has long been the kind of rallying cry of the global justice movement, another world is possible, that kind of slogan is become manifest in some ways. We, it exists and in some ways, the camps, as problematic as they were, were kind of a manifestation of that. They were their own kind of little microcosms, though there were many problems within them."

Contrary to many of the images portrayed in mainstream media, for participants the camp constituted a space for humanity at its best. In the quote leading into this chapter, Mac, a political science major and college graduate now in his late thirties expressed his frustration with the media's pejorative depictions of the campers. He juxtaposes his story of giving and community as a better representation of camp then the sensationalized stories rampant in the press. But the encampment was rife with contradictions. Perhaps surprising to Occupy participants, the occupation quickly became about meeting the immediate concerns of those without shelter. Elayne, a Canadian activist drawn to Portland for its "thriving food security community," explained that participants struggled to keep the encampment "politically focused" as the camp became consumed with other issues brought about by the inclusion of a growing constituency of homeless persons. She explained many folks were there to have "their basic needs met." Thus the camp met the challenges that more permanent communities face. Almost everyone interviewed in this project generously owned the problems of houselessness (a term preferred by some and used by the authors in this text), uncared-for mental illness, and drug abuse as symptomatic of the very economic disparities to which the movement drew attention. Allen explained,

> I think a lot of us felt that having these, for example, there were some drug issues or some alcohol issues that the camp kinda helped bring to the forefront that society does have this problem. And so we weren't, I guess people weren't really angry at the fact that there were drug addicts there but the fact that the situation of society allowed that to happen.

Accordingly, Occupy participants struggled with their newfound responsibility. Many participants admitted, "we're not mental health professionals." Their time in camp began to reflect the growing tensions pulling them toward immediate social needs in the midst of a political act of resistance. Elayne explained,

> Everyday there was [sic] new problems to report and so it really threw us off and most of the energy went from trying to really, you know, people were like, "What does Occupy want?" and like, we were trying to respond to the question about where we put poop.

These material challenges would fuel the city's argument for the undoing of the camp (see an analysis of the mayor's speeches in mcclellan's chapter 9).

Divisions among participants were fueled by the DIY culture. For example, there was the immediate problem of what to do about monetary donations that were coming into the camp from the greater community. In an early, perhaps well-intentioned but naïve effort, an individual volunteered to collect and deposit money on behalf of Occupy Portland and hold it in a PayPal account. This created all sorts of suspicion, cultivated distrust, and led to wild rumors that were repeated to us in the interview process in various versions. Too quickly, the well-intentioned DIYer realized (with legal advice) that without the protections granted by a nonprofit designation, this individual would be paying personal taxes on all donations made to Occupy. However, while this drama unfolded, strong resistance was voiced regarding the efforts to organize into anything that resembled the corporate structures that the movement resisted. Jake, a twenty-something, self-identified anarchist, in an interview conducted the second week of the encampment complained, "they [other Occupy campers] actually have an economics committee now." Later he said incredulously, "You know the name's [Occupy Portland] copyrighted now. Like copyrighted into everything; there's a corporation being created." Because the movement provided little direction or formalized structure, and was sensitive to honor the autonomy of others, the DIY culture was bound to surface conflicts and contradictions of vision.

As the camp droned on, and press coverage tended toward the sensational and arguable—a drug overdose, physical confrontation with the police, deterioration of the city grounds—general public and city support waned. However, despite what appeared to be a general fatigue with Occupy, at least according to the media (see Lovejoy and Brynteson chapter 8 in this volume for more on Portland's media coverage), the final night of the encampment drew by some accounts ten thousand supporters in a night of celebration, festivities, and music.

The eventual disbandment of the camp thirty-eight days after its commencement once again spurred fragmentation, in which case the need and desire for space as a way of facilitating the movement manifested in the leasing of an office at St. Francis Catholic Church. Questions arose as to how authentic the Occupy movement could be if they were now *renting* as opposed to *occupying* space and splinters among the worldviews of participants were revealed as political reformers tended toward structure and organization, and those with anarchist identities tended to distrust the creation of newly formed governance structures.

In the weeks that followed the campers' eviction, Occupy suffered heavy criticism in the media for the destruction of the two parks with damages alleged to reach $85,850 by the Portland Parks Bureau (Theriault 2011). The general assemblies, with attendance in the hundreds, had waned but an incredible infrastructure lay in its wake. By some accounts (even Occupy participants have failed to come up with an accurate mapping or count of their subgroups), more than one hundred committees or affinity groups flourished. Some of the committees were no longer necessary such as those associated with foci specific to the camp (the kitchen, peace and safety, etc.). But new affinity groups aimed at more specific issues such as healthcare, feminism, and political action remained a vital and still vibrant part of the Occupy infrastructure.

Occupy activism continues at this writing. Marchers were controversially sprayed with pepper spray by Portland police in November 2012. And some activists argue the movement is larger now than it was in its first year due to its social media and affinity group infrastructure (see similar claims regarding Occupy Wall Street in Tewksbury's chapter 10 in this volume). Its more ambiguous form is apparent in the data that follows as some participants refer to it in past tense (primarily referring to the camp) and others still consider Occupy a flourishing movement. We decided not to edit the tense used by our participants as their interpretation tells a more accurate if not complex story.

METHODS

Data for this study were gathered from the first week of the camp, October 2011, to winter of 2013. A team of trained researchers including three professors, two graduate students, and three undergraduates visited the field, writing copious fieldnotes, observing and interviewing Occupy participants. This launched a unique ethnographic project that allowed us to witness the Portland movement from its physical inception to present day. Once the camps closed, three researchers, Renee, Ricardo, and Vail, continued to attend general assembly and other meetings. For more than one year, our team had a weekly presence among Occupy activists as observers, participants, and interviewers. Each of the primary researchers, Renee, Ricardo, and Vail participated to various degrees in the movement (Lindlof and Taylor 2011). Renee and Vail were primarily observer-as-participants—their principal activity was observation with occasional interaction with participants, such as when they marched with participants in rallies (147). Renee and Vail also conducted the majority of the formal interviews. Ricardo, on the other hand, evolved from an observer-as-participant during the encampment, to a complete participant (145) when he joined the facilitation team after the camp's disbandment.

Data Collection

We initially met, observed, and interviewed participants by visiting the Occupy Portland campsites. Participants in our study ranged in age from eighteen to sixty-five and we were careful only to interview people who were at least eighteen years of age to fulfill our obligation to the Institutional Review Board (IRB) that approved our study. Participants were asked whether they affiliated with a political party. Many participants rejected affiliations to traditional parties and identified as humanitarian, communitarian, or anarchists. Some rejected labeling themselves at all. Indeed, when we began the study we hoped to track participants' demographic data—at least those whom we interviewed—so that we could later try to make sense of, and answer the question, "Who was the average Occupy participant?" Looking back we now realize that there was and is not an average profile of participants, generally speaking. The scope of involvement was too wide to capture an average participant—unless we could authentically attend and observe the dispersed network of Occupy activities—a physical impossibility as many Occupy participants were not even aware of some of the other Occupy activities we learned of through the interviewing process. These included reading groups, alternative living arrangements, and cross-country journeys to other Occupy sites and rallies. This does not even include the dispersed social media network of participants. And it would be inauthentic to collect data solely from the general assemblies (our original intent) because many participants did not attend these meetings (and we did not want to contribute to the plethora of mediated stereotypes already in existence). Perhaps more importantly, we asked ourselves how we could justify finding a typical participant in a movement that's very fabric resisted generalizations. Thus we abandon this question as the study progressed, accepting that our data was incomplete and fragmented, as is the movement.

Most of our interviews happened on location, beginning at the camps and then following the movement into the more formalized indoor location at St. Francis church, or in local coffee shops. We often interviewed at rallies and general assembly meetings, and asked participants to recommend other participants. Because we used a snowball style of sampling after the camps disassembled, we frequently interviewed people who were seen as visible "leaders" (our word not theirs) in the movement. They ranged from students to medical professionals and paid union activists. During the encampment and after we also interviewed people who identified themselves as houseless, rejecting the term homeless as it conjures notions that lacking a house means lacking a sense of place, friends, and other images of what "home" means. Our data did resemble some of the data collected from the Occupy Wall Street movement by Milkman, Luce, and Lewis (2012), specifically many of our participants (a) acknowledged that they were carrying significant debt, often as a result of educational achievement; (b) were underemployed and/or had recently experienced a layoff; (c) had skepticism about the current political system's ability to be used to effectively create systemic change; and (d) felt the movement was connected to a larger, global unrest over inequality. Toward the end of our data collection in the winter of 2013, participants began recommending that we interview people we had already interviewed, thus we felt confident we had captured a core group of active participants in our data.

More than seventy-five participants were interviewed either informally or formally during the course of this project. Interviews were originally conducted spontaneously in the encampment based on participant willingness to talk to a researcher and notes were taken, or if granted permission, interviews were audio-recorded. According to our IRB approval we did not collect consent forms so as not to accumulate any record of participant names that could eventually be subpoenaed. This was a deliberate decision as many of the people interviewed may have potentially been involved in illegal trespassing, resisting arrest, or in rare cases, destruction of property. With verbal participant consent we audiotaped and later transcribed forty-eight formal interviews. Participants were assigned pseudonyms. Participants who figure significantly in these analyses were later contacted again to give feedback on our manuscripts and provide written approval to utilize their insights. Additionally, three panels totaling eleven participants took place at the University of Portland, where interviews were conducted in conjunction with an audience of students, faculty, and community members. These panels were videotaped and transcribed. Also included in these data is a transcribed meeting in which case twelve Occupy facilitators, including Ricardo, reflected on their own processes. Occupy participants—not the researchers—organized this meeting, referred to in this book as the *facilitators' debrief*.

The interview protocol loosely attended to constructs of consensus, identity, organizing, and leadership. We employed an ethnographic style, defined as a conversational style of interviewing (Lindlof and Taylor 2011, 176). The interview format was loose enough to allow interviewees to take the conversation in relevant directions based on a core set of questions including: How did you become a part of this movement? Why? What are you trying to accomplish? What has been accomplished? What have been the highs and lows/strengths and weaknesses of the movement? What committees or affinity groups do you belong to? How do you participate? What do you wish we would ask you? Additionally, several questions attended to process issues associated with the movement. We asked participants to describe and evaluate their decision-making processes and discuss their own philosophies of leadership as it pertained to Occupy. Informal interviews could be as short as a few minutes. Formal interviews ranged from one to two hours, with the average interview lasting about one hour and twenty minutes.

Data were made available on a secured website that allowed researchers to pool raw records. In addition, textual data such as Occupy pamphlets, booklets, articles, etc., were added to the website randomly. Occupy Portland also did an excellent job of archiving its own data. Livestream of meetings, and notes from general assemblies and spokescouncil meetings were available to the researchers. Local interviews with Occupy participants were archived on the radio station KBOO.

Analyses of Data

The abundance of data and the number of researchers gathering data both fostered and hindered analysis. Because of the ubiquitous use of social media and technologies, Occupy data is seemingly unending and unwieldy, with data being collected across numerous social science and humanities fields, and new data being added with regularity to countless local and national Occupy data listservs (google "Occupy Data" for a sample of what has become available). For example, Berkeley Journal of Sociology (2013) has acted as an online hub to many recent interdisciplinary perspectives on differing aspects of the movement. While Renee and Vail were able to collaborate on their analyses, because of Ricardo's embedded presence, and because he was no longer physically in Portland during the peak of the writing period, he reduced data using an entirely different method. First we describe the Spradley (1980) approach used by Renee and Vail. We then describe how Ricardo used a phenomenological (Van Manen 1990) approach to arrive at his themes.

Renee and Vail initiated their analyses at the level of participant voice. Meaning, they first transcribed and coded *interviews*. Initially they worked together to initiate the coding process. They first printed and read all the fieldnotes and transcribed interviews several times. They then separately coded the interview documents for emergent categories such as "leadership," "co-opting the general assembly," and "visions for Occupy" beginning with the interview data. Next data were categorized using Spradley's (1980) domain analysis. Domain analysis uses specified roots that aid in the researchers' interpretation of the data, such as attitudes of, reasons for, etc. Some of the domains included "reasons for Occupy," "ways of conducting meetings," and "attitudes of participants." These domains were later used to categorize other data such as fieldnotes. Textual data, such as training manuals, were later used to supplement established domains.

In order to arrive at the claims detailed in the forthcoming chapters, they independently organized the domain categories around their *own research questions*. For example, Renee's chapter looked specifically at the data relevant to consensus processes and participative decision-making, while Vail considered identity and intersectionality. The data presented in the chapters that follow were also further analyzed as to how they pertained to romantic, functional, and critical interpretations of Occupy. For example, Renee found in the domain of "attitudes of participants" that the anarchist attitude could also be understood as a romantic understanding of democratic processes. Thus a subsequent collapsing of data occurred around Trujillo's (1992) romantic, functional, and critical lenses.

Ricardo reduced data using a very different approach as he had the benefit of being immersed in the project as a participant. He conducted a process of hermeneutic phenomenology throughout his field work: a research attitude that aims to "transform lived experience into a textual representation of its essence—in such a way that the effect of the text is at once a reflexive reliving and a reflective appropriation of something meaningful" (Van Manen 1990, 36). Doing phenomenological research is an act of writing and rewriting—translating the life of the scene into speech in a continuous process of relating the specifics of the scene with the larger textual world surrounding a phenomenon. Ricardo consistently wrote and reflected on fieldnotes and consulted the activist-related literature. He learned facilitation by doing, e-mailed facilitation team members with meeting observations, engaged in casual discussions, and generally engaged in the lived experience of being a member of Occupy Portland. This engagement was essentially hermeneutic: The meaning of a produced text is not fixed but is rather "an opinion or a possibility that one brings into play and puts at risk" (Gadamer 1975, 390), with each iteration being a refinement towards an understanding of the scene as new questions arise from earlier reflection. Ricardo revisited earlier texts he wrote and modified them to account for deeper understandings gained in the process. Prior writing about a phenomenon contributed to the understanding of the scene in which he engaged in the production of texts (Gadamer 1975). Thus existing texts on activism and anarchism "to which the phenomenologist may turn to increase practical insights" (Van Manen 1990, 70) contributed to the understanding. Themes that resulted from this process were grouped in relation to these prior texts that allowed a fusion of the present with the past (Gadamer 1975) as the understanding of the phenomenon evolved.

Thus, each author in this section of the book had the freedom to reduce data differently and will briefly discuss this in the subsequent chapters. To the extent that we could, we have leaned heavily on participants' own words to aid in our understanding of Occupy.

CONFESSIONAL TALES

We decided to approach this chapter with confessional tales as a method for making the research process and our own positionality transparent. Van Maanen (1988) argued the confessional tale reveals the fieldworker's rapport and sensitive contact with others in the world. We have written these tales in response to the Occupy movement's own commitment to transparency, and our commitment to more fairly distribute power in the research process (Dempsey 2010). In the confessional tale, concrete cultural particulars that baffle the fieldworker are revealed. Confessional tales also accomplish other tasks as they present the fieldworker's point of view and make public the fieldwork process. They may potentially account for some if not most of these things: missing data, incompleteness, blind spots, and various other obscurities; preconceived understanding and own interests in studying the scene; modes of entry into site; sustained participation or presence; responses of others on the scene to the researcher's presence; the nature of relationship with informants; and modes of data collection, storage, retrieval, and analysis (Van Maanen 1988, 73–81). Because we were involved in different ways in the collection of data, the challenges and opportunities of this project are detailed next in our own narrative tales.

Renee's Tale

I am committed to acknowledging our own positions of privilege and worldviews that affected how we approached this research, yet I find it awkward to write this section. However, Van Maanen (1988) assures me that my confessional tale is not alone in its "highly personalized style and self-absorbed mandate" (73). My own research and politics align well with the broader concerns of Occupy especially in relation to a growing divide among the wealthy and the poor stemming largely from corporate power and influence. I dragged my husband and three children to march among thousands in one of the first large rallies of Occupy Portland. I teach classes on environmental collaboration and diversity, and have a nonacademic history in the nonprofit world working on behalf of at-risk children and the elderly. My activism, if you can call it that, is largely reduced to occasional calls to congresspersons (I have Congress and the White House numbers saved on my cell phone). I also sign petitions and forward e-mails every once in a while. I donate to a few campaigns. As a teacher I try to keep partisan political conversations out of the classroom and focus on educating students and teaching them how to ask useful critical questions.

Whatever kinship I felt to the Occupy movement, I became acutely aware of my own differences and privileges compared to many of our participants when I started in-depth interviewing. First of all, at the time I drove a Lexus. I felt hypocritical driving this luxury vehicle to an interview with an Occupy participant as many shared their stories of humble origins with me. Most times I opted out (or chickened out), and drove the family sport utility vehicle. Not really a much better option but at least more understandable given my need to shuffle three children around. And together my husband and I own three properties, which is hard to reconcile knowing my participants were championing the rights of the homeless and those being thrown out of their homes by banks. Surely the system has worked for us. So am I really the 99 percent? Is there enough room in this movement for me? I struggled with my desire, more than any other research project for which I have been a part, to be a *participant*—part of the 99 percent. I suppose I deemed it lent to my credibility, after all I am a scholar of democratic communication. Certainly my husband and I do not having earnings in the 1 percent of all Americans (see Barnes in this volume for a detailed description of the 1 percent) and at any time we are just one major medical illness from bankruptcy. But who was I to claim an understanding of Occupy participants?

Reconciling my economic privilege is more complicated than recognizing my white, heterosexual privilege. I readily admit I know nothing about what it means to be racially or sexually marginalized. But as for my comfortable life now, my children are certainly growing up with greater privileges than I had. I am the oldest of six children. My parents worked hard to educate us in Catholic schools but we were always on scholarships. I did not receive any financial help from my parents for college. I was however able to benefit from Pell Grants and student loans. My debt after one year at a community college and four years at Oregon State University was only ten thousand dollars, and that included the opportunity to spend one year on exchange in Australia. I have worked steadily since I was sixteen. I later received teaching assistantships, which supported both my master's and doctorate degrees. Of course, I believe my economic comfort has been so-called earned. That said, these thoughts were constantly in the forefront as I interviewed Occupy participants.

Many of my new friends in Occupy do not even have the opportunity to succeed in this economy. As Elizabeth Warren, newly elected Massachusetts senator, said at the 2012 Democratic National Convention, "the game is rigged." Some people I interviewed carried so much student loan debt it was impossible for them to envision when they could afford to live on their own. Their repayment amounts equaled a mortgage payment. Clearly I benefited from a different system—a different economy—perhaps a more just democracy. Understanding this increased my commitment to this project and my aim to create an authentic, comprehensive analysis of Occupy Portland.

I also had to come to grips with another difference I held with Occupy participants—my "intolerance" for violence. I knew that some of the tactics of Black Bloc[3] and other affiliative strategies associated with Occupy called for violence against *things*, like BMW and Lexus cars, to draw attention to the *violences* committed against the earth and people by corporations in so many unacknowledged ways (of which they would argue I am tolerant). While I can comprehend the injustice and subsequent logic, the whole idea of physical destruction violates my own beliefs in dialogue and openness to the other. I understand that resistance tactics can force societies to have tough conversations but they are tactics that I do not condone. And yes, I was afraid my car would be keyed. While to my knowledge I did not interview any person that supported violence as a tactic, many of the participants admitted a greater tolerance for it than I was prepared to accept. My heart always sunk a bit when the topic turned toward acceptance of Black Bloc. I fought my urges to teach and struggled for the strength to listen as objectively as possible. I challenged myself to ask questions without judgment.

While my own positionality in the movement was ever-present in my reflections and writing, it also had material consequences for how I collected data. As a full-time professor, and mother of three school-aged children and a traveling husband, I could not easily attend evening meetings. I accepted that my role in this ethnography was less than pure as I could not fully observe; the movement was too dynamic and challenging for me to immerse. I acknowledge my roles as trainer of research assistants, occasional observer of general assemblies, and participant of rallies. But my chief role was in organizing the project and formally interviewing participants. Even my interview schedule was oft interrupted by the schedule of life. I began interviewing participants the first week of camp and continued until January 2013. However, I was not present during breaks and the busiest parts of the semester. For this incompleteness in data collection, I turned to participant recollections, and my embedded partner Ricardo. I was reassured by the fact that most of our participants could also not claim full, uninterrupted participation in the movement. It turns out, ironically, that activism in this form is a full-time endeavor that few can fully execute without great resources.

Data collection in this collaborative project also presented challenges as we relied on each other to pool and post documents. As we independently collected data we were less familiar with the volume and comprehensiveness of what those data constituted. Initial data analysis meetings proved essential to our own understanding, processing, and for simply finding of our data. The collaboration among researchers certainly increased the comprehension of data and perspective, but it also contributed to an immense organizing headache of collecting, creating access, maintaining confidentiality, etc. While we followed similar protocols and shared our experiences in fieldnotes and dialogic meetings, we are certain our data reflect our disparate trainings and worldviews as well.

Ricardo's Tale

I approached this site from an ironically nuanced perspective. What I am inside: Spanish but not from Spain. Filipino, but really not accepted as such by native Filipinos. Privileged, but in a way that can only be described in terms of colonial relationship: not just white, but *conquistador* among the formerly colonized who still carry that memory. Back home in the Philippines, I can expect a large measure of privilege bestowed on me by history. My position in Occupy is thus ironic; back home, I'm from a 1 percent family, not just economically, but culturally. But this fact has little importance while I am living in the United States. What I am certainly not, but can certainly pass for while in the United States, is White-Anglo. Americans I speak to are eventually surprised when they find out that I'm a foreigner; my English is barely accented (from their perspective). I find that ironic because I can claim more career success from my use of English than any other personal characteristic, yet English is not supposed to be my native language. So, by effect and affect, in this country I am privileged—to a degree. It's a different form of privilege from a different history, but it still counts for something when people make assumptions about me.

What really matters though, a fact that constantly hovers over my head, is that I am a foreigner with no permanent right to live in the United States. My stay here is only as good as the conditions of my F1 visa: I can only work on campus and cannot seek other employment. After I obtain my doctorate, I will not have an automatic right to stay in the United States even while seeking employment. Being a foreigner in the United States has multiple constraints on what I am able to do politically. I cannot cast a ballot or run for public office. I have to take a driving test because my driver's license from home is not recognized. I need to have my passport and I-20 form handy whenever I engage in business with my school or the state. This flaw in privilege is not very problematic except for one important aspect about this project: If I am ever convicted of a felony, I can be deported and not allowed to legally re-enter the United States. That status has consequences when choosing to engage in political activity that involves civil disobedience. Because this is a political project as much as it is a project about politics, engaging Occupy as a participant is to engage in political action that challenges assumptions about power relationships. In joining Occupy Portland, I am assisting in political acts that threaten a status quo with real consequences and real potential for jail time. If I wish to continue studies here, I cannot afford to be arrested even if my political beliefs warrant civil disobedience. Thus, I have to be careful where I place myself in relation to the police when engaging in activism.

This position in relation to the police was one reason I chose to facilitate meetings instead of joining protest marches. In that role, I could afford to contribute to something I believed in while minimizing the risk of arrest. I freely acknowledge this to other Occupy participants and most of them are sympathetic to my reasons. Although they don't fear arrest as much as I do, and in fact many do get arrested to openly challenge the police in order to expose that violence, they understand its consequences and what that means to others who lack the privilege of being allowed to live here. This relationship thus revealed one disadvantage; in removing myself from the danger of being arrested I could not express that very important aspect of organization in my notes. Challenging authority in order to expose it is one reason why activists choose to march. It is one aspect of the activist's lived experience that I cannot express.

My fellow activists also acknowledge and understand why I am engaged in this study. Horizontal organizing is ideologically important to the movement and its processes of inclusion, diversity, and self-management are what primarily interest me. Thus, my role as ethnographer, especially as someone with an expressed affinity for these sorts of issues in organizing, was not only acknowledged but also encouraged by fellow Occupy participants.

The facilitation role also has some advantages for an ethnographer. As a communication scholar, I feel at home in the role. I could keep an eye on the meeting even as I was gathering headnotes[4] about the meeting to incorporate later into fieldnotes. And because we are physically up in the front of the room or public square during meetings, facilitators become known by the community fairly quickly, which helps establish credibility with participants and encourages access. People often thank facilitators after a meeting; they know it's a hard job to keep a meeting democratic while on schedule. I spent much time socializing with activists as a result, which helped when listening to organizational processes that are inaudible to an unfamiliar ear. From my position, I learned to sense the organizing going on and express these in my notes.

But my embeddedness was sometimes problematic because I had occasionally "gone native" during the process; that is, "over identifying with a group's ideology" and "failing to document what is happening" (Lindlof and Taylor 2011, 146). There were many occasions when I failed to construct fieldnotes; thus, there are facets to the experience that went undocumented. I would sometimes be uncritical in my reflection of events; this is one danger of being so enclosed within the scene—the friendships you establish with other participants are real and I came to value them. As the participants and I mutually constructed an understanding of the phenomena, our shared perspective began to predominate over other scholarly needs. Thus, standing back from the native aspects of my descriptions was sometimes difficult. Going native also meant that I absorbed and performed an anarchist ideology—mostly as horizontalist organizing methods (see my chapter in this section for a description)—in my day-to-day interactions even after I had left the scene. I became an anarchist and I still consider myself an anarchist today. As descriptions of anarchism emerged from the experience, the themes presented in the texts therefore reflect my anarchist attitude. This was ultimately beneficial to the project as these anarchist themes flavor the understanding of the text as a phenomenon in itself. I also had the advantage of working with a team of researchers who challenged my native status from time-to-time, aiding in the reflexive aspects of my analyses.

Vail's Tale

I initially learned about the concept of positionality and white privilege during the first year of my doctoral program in a critical cultural studies class. What followed this new knowledge was a deeply reflexive period that ended with me undertaking an auto-ethnographic study of my own understanding of what privilege had meant in my life. And I have struggled intellectually with similar variations of the tensions created by my upbringing and positionality (i.e., white, middle-class) since. Still, as life swirls in a seemingly never-ending series of deadlines and bills and trips home to visit family and friends, my reflexive time and energy has waxed and waned. Occupy brought me to another pivotal juncture, not unlike my first year in graduate school, as it forced me to reconsider (and in some real ways, consider for the first time) income equality, specifically, and inequality embedded at every layer of society, generally.

I grew up in middle-class suburbia in Upstate New York, surrounded by embedded messages of "The American Dream." There was little questioning of the status quo, and I believed the mantra of "you get what you work for." In many significant ways, I have practiced my life according to what is often told to any citizen or immigrant in the United States via the media and cultural doctrines; that is, if you work hard and attend college, you will be financially rewarded. Fast forward to my thirty-third year on the planet and I am employed in a tenure-track position as a university professor, I own my own house, and I travel abroad at least once a year. Similar to Renee, my entire graduate education was funded by my teaching and research assistantships. Also, my partner is from Great Britain, thus lending another unique lens to our conversations about nationality and citizenship and the opportunity that is often awarded or assumed by association with our homeland, historically and modernly. This is the short list of my tangible privileges.

Still, when the Occupy movement spread so ubiquitously throughout the national and global scene, I was amidst a personal family crisis related to my father's ten-plus year struggle with bipolar disorder (which contributed to my uncle, his brother's, death by self decapitation, just a few years earlier). In October 2011, at the very beginning of the Occupy movement, my father had an emergency quadruple bypass surgery for his largely untreated heart disease (exasperated by fifty years of smoking). My brother and I flipped a coin to determine who would be the first to drop everything and travel to New York to help during his recovery. I picked heads and was scheduled to fly standby a few days later (aided by a pass from Renee's airline pilot husband—privilege, eek!). In my immediate past trip to visit my father, I became infected with scabies after spending a week in his house (which took nearly four months to diagnose, for reasons that I speculate may be associated with my socioeconomic status), so I was uneasy about what I would find. As is often the case for individuals with bipolar disorder following a serious surgery, my father spiraled into the most intense manic phase to date, and for the following six months we did our best to dilute his sleeplessness, wild ideas, spending sprees, and general irritable excitability. He lives alone and getting him to take his medicine from afar is impossible and thus we plead daily with his pharmacist, psychiatrist, and heart surgeon, to help us, often to no avail (my father is generally belligerent when he is manic, and therefore alienates most individuals he comes into contact with—leaving us few or no allies). There were several weeks when he would call me ten or twelve times a day, and often in the middle of the night. He tracked me down at research conferences and called my hotel room; Facebook-messaged a couple of my ex-partners and asserted why it would never have worked out for us; bought me a $10,000 hot tub, two printers, two clocks, two Keurig coffee-makers. I could go on and on. His illness was inescapable.

So, when Renee, Ricardo, and I entered the Occupy encampment in downtown Portland during this same time period, I felt viscerally connected to the plight of many of the participants we faced (particularly the mentally ill and houseless)—and simultaneously disenchanted with the possibility for any real change (I was truly emotionally fatigued). At that exact moment, in fact, I was deeply embedded in a period of my life (that I think I still inhabit today) where I felt that generally speaking life was and is largely unfair and full of a lot of heartache and tragedy. To me, though I was (and am) inspired by the virtues of the movement, I ebbed and flowed between a place of optimism and dark cynicism—my own life felt like it was similarly teetering on the edge of the same unknown cliff that many participants reflected in our interviews. I felt like everything in my life was just one poorly orchestrated event away from bankruptcy. I was also afraid of losing everything I had worked for, yet questioned the validity of my own accomplishments given the privilege I had been afforded. What is truly authentic in life, I'd ponder. And, perhaps similar to others who have a parent suffering from a severe mental illness, I was worried that something might be wrong with me—that I, too, would eventually begin to display the manic and depressive phases inherent to bipolar disorder. At the rallies and general assembly meetings, which were often filled with individuals that knew intense personal hardship, I felt both numb and intrigued, and sometimes perplexed as to what keeps individuals' hope alive when so many had shared deeply personal stories of defeat and loss not unlike those in my own family. There was definitely recognition of *self in other* happening for me at these meetings; I felt at times comfortably and uncomfortably connected to the participants.

Looking back over the past eighteen months of sporadic data collection and analysis, which jibed with the movement's own seasonal and high maintenance nature, I feel that this project and movement have challenged me in a variety of ways. And in some very profound ways I feel moved. It provoked me a researcher, especially as it seemed to change form before my eyes, and as a citizen. The project often felt overwhelming and hard to fully grasp, particularly as an observer, as each participant articulated the movement's goals and ideologies in slightly different ways. Although I do not fully identify with Ricardo's newly anarchist identity for myself, I can relate to the integral ideas that come with an anarchist lens. I feel that in many ways humans are sincerely flawed and limited by their own inherent needs and desires—and as such society cannot be changed from within in its current iteration and thus must be completely revamped.

Overall, the process of data collection and analysis has taught me new things about humanity, and a lot more about my own limitations as a researcher and academic. In the spirit of Van Maanen (1988), I had to learn how my own personal experiences informed, blinded, and/or transformed my own abilities to make sense of the data. If my own vulnerabilities and lived experiences are simultaneously being further revealed and also informing my interpretation of the data, how may I also account for this in any true way? I think we do suffer our way to wisdom and this data collection was about me finding balance between my own understandings while also acknowledging and honoring the fact that others' experiences, whilst having apparent threads of overlap, are intrinsically unique experiences. Thus, I tried to account for my own limited positionality through active listening. By listening to participants' voices, words, and feelings, and trying to intentionally remove what may feel most comfortable to me in terms of sense making, I instead tried to lend authenticity to the idea that everyone's experience is different and therefore must be given the benefit of the doubt.

The movement also reified some prior beliefs of mine, while adding new knowledge. For example, I now understand more clearly that people *really* need to feel purpose and a sense of belonging—the feeling one gets from being connected is irreplaceable and our current society makes it quite easy for many to become fragmented or disenfranchised. I talk about this in my analysis of the identity roles fulfilled by participants in Occupy Portland in my chapter. In that same vein, I think Occupy Portland became quite a personal experience for me, and I now find myself defending its core ideals in conversation with students, colleagues, and family members. I feel strongly that my privilege and positionality and subsequent lens afforded me a unique relationship with the mentally ill participants (even from afar), yet in other ways I often felt restrained in relating to the movement by my need to maintain (emotionally and literally) my "day job." I think I ultimately realized how much of my own life is lived with fear as the backbone—what I have not been able to fully determine is whether the participants were also acting out of fear or against fear. Again, throughout this ethnographic journey I have strived to account in the research process for any highly situational perspectives I have by explicitly owning and making visible my privileges when possible and necessary.

CONCLUSION

The remaining chapters in this section of the book are the result of this ethnographic project. Our aim in writing this chapter was to better prepare the reader to understand these forthcoming chapters after having learned more of Portland, the Occupy camp and its participants, and our own methods and experience as researchers and people. The methods described in this chapter support our independent analyses. We hope that descriptions of our different positions as researchers facilitate the readers' ability to assess and contextualize the claims that follow.

DISCUSSION QUESTIONS

1. What details written in the section of the site and participant description stand out as most relevant to your understanding of Occupy Portland? Return to this question after you read the studies in this section of the book. What details seem relevant now?
2. Professors Fletcher and Heath used Spradley's (1980) domain analysis to reduce their data, while Munoz employed the phenomenological methods described primarily by Van Manen (1990). How are these qualitative, interpretive methods of analysis different? How might they be similar? What might they reveal differently in the data?

3. Why do you think the authors chose to use confessional tales particular to the study of Occupy? How do you acknowledge your own positionality in your research?
4. Given the admissions of the authors described in their confessional tales, how do you think they each approached their research differently? What did they have to account for in order to arrive at the most plausible claims?
5. How did the authors achieve "validity" and/or fidelity? Meaning, how do they achieve authenticity in their claims?

NOTES

1. For a key timeline of significant events in Occupy Portland's first year see Helen Jung's article www.oregonlive.com/portland/index.ssf/2012/10/occupy_portland_a_timeline_of.html.

2. David also wrote the foreword to this book.

3. In a blog piece, Arlo Stone (Stone, 2012) describes the Black Bloc as "people who have calculated that specific property damage and engag[e] in confrontations with police directly in specific situations." Black Bloc activists wear all black clothing, including face cover, and engage in a variety of tactics during demonstrations. These tactics include the purposeful spray-painting of the anarchist "circle-A" logo on public spaces that include buildings and parked automobiles, as well as the deliberate breaking of storefront windows. They also practice "counterviolence" tactics such as distracting the police to "de-arrest" fellow activists being held by the police.

4. In ethnographic methods, headnotes are used when researchers "focus their attention to specific events. . . . They then commit these impressions to memory through an act of will" (Lindlof and Taylor 2011, 156). Headnotes must often serve when the taking of scratch notes would be difficult (or impossible), such as while facilitating a general assembly.

Chapter Five

Finding the Space Between

Participative Democracy, Consensus Decision-Making, and a Leaderful/less Movement

Renee Guarriello Heath

> I just remember the first couple meetings when we were having to mic check everything because there were hundreds of people. And what was fascinating about mic checking is that it slows down your process and it slows down the entire group process to where you have to slow down the pace and you really have to listen. And you have to pause. And you have to breathe. And it takes a whole minute to get out a couple sentences and I think that that pacing rocked my world. I went to bed the first few nights and it was like a fucking fantasy.—Ivy, Occupy Portland Participant, intensive care unit nurse, feminist, February[1]

A meaningful feature of the Occupy movement is the centralization of participative and consensus processes. Social movement scholar Donatella della Porta (2008) traced the phenomena of consensus, noting activist movements throughout the world have expanded to include consensus as a cornerstone of their espoused mission. She posits that prior to the 1990s social movements were more likely associated with conflict than consensus, but that has since changed.

> If the presence of conflicts is certainly not denied, nevertheless, especially since the 1990s, the conception of politics as an arena for the expression of conflicts has been challenged (or at least balanced) by an emerging attention to the development of political arenas as spaces for consensus building. In political theory, a focus on consensus emerged within the debate on deliberative democracy—stressing in particular, the importance of the quality of communi-

cation for reaching consensual definitions of the public good in democratic processes. (Della Porta 2008, 3)

Della Porta (2008) examined the missions of 250 organizations associated with Global Social Movements (GSM; for examples, the British Wombles and *Dissent!—A Network of Resistance Against the G8*) and identified the specific values of consensus, participation, inclusion, autonomy, and individualism. She noted many of these organizations credit the Zapatista's experience for their inspiration (discussed in detail in Kapoor chapter 1 this volume).[2]

A social movement's turn toward consensus demarcates more than a trend. Others have linked consensus to activism dating back to the 1960s and 1970s in the United States (Cornell 2012). Anthropologist David Graeber, dubbed by many, especially outside the movement, to be the father of Occupy, argued the anarchist attention to consensus processes in the global justice movement "is about creating new forms of organization. It is not lacking in ideology; those new forms of organization *are* its ideology" (Graeber 2002, 70).[3] Meaning, participants commit to an ideology of consensus rather than view consensus as merely a tool for accomplishing an ideological agenda. This commitment to consensus and participative processes in contemporary social movements constitutes an opportunity for communication scholars who seek to understand the successes, challenges, and paradoxes of consensus in participative democracy ultimately contributing to communication and leadership theories.

Accordingly, this chapter attends to the communication structures and processes embedded in participative democracy as found in the case study of Occupy Portland. I proceed with a review of the relevant literature including explications of participative democracy, consensus, and horizontal leadership, drawing out the role of communication. Next, I discuss the features of the camp and other Occupy Portland activities germane to consensus and participative democracy. Finally I present findings from our ethnographic project that advances our knowledge of these concepts.[4]

COMMUNICATION AND PARTICIPATIVE DEMOCRACY

Participative democracy may be best described by political theorist Benjamin Barber (2003) who fleshed out various forms of democracy. For our purposes I will discuss two forms most relevant to this study: liberal democracy and participative democracy. Barber also referred to these as representative democracy and strong democracy, respectively. Liberal democracy is most visible in political structures in the United States and other western nations where voting, representation, and freedom of expression are central. Barber critiqued liberal democracy for stealing the voice from the individual by abdication to a representative politics. Barber advocated instead for participative democracy in which case conflicts are recovered in meaningful discussions and individuals make decisions together at local levels. In the purest form, participative democracy manifests as direct democracy, "the process of making collective decisions without delegating power to representatives" (Cornell 2012, 165).

Stanley Deetz (1992) developed a communicative understanding of these types of democracy. Accordingly, liberal democracy results in an emphasis on forums for expression and persuasion such as ballot boxes and debates. However, these forums and modes of communication fall short in a diverse society because they rely somewhat on agreement and alignment of values. Given the complex societies of the twenty-first century, participative democracy has the potential to surface constructive conflict by staying open to the "other" and negotiating meaning among participants to arrive at temporary decisions (Deetz 1992). Any enduring consensus (agreement) would be viewed as suspect in a strong democracy as it would always privilege some peoples' interests over others (Friberg-Fernos and Schaffer 2010). Drawing on philosophers of dialogue such as Hans-Georg Gadamer (1975) and Jurgen Habermas (1990), Deetz (1992) argued participative democracy would include "genuine conversation" that produced learning, generating new meanings among interactants (Gadamer 1975 in Deetz 1992). He also argued that the ideal speech situation posited by Habermas (1990) provides the best normative hope for participation. Habermas contended decision-making situations in the public sphere require competent actors who behave reciprocally and cooperatively and must allow for the *contestation* of claims of truth (knowledge), the questioning of social relations, and the sincerity of speakers. In the ideal speech situation, conversations would be free of distorted and unseen power.

Consensus

Consensus *processes* are vital to participative democracy and necessary to facilitate contestation (Barber 2003; Graeber 2002). Andrew Cornell (2012), writing about Occupy, claimed the word consensus "means, generally speaking that all parties involved in discussing a topic or making a decision have reached an agreement or have come to share an opinion" (163). Della Porta, Andretta, Mosca and Reiter (2006) argued, "The consensus method in GSM thus builds 'agreement within disagreement', since any particular disagreement is always set within a framework of more general agreement, based on respect and reciprocal trust" (quoted in Della Porta 2008, 53–54). General understandings of consensus frequently conflate its role as a decision-making process with its role as a decision outcome. Most people are probably familiar with the colloquial use of the word consensus as unanimous agreement, that is, an outcome in which all participants agree or can accept a decision at some level (McKinney 2001). However, McKinney, a scholar and practitioner of community-based consensus decision-making, also described consensus as a process that elicits conflicts and differences in a respectful deliberation (see also Daniels and Walker 2001). In this sense, consensus-based deliberations are more about discourse than unanimity (Min 2012; Polletta 2002). Political deliberation precedes collective decision-making by informing and preparing "citizens to determine which collective action they support" (Yack 2012, 41). Political deliberation may or may not incorporate the values of consensus processes.

Consensus processes honor the egalitarian values rooted in Quakerism (Cornell 2012) of including the diverse ideas of individuals in the group, acknowledging dissent (Sheeran 1996), and laboring (Heath 2008) through differences until an outcome can be agreed upon. It is both possible to arrive at a consensus agreement without invoking a consensus process, and to utilize a consensus process and not arrive at a consensus agreement. How an acceptable agreement manifests in the communication process can vary widely. Most consensus scholars are careful not to prescribe a particular consensus process as this philosophically runs counter to the idea that the participants create their own processes (Innes and Booher 1999; McKinney 2001). That said, Graeber (2002) suggested a number of techniques that are visible in the Occupy movement including suggestions for how to submit proposals and when people should stand aside and not block consensus. Della Porta's work (2008) described how GSM organizations utilize facilitators and hand signals to facilitate discussion and measure agreement. These consensus processes and techniques have made their way in various forms to the Occupy movement and complicate the role of leadership and structure in GSMs.[5]

Leadership and Structure in Participative Democracy

Graeber's (2002) "new" anarchist writings ubiquitously reproduced (though not always cited) throughout Occupy literature and handouts, tout antiauthority and autonomy as central organizing principles within the global movement. However he defends that GSMs are not opposed to structure and organization; instead they are about creating new forms of organization. Graeber argues for plurality and difference and the basic understanding that underlying GSM practice is the assumption that "no one will ever convert anyone else entirely to their point of view" (2002, 72). This philosophy holds firm the idea that participants do not expect to alter diverse perspectives but to expand them in order to make decisions together. Participants are suspicious of representation as a replacement for direct, participative democracy (Graeber 2002). He contends that this commitment to process rather than ideology has been misunderstood and misconstrued by the media as being antistructure [or leaderless].

Indeed social movement literature is informative on the matter of structure and leadership. Jo Freeman's (1972/73) essay, "The Tyranny of Structurelessness," is one of the most influential discussions of structure that emerged from the feminist movement. Freeman's essay argued "there is no such thing as a structureless group" (152). She warned of the dangers of informal groups wary of hierarchy as they are likely to mask power, avoid accountability and responsibility, and foster elite informal groups of control. Freeman argued, "informal structures have no obligation to be responsible to the group at-large. Their power was not given to them; it cannot be taken away" (157). That said, rife with tensions and contradictions, leadership and structure theories remain underdeveloped in our understanding of participative democracy. For example, under Graeber's vision of direct democracy accomplished via consensus processes, he claimed,

> The result is a rich and growing panoply of organizational instruments—spokescouncils, affinity groups, facilitation tools, breakouts, fishbowls, blocking concerns, vibe-watchers and so on—all aimed at creating forms of democratic process that allow initiatives to rise from below and attain maximum effective solidarity, without stifling dissenting voices, *creating leadership positions* or compelling anyone to do anything which they have not freely agreed to do. (2002, 71; emphasis added)

In this articulated vision, leadership positions are lumped in between thoughts of stifling dissenting voices, and compelling people to do things against their will. It is no wonder this philosophy, fostered by the work of young and often unskilled passionate people (Graeber 2002), has come to construe leader as a pejorative term. Ganesh and Zoller (2012) warned, "While sensitive to the rhetorical significance of 'leaderlessness' in constructing the communitarian character of activism, we suggest the notion of a formally leaderless activist group could prevent identifying novel ways in which leadership is enacted in social movements" (74). And, although Barber (2003, 238–241) shares Graeber's skepticism of leadership, he theorizes four types of leadership that can contribute to participative democracy: transitional leaders can create participative institutions but do not linger in leadership positions. Natural leaders possess leadership and communication competencies that will affect even egalitarian communities. Facilitating leaders maintain neutrality and mind the integrity of processes, and moral leaders act publicly but not politically, meaning they should not be controlling the processes but publicly inspiring the vision. This chapter seeks to understand the role of leadership in a consensus-based participative democracy by asking: What are the successes, challenges, and paradoxes associated with commitments to consensus values, structures, and processes in the Occupy Portland movement? I next explore the site and briefly discuss how I reduced data during the analysis stage of this study.

THE SITE: THE CAMP AND PARTICIPATIVE PROCESSES

The Portland camp and the worldviews held by its participants (discussed in greater detail in the previous chapter), influenced how participative democracy and consensus processes would be understood and enacted. In many aspects, the camp was an idyllic community grounded in communitarianism and fueled by an organic do-it-yourself (DIY) culture that was based not on social class or position, but on individual interest and skill. Eric, an illustrator from New York and cofounder of the camp's library argued, "We were building this community and trying to develop best practices for small democracy building and community building . . . getting to know each others' talents and strengths and congregating around the pet issues that put us here in the first place." Indeed the DIY culture was no doubt cultivated by the consensus values oft attributed to GSMs of inclusiveness, individualism, participation, and autonomy (Della Porta 2008). For example, Elayne had experience in web development and therefore ended up managing web content. Allen saw the need for an information booth and literally hung a sign that became the information hub of the camp. Eric teamed up with local librarians to create a library space both virtually and physically at the camp. Mark, a self-proclaimed "houseless,"[6] culinary school graduate, with more than $100,000 in student loan debt, was skilled at running kitchens and quickly organized the camp's food service, resulting in its distributing more than six hundred meals a day at its peak.

The camp also cultivated a growing intellectualism fostering the ability for individuals to participate in direct democracy, meeting the competency requirement theorized by Habermas (1990). Participants told us they were frequently visited by academics including economists, social movement professors, conflict meditation experts, and healthcare professionals. They attended learning sessions on legislation, nonviolent protest, and other substantive subjects that contributed to the movement both by igniting passion and informing action. Allie, a regular facilitator in the Portland movement, described the camp as a hub for political education. "Every night there was the major actions meeting to bring awareness to corporate money in politics [such as] through the body of ALEC. The American Legislative Exchange Council is the acronym . . . So exposing it for what it is." Thus the camp functionally advanced the political movement with organized educational sessions. Its structures such as the library, which was staffed on the weekends by master's level librarians, and the ease of access that campers had to each other's knowledge fostered learning and education on such subjects as the environment, watershed communities, and *Citizens United* and corporate personhood (for definitions see Barnes in this volume). Occupy activists spoke of the oppressed poor, marginalized voices of women, and the invisibility of minorities, even in their own movement (further developed in Fletcher chapter 7).

However, divisions and fragmentation also existed. The most obvious division was in the worldviews held by campers that resulted in pejorative names used by some, such as the "poly-sci kids" and the "anarchists." If reformists of the current political system were to be on one side of the continuum and revolutionaries who wish to discard the current system as hopeless were to reside on the other end of the continuum, Occupy participants would fill all gradations of commitment to these various ends. These worldviews become especially relevant as we try and understand the movement through the lens of participative democracy. In particular, the creation of structure such as rules and regulations (discussed later in this chapter) made visible the splinters of the Occupy movement.

Some also viewed the camp as a stifling structure to the movement. One experienced organizer credited the battles that erupted as a result of the camp occupation as a "cancer" that socialized and skewed participants' understandings of how to orchestrate a movement. As a veteran facilitator who contributed most of his energy and experience to *InterOccupy.net*,[7] Walt believed that habits of interaction formed in the management of the camp eventually undermined the movement's potential. "The camps were rife with all kinds of challenges of drugs and interesting subcommunities trying to get along . . . and because of the 'inclusion' . . . 'we can't be hierarchical,' and, 'we can't be domineering,' there was no way to shut down the pathology. It was a cancer, an incongruence and incompatibility that we didn't have the means to stop."[8] Thus the structure of the camp influenced worldviews, which in turn influenced the way participants were willing to interact with each other. Anarchists were mired in the conflicts of camp and as a result were sensitive to marginalization and oppression. But political activists were equally committed to organizing, which brings with it structures traditionally laden with power.

The general assembly (frequently called the GA)—the primary open meeting—initially served as the decision-making body. Iconic video of mic checking, the process of using the crowd as a human microphone,[9] vividly depicted what many described as "experiencing democracy." In Portland, the early days and weeks of the movement brought crowds of two hundred to four hundred (thousands in the first few days) drawing people from the nearly six hundred campers, the city, and the suburbs. Given its size, the GA was not a good decision-making structure and so the consensus design and process morphed many times during the camp's peak and in the months that followed its disbandment. Following leads from Occupy Wall Street and the

Puerta Del Sol camp of the "15th May Movement" in Spain as documented in their own manuals, a spokescouncil model was implemented seeking input from interdependent affinity groups and committees whose individual spokes contributed proposals and ideas on behalf of their groups. In this model, consensus was first built in small groups who then took their proposals to the GA once they had garnered support from enough participants. Although rumor has it that there were as many as one hundred committees and affinity groups, one website (at this writing) lists thirty-one spokes participating in such diverse committees as the Solutions Committee, Our School (formerly the library), and the Elder's Council. As the camp disassembled, some of the committees were no longer needed, such as the Sanitation and Food committees. Other committees and affinity groups grew stronger and decentralized facilitated by social media (see similar findings in Tewksbury chapter 10 in this volume).

In response to the question of what were the successes, challenges, and paradoxes associated with consensus and participative democracy in Occupy Portland, I first analyzed data that emerged from interviews and (later observations) by collapsing them into common themes and categories. I next attended to those data that responded to my research question regarding communication practices and structures associated with consensus and participative democracy. Finally, in keeping with the book's theme and our desire to complexify any single narrative that would be tempting to draw from our findings (Trujillo 1992), data were organized around romantic, functional, and critical understandings of the outcomes associated with participative, consensus decision-making.

FINDINGS

Romantic Perspective: Democracy and a "Leaderful" Movement

The romantic view of Occupy Portland illuminates the dream of an idealized society (Trujillo 1992). In this case consensus and participation breathed life into a new paradigm of democracy—one that looked quite like the participative democracy Barber (2003) and Deetz (1992) described. The consensus structures also facilitated a "leaderful" movement grounded in horizontal leadership.

Consensus processes constituted a new and romantic democratic paradigm. For example, the GA, which was the most visible space for consensus decision-making, was guided by a philosophy explicated in Occupy Portland's own materials that sounds much like a description of the genuine conversation—dialogue is generative and creates new meaning among the interactants (Gadamer in Deetz 1992). Explained in The Facilitation Team User Manual and Orientation!: [10]

> The consensus process is diametrically opposed to the kind of thinking propounded by the present system. The normal response of two people with differing opinions tends to be confrontational. They each defend their opinions with the aim of convincing their opponent, until their opinion has won. The aim of consensus, on the other hand, is to construct. Two people with differing ideas work together to build something new. (*Portlandgeneralassembly.org* 2012, 1)

Many participants credited their initial experiences with consensus decision-making as profound. Ivy explained:

> Consensus was a really big high for me, I really like the model of consensus; it's really fascinating, especially when we were first starting it. To be able to come to a group of complete strangers, thousands in the beginning and then hundreds, and come and propose your idea and your passion and your desire to the group facilitated a really interesting dialogue and a really fruitful dialogue where people are saying things from their experience or maybe really good intellectual juice, you know? And then having a consensus and a sort of solidarity getting behind an idea or an action of somebody is really fascinating to see that we can actually have a say on what goes on within our community of Occupy.

The processes associated with the movement became symbolic of a political paradigm shift. "This is what democracy looks like!" was the chant of the early days of the movement. David,[11] a part-time instructor teaching courses on social movements at Portland State University, and co-architect of many of Portland's processes, described the dynamic of the GA as symbolic of democracy.

> Just the extraordinary amount of conversations, discussion, there is actually a civic space, a public sphere, in which people are talking about these things. I mean, time and time again when I was facilitating meetings as frustrating as they could be sometimes, and as problematic as our process is sometimes, I was very moved sitting in Terry Shrunk Plaza by the fact that every single night hundreds of people were gathering and debating both problems and solutions. And that's extraordinary. And so I think in some ways, we're having a conversation about what is a democracy? What does it mean to be in a democracy? Are we even living in a democracy? I mean, I would pose that question and I, for me the answer is no. Um, and I think we're discovering what democracy actually looks like when we engage in these kind of participatory, really open, horizontal decision-making structures that we have in this movement.

What began as a modeled process at general assembly meetings became a different way of thinking about interaction in a democracy, captured in Elayne's, a food activist, admission, "I don't want to march anymore."

True to the intellectual thread that ran through Occupy, several facilitators initiated by David organized themselves in a reflective debrief in August 2012, almost one year after the initial organizing meetings for the Occupy Portland movement. They acknowledged communicative norms developed around consensus values and processes resulted in alternate ways of thinking. Bonnie (facilitator) said,

> I remember after the eviction, and I remember someone there, I think from the homeless population and this person had said, "You know you're not following process and here's why." I mean it was a very subtle point and when she said that, you know, I just felt so moved that people really had buy-in into this idea of how to do the process. And even though, you know, there were a lot of people who didn't have buy-in or wanted to bite, there was that consensus, that at some deep level, and there were numbers of moments like that, but mostly I saw, I mean, I saw it during the encampment. But I saw that afterwards and people were still sort of hanging on to this idea that this [consensus] is important and I thought that's really quite amazing. That really struck me a lot—a big takeaway.

Consensus processes were constitutive of the change in paradigm to a more participative democracy.

The romantic lens also foregrounds the possibilities of horizontal leadership structures to encourage citizens' participation directly in making decisions within their community (Barber 2003). In the romantic perspective, the autonomous DIY culture and the GA and its associated process of facilitation, spokes, and consensus decision-making, constituted horizontal hierarchy fostering the notion of a "leaderful" as opposed to leaderless movement, suggested by Lionel, a former nonprofit professional and active Occupy participant. Neutral facilitation modeled horizontal leadership perhaps more than any other intentionally designed structure. The facilitation team members, whose active membership waned "between thirty and three" (Allie, facilitator), were trained to suppress their own opinions as two to three led crowds of hundreds early on, and tens (later, after camp ended) through the decision-making process.[12] Horizontal leadership was held in check by self-monitoring and negative sanctions from other participants. For example, if a facilitator had helped guide a number of meetings, he or she would voluntarily step aside so as to allow another facilitator to lead the processes. When facilitators did not stand aside, peers exerted pressure or individual facilitators lost credibility.

Teresa, a respiratory therapist and long-time activist, likened the leadership process to migrating birds that organically take turns leading in flight, shifting positions with shifts in directions along their path. In this metaphor the ideal is shared leadership, or perhaps a better description would be seasonal leadership, which David described as "people come in and out" of leadership roles. Many of the people interviewed in this project were identified because they had served in a leadership role using the horizontal decision-making structure to propose actions and rally supporters. Mark organized a march that drew one hundred protestors. Jessica planned a day of action, education, and protest on health care issues. Chad mobilized action in the antiwar movement. Walt served as a facilitating bridge among other Occupy groups around the country. Elayne was part of a group that began an Occupy electronic newspaper that could write opinion pieces. David helped initiate Occupy Portland, taught facilitation, and was vital in the organization of a very effective spin-off group call Action Lab. This leadership was cultivated by the processes that both centralized information and decentralized action—the camp and general assemblies initially, and the committees and affinity groups, eventually. Within the romantic lens consensus values, structures, and processes constituted a new way of understanding communication and decision-making and supported a leaderful movement laying the foundation for a flourishing participative democracy.

Functional Perspective:
Communication Training, "Tethering," and Leadership Cultivation

The participative values, structures, and processes in Portland also provided a very functional role in the advancement of the movement. Consensus processes were training individuals how to communicate in a participative democracy. The meetings and subsequent committee structure served as a place for networking, facilitating inclusion and connection among diverse groups and already established activists. The movement also served as a training ground for sustained leadership in activism.

The microprocesses associated with consensus facilitated the communication conditions necessary for participative democracy. The Occupy processes that centralized dialogic principles appeared to be teaching a whole new generation of people how to slow down conversation, listen, interact, honor diversity, and make decisions together, demonstrating what communication looks like in participative democracy—competent, reciprocal, and open to the other (Deetz 1992). I invited two panels of Occupy participants to share process experiences with the students and faculty of the University of Portland. Panelists impressively modeled active listening, validating of diverse perspectives, and patience when listening so as not to interrupt their peers. In another example, Ivy described the personal effect the human microphone practice had for her:

> These echoing of voices you know and like the pace of conversations was really fascinating and a way to process because if I'm talking a hundred miles an hour but if I speak with intention and points with emphasis and pause, it allows space for people to think. And if you're an active listener it allows the

space of silence within your thoughts because then you're actively listening and not trying to formulate your own thoughts. That leads, what I think, to a space of contemplation and control. Like, contemplative thought, which I think is one of the more radical things about mic checking and so that was a really fascinating group dynamic.

Accordingly, the processes were constitutive of communication skills necessary to enact participative democracy. Lionel, Ivy, Elayne, Eric, and Allen all talked about teaching one another, hosting dialogue groups, and creating spaces for learning in the community. Lionel claimed, "It's [Occupy] becoming so much more about building relationships between each other and empowering communities to actualize. Not about political revolution, but social revolution, replacing oppressive structures."

The general assembly meetings were also the first site of connection that facilitated the networking or "tethering" of diverse groups of people, fostering inclusiveness. Jessica, a health activist, said,

I went to the first meeting that happened down at the waterfront and total chicken-skin goose bumps the whole time! I was so excited to see a couple thousand people there. All different people so excited to see [people talking about] issues that were hurting Americans and families. And it wasn't like a bunch of hippies or homeless people it was everybody. . . . it tethered all the activists together.

Despite much frustration about the effectiveness of the large general assembly meetings, which is discussed in the next section in length, the processes—especially the spokescouncil and the general assembly—inescapably served the initial functions of connecting people. The act of breaking into committees, caucuses, and affinity groups facilitated the organizing of people who cared about similar things and could organize actions around those things. Teresa said, "It's [Occupy's] strength is its inclusiveness that it's a bit like the Catholic Church you know . . . it's like anyone can come in and worship here. You can step up and be a leader, it gets people, it makes people feel empowered. I think that's its biggest strength. It gives a sense of community and family—it's a source of support, and family, and connectedness."

In processes set up via the facilitation team, committees and affinity groups could propose an action and bring it forth to the general assembly meetings to recruit for resistance actions, or other specialized projects important to them. The general assembly initially served as a hub for the activity that introduced folks to one another. As attendance at the general assemblies waned, the spokescouncil and affinity groups sustained that action by allowing people to spend their time and energy with others who shared their values. Teresa, who in August 2012 stayed involved by attending affinity group meetings, explained:

> I am getting less involved with groups that have taken that [militant perspective] . . . And what I do every day is get behind groups who I wholeheartedly feel that I can connect with and not compromise what I believe. However, I have great respect for those who are able to cobble together, in a better way than I do. I have my own ideals and my own reasons for getting involved.

Teresa continued to work on Occupy causes that were important to her. The affinity group structure connected her with like minds but allowed a loose affiliation to the Occupy movement with those she shared less in common. Thus, the consensus structures of the general assembly, committee and affinity groups facilitated the tethering of diverse groups honoring the values of diversity and inclusion. Finally the consensus processes and structures of the movement provided not just leadership structures and opportunity (mentioned above) but the practical leadership *training* necessary for the sustainability of the movement, once again constituting the competency necessary to enact participative democracy. Given its grounding in horizontal decision-making and organizing, participants (especially those who were not already experienced activists) were highly resistant to the notion of leadership. However, the structures and processes associated with decision making developed shared leadership skills, particularly among Occupy facilitators who practiced facilitative leadership (Barber 2003) in a very visible way.

David acknowledged shared leadership development in a question he posed to the trained facilitator team during their reflective meeting. "Do we understand facilitators as leaders and if so, is this, or was this leadership owned in a way that was . . . accountable and horizontal? And just to give my own thoughts . . . I think that some of us were acting in the role of leaders in a very particular kind of way—kind of shared leadership kind of way." Jessica, who was not a facilitator, explained how important facilitation as leadership was to the movement. She shared the story of a mentor and female activist in the antinuclear community who also was not an Occupy facilitator but frequently collaborated with Occupy participants.

> She's really built a great relationship and energy with the activists. She has a great way of speaking and she has a good manner. She's a really good facilitator. She has a way of cutting people off politely when they're talking too much. Being an effective facilitator is definitely something that could make you a better leader. She's also a good speaker. Because if you're being respected as someone who can contain a meeting and make it a successful meeting and worth your time, then you are worth so much because you are going to make things happen.

Jessica viewed the meetings and participation in Occupy as a training ground for future activists. She said, "Kids are going to have to learn how to be better organizers and leaders even if they make mistakes."

The tethering structures and leadership training opportunities were also related to one another. Participants of Occupy, when asked what they accomplished, frequently credited the movement in creating a communication infrastructure that facilitated further action. The structure allowed diverse groups to loosely connect and affiliate under the larger Occupy umbrella. Through the committee and affinity group process, the meeting process, and social media processes, activists that now knew each other, and had some experience in organizing actions, had a new network of resources and leadership tools at their fingertips. Teresa explained,

> And it's kind of a self-generating thing in that the more you stay involved, the more you realize hey, anybody can organize anything. Anything you're passionate about, I can learn the tools, like you can learn how to do facilitation or you could form a group and I don't see individuals being responsible, like leaders. There isn't. There's no one leader. There's a huge number of people and I think there's this amazing interplay between individual passions and group and your ability to inspire others. You know? And we found that the most unlikely people are leaders.

Hence the consensus processes of Occupy were a fertile training ground for participative leadership, even if participants were not ready to claim their leadership status.

Critical Perspective: Expression, Proceduralism, and an Underdeveloped Theory of Leadership

A critical lens complicates the romantic and functional understandings of a phenomenon by bringing forth tensions, ironies, and contradictions especially as they relate to ideology and power (Trujillo 1992). While the romantic and the functional remain as "truths" of the experience, the critical illuminates other truths that paint a less coherent story of consensus and participative democracy. In the critical perspective we found the idyllic chants of "this is what democracy looks like" were replaced with personal "irritation" with messy general assembly meetings that did not do a good job of facilitating decision making. The prioritizing of particular participative values over others worked against consensus decision-making and contributed to a local underdeveloped theory of horizontal leadership that cultivated distrust.

Predictably, the large general assemblies did not facilitate consensus decision-making in part due to the primacy of expressive modes of communication and the varied competency and attendance of the crowd. Meetings were too big, too long, and often co-opted by personal agendas. In their reflective debrief, facilitators likened their experience of facilitating general assembly meetings to a plethora of vivid metaphors all depicting the messiness of the process: "It was like taking a fire hose to a tea cup," Mike said. Lana and others described it as "hairy." Walt described managing large group dynamics as trying to "put toothpaste back in the tube." And several facilitators expanded on the metaphor of a plane in flight, "but once in the plane, you realize it isn't actually bolted right yet [laughter from the group] and we didn't have the tools we needed once we were in the air" (Brandt).

Brandt (facilitators' debrief) admitted, "it was not really consensus, but mob rule." Early general assembly meetings held during the encampment were three-hours long and fraught with the emotion that accompanied the very serious problems of the camp such as safety, drug use, mental illness, and homeless issues. Brandt complained it was "insane" to try and arrive at two or three consensus decisions with two hundred people in a three hour meeting. He described the chaos of these early, irritating meetings. "The first couple GA's that I went [*sic*], the ones that we all were facilitating, I was like, I don't know what to do with this. This is just terrible. People have no respect for each other. People are not doing anything good, you know, meaning habits wise. And it's very hard to field anything with those kind of dynamics. You know? I mean, it was just a mess."

Lana (facilitators' debrief) reflected with her peers that the process was not supposed to be about "expressing an individual opinion but [rather] an idea." Instead, the general assembly meetings tended to be redundant because people vied to express their individual opinions resulting in what she called, "the tyranny of the minority." Deetz (1992) argued that liberal/representative democracy as opposed to participative democracy (Barber 2003) relied on linear one-way forums for communication, where persuasion is the dominant mode of expression. As it turned out, the general assembly was not a bad place for linear expression. Anyone attending a meeting could be included in the processes to make their announcement of solidarity, propose an action, or emote their concern. That is unless they started to take too long, at which point the congregate would roll their fists to move the subject along. Bonnie argued in the facilitator debrief that, "The GA was a fundamentally flawed model for doing much besides what it does, or has done, you know, in 2012, which is a good place for discussion, political ideas, and endorsements. It's a great place for soap boxing . . . ." Brandt claimed, "The GA really didn't in my mind accomplishing nothing [*sic*] besides giving people a chance to speak who had never spoken in that kind of forum, which is great, but it could have been done in other settings as well."

Deetz (1992) would not be surprised that many participants lacked the communication competency that is required for participative decision-making. He argued that people often default to "native," expressive practices in communication because we are most familiar with them. These native communication habits prioritize the expressing of opinions rather than integration of diverse perspectives into decision making, which demands greater openness, listening, and inquiry skills (Deetz 1992, 2007).

Following the lead of Occupy Wall Street, facilitators adapted to the rapid changes in the movement and the constant flux of participants and their varied understanding and skill levels with consensus, by adding and changing processes. Steps and procedures were codified and the processes associated with consensus and the general assembly meetings became laden with rules about what types of topics were appropriate for the larger meetings, what counted as a proposal, and how communication would happen within the meetings. The facilitator's manual was an eleven-page booklet layered with no less than eight Internet links to other instructive resources such as: "The Facilitator Checklist for all Meetings!" and "The committee spokescouncil model implemented by OP" (Portlandgeneralassembly.org 2011, 2012). At one point spokes from affinity groups and committees were expected to attend one weekly meeting while the later weekly general assembly meeting was reserved for larger group decision-making. The processes were confusing and convoluted as steps were added, manuals were created, and participants felt defeated by procedures, further alienating them from the consensus skills needed to partake in participative democracy. Jessica explained, "In order to speak up at a GA you had to have a certain amount of people with you, things had to be approved through Occupy, yet I didn't even know who these Occupy people were. Who were making these decisions? It made me want to work separately but work with Occupy." Even facilitators admitted "the rules made it really fucking complicated" (Bonnie, facilitators' debrief). Many of the participants we interviewed admitted they stopped attending the general assembly meetings early in the process. Barber (2003, 242) argued, "Without loyalty, fraternity, patriotism, neighborliness, bonding, tradition, mutual affection and common belief, participatory democracy is reduced to proceduralism." He couches this argument in a discussion calling for the need for moral leadership *as well as* facilitative leadership in a strong democratic system. Accordingly facilitators' ability to address communication incompetency and the tendency for the participants to rely on expressive rather than generative communication was further hampered by an underdeveloped ideology and acceptance of leadership.

Caught in a young ideology of horizontal leadership, facilitators lacked the support to provide leadership in the way of design and managing. Although they were gaining experience regarding how to best run meetings, the leaderless philosophy often prevented them from providing the direction necessary to progress toward specific goals. Leslie commented on the frustration she felt as a facilitator and the toggle she experienced between having some expertise and managing a group that did not. The values of inclusiveness and diversity visibly bump up against the need for communication competency and adherence to a leaderless philosophy. This excerpt captures the paradox that facilitators experienced managing these competing values:

> And for me, I had many points where I actually like, wanted to just yell and tell people like, listen, everyone up here or everyone that has these couple of points has done this before. Like, so we're going to give priority from this part of the discussion to the people that have done this before, which is totally against everything that I'm trying to do there. But that, there were definitely several hairy nights where I was just like, "Why can't I just tell people what to do for one second? Why can't I tell everyone to shut up and listen to the people that have done this before?" And it goes back to why we're doing this and not having to reinvent the wheel. But I feel there were some hurdles that we could have overcome if the facilitation team could have stepped up and been like, just trust us. Fucking trust us, and we're going to do it and try it and if it doesn't work, do whatever you want to do. (Facilitators' debrief)

Rapidly changing processes without explicit reflection on philosophy, as David noted at the facilitators' debrief, left the congregate distrustful of leaders and methods. Certainly some of the chaos of early meetings could be attributed to a reluctance to accept leadership and a clear miscalculation by many that leadership, rather than concentrated, unchecked leadership, was a dirty word. Both the desire to be inclusive of everyone, and the refusal to appear like one was leading the group, meant that meeting management had to be conducted via processes rather than any overt direction. But the changing and cluttering of processes worked counter to growing the movement because it often turned people off. In Jessica's words, the meetings "dissipated because people got sick and tired of the stupidity of it, not working. Then they went into the neighborhoods."

Those facilitators who did provide leadership eventually came to understand how the hesitancy to embrace leadership hurt the movement. David posed the question of ownership to the facilitators' debrief group.

> And I think it would have been important to actually name that [facilitation] as leadership. And this obviously much, is embedded within a much larger, I think that our horizontal movement's conception of this kind of shared or horizontal leadership is total shit and completely undeveloped. I mean, I remember distinctly a point when in some news articles and then other people started to use facilitator as the word for leader, because facilitators were the most visible form of leadership. But there were many other forms of leadership that were happening but because of the nature of the GA we were in a very visible location and so I think that, I don't know, I think that's a question. And from my perspective there's more to directly engage that could have been useful and I think some of the distrust that's happened, or the push back I think came in part because we didn't fully own that we were acting in a certain model of leadership, when we clearly were.

Indeed, Jessica attributed some of the chaos to the leaderless ideology. She said the general assemblies were "terribly frustrating because people wanted to work on things and there were already these causes going on and having a leaderless movement. Going to a meeting was like sitting down with ten-year-olds that were full grown men. And it was irritating." Jessica was impatient with the emphasis on inclusion and the refusal by others to lead, that is, to step up and not allow meetings to be co-opted by competing agendas.

Occupy Portland appeared to prioritize particular participative values more than others. Specifically inclusion and autonomy challenged participative decision-making with some rejecting any attempt to organize or add structure to either the camp or the movement. Walt, a professional facilitator, who spent most of his energy in InterOccupy.net, juxtaposed the success of InterOccupy.net with Occupy Portland in his interview with me:

> For example hierarchy, this—"Oh hierarchy is bad. Occupy is against hierarchy"—[was problematic]. [Instead, *InterOccupy.net*] provided a space and the space was created consistent with the norms of how things get done in Occupy. . . . In the greater Occupy, the general assembly and the decision-making process for inclusion and what-have-you was [sic] way lopsided and it needed to be bolstered by, "And what is the structure and process for getting shit done?" And [Occupy needed] a champion for productivity that would bump up against and find a way to be honoring inclusion but drawing a line. So we [*InterOccupy.net*] figured out how to do that. I was a champion of, "We need to be high performing and high inclusive." We need to have something like consensus and we need to make decisions in a timely fashion and we came up with our structures and processes for, much more complete and much more healthy than the rest of Occupy.

InterOccupy.net, a successful collaboration of Occupy sites across the nation, did this by designing protocols for interaction by consensus and within a participative philosophy. However, they did not dismiss the need for or idea of structure and protocols. Walt posited that an organization that spun of off Occupy Portland, The Portland Action Lab, was a "brilliant example" of how to balance inclusion and action. It is no surprise that some of the same leaders of Occupy Portland brought their skills to the work of Portland Action Lab. But Occupy Portland appeared unable to overcome the stifling battles over structure, process, hierarchy, and leadership.

The division among competing participative values coupled with an underdeveloped theory of leadership manifests in participants' responses to an example of consensus decision-making that took place during the camp. We asked in almost all interviews for participants to describe personal high and low moments in their experience. Elayne described as a high moment the event in which the rules she helped draft, regarding respect and drug prohibition, were adopted by consensus at the general assembly:

> So I wrote guidelines for safety and health, which is a really challenging thing to do and get passed at camp because, you were there, like, okay, maybe we shouldn't be allowing alcohol and drugs and this zone that we created [unintel-

ligible] created all these rules and that was a really big deal and it sort of resulted in pouring over our values and trying to create a document that would represent the values of everyone at camp. And uh, getting that passed through the general assembly was a really high point because I didn't think it was possible, but it got done. And in that moment I saw everyone's hands go up for this thing, [I thought] "oh my God, maybe we can do this."

However, Mark described the very same event as one of the lowest moments in his experience as he found the rules symbolic of exclusion. Thus, Elayne's high of being able to create rules for society, albeit through consensus, became Mark's low as he contested the very notion of rules being used to exclude members of society. Occupy Portland's fear of hierarchy and power prevented many participants from accepting any type of structure or leadership that potentially limited the autonomy or inclusion of others.

CONCLUSION

A first goal of this analysis sought to identify the communication values, structures, and practices that constituted the successes, challenges, and paradoxes of a consensus-driven participative democracy. These findings were further contextualized through romantic, functional, and critical interpretations of Occupy Portland attending to a second goal of this analysis, to demonstrate no single narrative is sufficient to tell the story or understand the contributions of this movement. Attention to the lived experiences of participants practicing participative democracy facilitates the development of theory relevant to leadership and structure. After describing the contributions of Trujillo's interpretive lenses, I next argue that consensus-based participation must hold in tension the values embedded in its ideology by heeding the communicative practice of contestation.

The romantic perspective of consensus structures and processes makes visible what a society may look like with a different paradigm of democracy that is grounded in participation, realizing the new anarchist's vision. The chant, "This is what democracy looks like!" is telling in that it expressed the feeling that somehow participants had not really experienced democracy until now. In the romantic lens the processes are symbolic, representing a new way of engaging in the politics of our society. The general assembly is a vibrant public sphere facilitating inclusiveness and autonomy of ideas. The movement is not leaderless, but leaderful. Horizontal leadership is realized as people self-monitor their domination, and like migrating birds shift and change leaders based on the needs of the movement. This idea of leadership is consistent with Barber's (2003) conception of leaders stepping in and out of leadership roles in strong democracy. It supports more nuanced developments in leadership studies of leadership not just as a category of behaviors but as a "dialectic that questions sharp distinctions between leaders and followers" (Zoller and Fairhurst 2007, 1340).

The functional view demonstrates how consensus processes and principles worked practically in the movement. Many participants were gaining interaction skills and competencies. Dialogue, critical listening, and spaces of contemplation made their way into civic discourse and these principled practices were reproduced in other settings (for a similar study of Occupy Wall Street see Min 2012). The general assemblies also tethered activists in a very practical way creating an infrastructure that later facilitated the ability for affinity groups to quickly mobilize political action. The affinity structure supports Freeman's (1972/73) claim that homogenous groups will be more productive. Accordingly, affinity groups could loosely affiliate with the larger Occupy movement but work independently with less misunderstanding (Freeman, 1972/73) to design and craft proposals—or be task oriented, as Freeman would say.

Additionally, the functional perspective illuminates the very practical role that the general assemblies and associated structures and processes were fulfilling as they created an opportunity for leadership training both as facilitative leaders and transitional leaders. In this view, transitional leaders, those who design processes and institutions then step down (Barber 2003), such as Jessica, found role models. Jessica emulated the skills she learned when she designed her own day of education around health care. Leadership training is very important in the sustainability of the movement. Indeed, as we interviewed participants into the second year of Occupy, we found prominent figures in the early days were not able to participate as much citing reasons such as marriage, buying a home, getting a job, and avoiding arrest. Hence fostering leadership skills is essential if the hopes of Occupy are to flourish. Clearly the movement's horizontal structures led to sustainable leadership opportunities.

The critical perspective surfaces the contradictions and ironies of the structures and processes and considers them in relation to power. Facilitators were held captive to the tyranny of the minority. Despite much of the communication skill development that took place, the movement suffered from a problem of scale (Barber 2003). Large general assemblies were often sites of incivility violating the reciprocity and respect conditions for the ideal speech situation (Habermas 1990). Trust was lacking as claims lay uncontested as to the sincerity of the speaker (Habermas 1990). In particular, a healthy discussion regarding leadership remained latent and cultivated suspicion. The predicted paradox of this movement came from its commitment to a leaderless philosophy. Students of the feminist movement and its suspicion of structures could have foreseen the parallels with this movement in which case a refusal to recognize the benefits of leadership results in a lack of action, accountability, and responsibility. Leaders in the Occupy Portland movement appeared to lead meetings and lead themselves in projects. But the most sustainable parts of Occupy like InterOccupy.net did not deny leadership as a philosophy. Instead, breakaway groups and organizations such as Portland Action Lab combined philosophy with organizational leadership and design, according to Walt. Needed distinctions between leadership and unhealthy leadership, power and pathological power, were not made in time to save the general assembly but consensus philosophies did follow the movement as it dispersed into decentralized committees and affinity groups. It may be that the general assembly served its inspirational purpose to help those visualize participative democracy, but inevitably the movement would morph into the smaller groups that Freeman (1972/73) touted better serve social movements.

The critical perspective also illuminates power in processes. One may argue that the creation of rules that were labored over by its authors was an excellent example of participative democracy. By taking into account the many and diverse values that needed to be reflected in the rules, the authors generated something greater than they would have without including those diverse perspectives (Deetz 1992). The authors took their proposal to the general assembly, where it was open to contestation (Habermas 1990) and was eventually agreed upon by the community through a consensus process of deliberation, revisions, and eventual acceptance. And the authors did not control or lead the processes of decision making. This is an example of David Graeber's vision of consensus and direct democracy and Barber's (2003) vision of participative (strong) democracy in which case communities create their own rules for living. However, a camp-centric view, as Walt called it, privileged autonomy and inclusion over consensus and participative decision-making. By privileging individualism and inclusion over all else the community lacked the ability to govern itself as all structure, all rules, all formalization, were viewed suspiciously by many Occupy participants. Deetz (1992) reminds us that all decisions are temporal and should be open to reconsideration. However, he did not suggest we try and live without making decisions as a society. Neither does Graeber (2002), as he argues initiatives that others can live with must be brought forth for consensus. When any "ism" is dogmatic in its privileging of some values over others, be it egalitarianism or individualism, it is subject to the same criticisms of power as any other ideology (Friberg-Fenros and Schaffer 2010). Dogmatism of any philosophy or worldview is the absence of openness to the other. Dogmatic autonomy ignores the communitarian aspect necessary to live and participate with others. Dogmatic egalitarianism ignores the need for direction and responsibility and ignores inequities in communication competence. So even in a participative democracy that is inclusive, dogmatic inclusiveness prevents it from making decisions together. And democratic societies must make decisions. The trick in participative democracy is to hold in balance these tensions of values. The best hope for consensus-based participative democracy is respectful contestation—one that happens both in and out of the dialogic situation (Ganesh and Zoller 2012). Deetz (1992, 2007) reminds us that in the ideal speech situation decisions are always open to contestation. By institutionalizing mechanisms for contestation, and assuring continued opportunity for individual communication competency, leadership and structure remain open to the scrutiny of participants, balancing the inequities and finding the space between competing values inherent in consensus-based processes.

DISCUSSION QUESTIONS

1. Compare and contrast the communication practices associated with liberal democracy and participative democracy.
2. What are some of the values and practices associated with consensus?
3. According to Barber's four types of participative leadership, what types are visible in the case of Occupy Portland? What types are absent?
4. How does our understanding of leadership in Occupy Portland change with the different romantic, functional, and critical interpretations?
5. Do you think Occupy Portland succeeded in achieving participative democracy? Why or why not? How could Occupy Portland strengthen participative democracy?

NOTES

1. Interview printed with consent of participant.
2. Mexico's Zapatista Army of National Liberation is well known for its commitment to participatory and bottom-up democracy (Graeber 2002). It is described further in Kapoor's chapter 1 in this book.
3. David Graeber would reject the idea that he is the leader of the Occupy movement, as many researchers and writers have contributed to the ideologies of Occupy. That said, his writings and philosophies are influential and easily traceable to Occupy discourse and texts.
4. Methods of data collection and analysis are discussed in detail in chapter 4 of this volume.
5. Typical hand signals include: twinkle fingers pointed up for agreement; twinkle fingers pointed down for disagreement; rolling fists indicate the conversation needs to move along; fists across the chest indicate a block; and matched pointer fingers and thumbs indicate there is a question of process.
6. As mentioned in chapter 4 in a discussion of Occupy Portland participants, some participants claimed the label houseless as opposed to homeless, claiming they lacked a house not a home, which is symbolic of more personal things such as sense of place or belonging.
7. *InterOccupy.net* is a collaborative virtual facilitation and organizing site that works on behalf of all Occupy sites across North America.
8. Interview printed with consent of participant.
9. "How It Works at Occupy Wall Street 9/25/11," www.youtube.com/watch?v=xIK7uxBSAS0
10. "Facilitation Team User Manual and Orientation!" revision January 4, 2012. (Portlandgeneralassembly.org 2012).

11. Interview printed with consent of participant. David also wrote the foreword for this book.

12. The meeting facilitation process involved one person who led the meeting while others watched the crowd and organized stacks (a queue of speakers in which case four to five people are identified at a time and given a number until it is their turn to speak). Another facilitator monitored the crowd for consensus. A loose modified consensus was accepted when the crowd sentiment seemed to be in at least 90 percent agreement (this number varied in the Occupy movement from city to city). Measuring this sentiment was a precarious process of scanning the crowd for twinkle fingers of approval and downward twinkle fingers of disapproval. In a crowd of one hundred or more persons, this was a guesstimate at best.

Chapter Six

Globalization from Below

Discourses of Horizontalism, Direct Action, and Violence

Ricardo V. Munoz

One woman raised her hand for a clarifying question saying this wasn't really a question but a statement. When asked if it was pertinent to the discussion, she remarked, "sort of" then immediately started reciting a poem off her laptop on the theme of Occupy solidarity. After a few minutes of this (with no end in sight) some people started making gestures to speed things up but the woman's attention was wholly on her laptop. Julian, the facilitator, said aloud to folks making signs to move on, "It's your meeting!" As she finally paused for breath, others intervened and thanked the woman for the poem. "I'm not finished yet!" she demanded gently. They suggested to her that she could continue reading it first during the Announcements phase of the general assembly meeting, which she agreed was a good idea.—Fieldnotes, Portland, Oregon, February 2012

What do I dream about? I don't know. It's funny, you know before I was dreaming only about the future, and now I'm dreaming in the present.—Carina, an Argentine collective worker [1]

[What brought you here?] It was something deeper than I can really explain. It was a feeling like this is where I need to be if I want to change the world.—An Occupy Activist

Not only have the chains of the Law been broken, they never existed.—Anarchist Poet Hakim Bey [2]

The Occupy movement began life as a verb. When the *Adbusters.org* blog (2011) called to "set up tents, kitchens, peaceful barricades and occupy Wall Street for a few months" (note the small "o") it revealed to the public a set of grievances that had been largely hidden in the political discourse. These grievances were not only about the normal politics of control over the media, the banking system, and the state; the call also brought media attention to a new ideology about organizing around the distribution, rather than the accumulation, of power. As the #Occupy meme took the cities of North America by storm in the autumn of 2011, these new ideologies spread as part of that meme. It began in a city location, Wall Street in New York. Once established the idea swiftly spread through various cities including Oakland, Denver, Los Angeles, Washington DC . . . Portland, as each version declared itself "in solidarity with Occupy Wall Street." Each city reiterated the language of antiglobalization against corporate capitalism, as well as an ideology of coordinated modes of organizing around the equal distribution of organizational power.

The emergence of Occupy provides an opportunity to examine how organizing at the grassroots level is done in terms of the "interrelationships between communication, organizing, and alternative economic systems" (Ganesh, Zoller, and Cheney 2005, 185). The coordination of local resistance in order to contest global phenomena has been described by some as *globalization from below* (Ganesh, Zoller, and Cheney 2005; Portes 1997). The antiglobalization or *global justice movement* (Della Porta 2005) grew out of local, grassroots resistance to international trade agreements that developed its own network of localities and affinity groups capable of bringing fifty thousand people into the streets of Seattle during the third World Trade Organization summit in 1999 (Della Porta 2008; Starhawk 2002). Importantly, these assemblages of resistance are "complexly connected sites that weave the global with the local" (Pal and Dutta 2008, 44). Unlike earlier waves of protest action this was a *new activism* (Graeber 2002) that was not limited to national projects, was truly global in scope, and more targeted against global corporations (Eschle 2004). This new focus brought with it new methods of organizing centered on horizontal modes of democratic public deliberation (Della Porta 2005). These activist organizations not only opposed global corporations but also enacted alternatives to capitalist organizing, as activist David Graeber (2002) notes, by embracing horizontalist modes of organizing. Thus the hierarchical structures of global capitalism were challenged both materially and symbolically. Occupy is as much about these new modes of organizing as it is about how to imagine a world where corporate domination does not exist at the local level of resistance. Conversely, an attention to the local is important because it is in the local forms of resistance that these new forms of global organizing are expressed.

Local forms of resistance are not without their own sets of problem, such as a tendency to co-opt hierarchical organizational forms that are contradictory to their ideological roots (Ashcraft 2006). Thus, one also has to account for the self-reflexive character of local organizing as it resists organizational impulses towards acquiring the features of the phenomena that they oppose (de Souza Santos 2006). So as the Occupy movement inherits much from earlier iterations of the antiglobalization theme, these new activists draw on discourses of existing structures that recreate the very power asymmetries they were meant to oppose. Thus, Ganesh, Zoller, and Cheney (2005) have called on scholars to "investigate the possibility of hegemonic framing of 'internal' group discourse and examine connections between hegemony, counter-hegemony, and transformation" (183). In terms of Occupy Portland, this is an opportunity to understand tensions in the organizational constitution of new activism at the local organization level.

Thus, this work seeks to explore how ideology and power operate at the local level of organizing antiglobalization movements. I investigate this by two means: First, by describing relevant discourses and interpreting them through Trujillo's (1992) romantic, functional, and critical lenses in an effort to better understand them. Second, by describing how the meanings of the ideologies surrounding antiglobalization are expressed as locally emergent dialectical tensions within Occupy Portland. In this way, I hope to provide scholars of activism (especially activist-scholars) an opportunity to create a more clear understanding of some of the difficulties and problems that organizing globalization from below entails; and for more general organizational studies readers, a window into the world of Occupy that helps to question established assumptions about organization.

This chapter proceeds by explicating concepts of power and dialectical tension in discourse that provide a context for the analysis that follows of the general discourses evident in the antiglobalization literature. I follow with a description of the dialectical tensions evident in Occupy Portland. But all of the analyses and findings presented will be foregrounded by reminding the reader of Trujillo's organizational culture schema.

TRUJILLO'S ORGANIZATIONAL CULTURE LENSES

This work is about understanding the organizational culture of antiglobalization activism. Trujillo (1992) introduced an interpretive schema towards understanding organizational culture. While these are discussed more fully elsewhere in this volume (see the introduction of this book), it is best to remind the reader what these are and how they are applied here. *Romantics* view the organization as a set of timeless and idealized qualities. *Functionalists* look to the organization in terms of the everyday, useful, and the practical. *Critics* tend to see how the organization deals with issues of power—how the organization functions as a set of relationships where domination and resistance might exist. These interpretive lenses each provide a way of understanding organizational discourse as nuanced and capable of holding multiple interpretations. In terms of the present work, this interpretive schema will be applied to various discourses that relate to organizing within Occupy, thus allowing the reader to understand how ideology and discourse constitute the movement.

POWER, IDEOLOGY, AND DIALECTICAL TENSION

This study of Occupy will consider how discourse functions at an organizational level as it recreates Occupy Portland's ideological foundations. While the term "discourse" has no overarching definition within communication theory (Alvesson and Karreman 2000), it is useful to consider how the term helps to reveal relationships of power when applied across various scales (from everyday to organizational to societal). I approach this by applying concepts from Foucault (1972, 1979) that outline both a theory of discourse and a theory of power as emergent through discourse. Foucault's analytics form a substantial body of work that "denaturalizes" historically produced relationships of power by "exposing them as products of particular discourses" (Prasad 2005, 251). In Foucault's concept, discourse invokes power, thus "is less about everyday linguistic interaction, and more about historically developed systems of ideas that forms institutionalized and authoritative ways of addressing a topic, to 'regimes of truth.'" (Alvesson and Karreman 2011, 1129). Importantly, Foucault also identified neoliberalism as one such system of ideas that replaces the state with the market as a system of economic regulation (Lemke 2011). Neoliberalism is a "political discourse/ideology that recommends deregulation, privatization, and the dismantling of the social contract" (Starr 2000, 16). The antiglobalization movement draws many of its ideologies from this understanding of how global corporations exercise power through neoliberal ideology.

Ideology functions as the discourse of certain socially constructed power relationships, or "when a particular definition of reality comes to be attached to a concrete power interest, it may be called an ideology" (Berger and Luckmann 1966, 123). Thus, any understanding of the ideology of Occupy must also include how its discourses reveal power relations and distances within the movement as particular ways of understanding the world. Additionally, understanding Occupy ideology incorporates knowledge and awareness of the ideologies that the movement opposes.

In his analytics of power, Foucault views power and knowledge as mutually constitutive social constructions:

> We must cease . . . to describe the effects of power in negative terms: it "excludes", it "represses", it "censors", it "abstracts", it "masks", it "conceals." In fact, power produces; it produces reality; it produces domains of

objects and rituals of truth. The individual and the knowledge that may be gained of him belong to this production. (Foucault 1979, 194)

This formulation sees power not simply as a repressive or dominating force by institutions overlaid onto individuals, but rather as a network of relationships that constitute society. In the Foucauldian sense, society is defined by its power relations and there are no power relations that are not constituted without exercising knowledge; knowledge "operates" as a means of regulating power.

Additionally, it is fair to say that the ideologies of Occupy developed in opposition to, but also depend on, globalized capitalism in order to be apparent. As Portes (1997) describes it, "the process of capitalist globalization is so broadly based and has generated such momentum as to continuously nourish its grassroots counterpart" (19). This metaphor of nourishment invokes a dialectics of control/resistance (Mumby 2005) that "emphasizes the ways organizational actors create and renegotiate meanings for organizational processes" (Norton and Paveglio 2009, 159). One should also bear in mind that relationships are not simple dualisms wherein a power interest exerts a particular form of knowledge (or reality) on a dominated class; power may also be viewed in terms of dialectical tensions that are expressed as relationships between "a set of situated discursive and nondiscursive practices that are simultaneously enabling and constraining, coherent and contradictory, complex and simple, efficacious and ineffectual" (Mumby 2005, 38); that is, dialectical tensions are a complex set of discourses that are constantly being negotiated among interactants.

Dialectical tensions also emerge from contradictions within a discourse. "Discourse," Foucault reminds us, "is the path from one contradiction to another: if it gives rise to those that can be seen, it is because it obeys that which it hides" (1972, 151). That is to say, an analysis of what is apparent in a group of related statements should consider how contradictions between them reveal the mechanisms that reproduce relationships of power. The approach here, then, is to understand how ideologies are represented through organizational-scale discursive tensions that emerge from processes of organizing and sense making and towards the production of meaning (Weick 1995). I follow the discourse of Occupy Portland from the ideologies surrounding and influencing the organization to how these are expressed through local dialectics that display inconsistencies, tensions, and contradictions revealing how discourse creates the organizational meanings of Occupy. Then, in relation to the analysis of Occupy discourse, I demonstrate how localized discourses about an ideology of Occupy are revealed to be in dialectical tension. This will be done by first presenting the larger ideologically grounded societal-discourses that surround the movement. Accordingly, I begin with a description and analysis of antiglobalization ideology through writers closely associated with the new activist movements.

THREE DISCOURSES OF ANTIGLOBALIZATION IDEOLOGY

The discourses of Occupy are found in the ideas and scholarship surrounding *new activism* (Graeber 2002). Unlike traditional organizational models, new activism expresses an ideological opposition to hierarchical organizing and adversarial processes of deliberation (Della Porta 2005; Graeber 2002). Importantly for communication scholars and students, these practices express discourses about communication that represent "a break with these sorts of vertical ways of organizing and relating" (Sitrin 2012, 33). The break is visible in the ideology of new activism, which emphasizes the primacy of relationships through the discourses of *horizontalism, direct action*, and *diversity of tactics*. While these discourses are described separately, it must also be understood that these are mutually constitutive of new activist organizing: no one discourse can be expressed without invoking the others. What is common among them is how they describe action; and what is different is how their talk about organizing relates to power. I next describe these discourses and characterize them in terms of Trujillo's (1992) romantic timelessness, functionalist immediacy, and critical reflexivity.

"To Be Discovered in the Practice of It:" The Romantic Discourse of Horizontalism

In some manner or other, the various activist groups that identify as Occupy make claims to holding general assembly meetings (also called GAs), spokescouncil meetings (also referred to as SC), and other meeting formats using a consensus process as a representation of their horizontalism:[3] "processes in which attempts are made so that everyone is heard and new relationships are created" (Sitrin 2012, 33). These principles are frequently referred to as a feature of antiglobalization activist movements (Della Porta 2005) and form part of the collective strategies of the Occupy movement (Sitrin 2012). Horizontalism expresses a quality of *timelessness* as an approach to organizing, or "removing the temporal distinction between the struggle in the present and a goal in the future; instead, the struggle and the goal, the real and the ideal, become one in the present" (Maeckelbergh 2011, 4). In this sense, the horizontal discourse of organizing evokes the romantic sense of timelessness in Trujillo's (1992) schema, except in reverse. Horizontalism does not look back to an idealized past; it invokes a mode of equally distributing power in the present.

The timeless quality of horizontalism grew out of revolution but has no particular origination. The term is first encountered as *horizontalidad* as it made its appearance during the Argentine Revolt of 2001, which led to four successive governments in the space of a few weeks after the fall of then President Carlos Menem (Sitrin 2006). The origin of the term is a mystery:

> No one recalls where it came from or who first might have said it. It was a new word and emerged from a new practice. The practice was people coming together, looking to one another, and—without anyone in charge or with power over the other—beginning to find ways to solve their problems together. Through doing this together, they were creating a new relationship: both the decision-making process and the ways in which they wanted to relate in the future were horizontal. What this meant was, and still is, *to be discovered in the practice of it*. As the Zapatistas in Chiapas say, the meaning is in the walk and always questioning as we walk. (Sitrin 2012, 32, emphasis mine)

Discovery through the practice of it expresses an ideological principle included within horizontal organizing: a discourse of the possibilities of organizing around the local and emergent expressions of power through deliberation and consensus.

Thus, horizontalism is a way of being in an ideal present without attempting to prescribe an ideal condition for some future time. It is firmly rooted in a sense of discovery through deliberation in the present, as described by one Argentine worker:

> There's something dangerous about thinking that the purpose of *horizontalidad* is to replace something else. . . . The real question of horizontalidad is: What does it mean to organize ourselves? What will it be today? What does it mean for us? And it is possible to respond to these things in a concrete situation. . . . We don't think that horizontalidad should be thought of as a new model, but rather horizontalidad implies that there are no models. (*Collectivo Situationes*, quoted in Sitrin 2006, 55)

The phrase "no models" implies an assumption of the discovery of horizontalist community practice through deliberation in the present. This vocabulary recalls Trujillo's quote from anthropologist Victor Turner, "Communitas is spontaneous, immediate, concrete—it is not shaped by norms, it is not institutionalized, it is not abstract" (Turner 1974, quoted in Trujillo 1992, 359). As Carina, an Argentine collective worker expresses in one of this chapter's beginning quotes, she is "dreaming in the present."

Thus horizontalism is more than a set of consensus-seeking deliberative practices. It articulates a romantic sense of organizing that is decidedly counterbureaucratic (Ashcraft 2006) in principle, but makes no specific recommendation about the future structure of an organization. Rather, it enables communities to continuously discover how structure is to be accomplished. And as *Collectivo Situationes* implies in the quote above, what is being deliberated is not some permanent organizational form, but rather present and immediate action.

"Act as if You Are Already Free:"
The Functionalist Discourse of Direct Action

While horizontalism expresses a quality of timeless "dreaming" in the present, the ideology of new activism also invokes a functionalist attitude towards action, which the anarchist poet Hakim Bey perhaps best captures the flavor of in terms of anarchist revolutionary acts:

> Don't just survive while waiting for someone's revolution to clear your head, don't sign up for the armies of anorexia or bulimia—*act as if you were already free*, calculate the odds, step out, remember the Code Duello—Smoke Pot/Eat Chicken/Drink Tea. Every man his own vine and figtree (Circle Seven Koran, Noble Drew Ali)—carry your Moorish passport with pride, don't get caught in the crossfire, keep your back covered—but take the risk, dance before you calcify. (Bey 2006, 28, emphasis mine)

The grand (societal level) discourse, act as if you are already free, encapsulates the anarchist attitude of enabling change by directing the romantic horizontalist attitude of organizing towards the reality of action. It does so without waiting for organizing structures to accomplish action. Hakim Bey's phrase is not a mere bumper sticker; it is a quoted principle of action—an anarchist principle—as David Graeber explains in an interview with Charlie Rose:

> [With] normal political action you go to the governor, sign a petition, or you can even blockade their house, but that still isn't direct action. Direct action is you go off and dig the well yourself and dare them to stop you. So, in a way, anarchism is about *acting as if you are already free*. And I think that's—if you want to define anarchism . . . the short version is simple: anarchism is democracy without the government . . . I guess the longer version would be: anarchism is a commitment to the idea that it would be possible to have a society based on principles of self-organization, voluntary association, and mutual aid. (Rose 2006, emphasis mine)

In Graeber's description of "acting as if you are already free," the power from coordinated action and membership is voluntary and unconstrained by dominating political structures. Anarchist organizing breaks with modernist assumptions about revolutionary action that directly confronts authority. Instead it attempts to contest domination by ignoring it and assuming it no longer has power over society or, as Subcommandante Marcos of the Zapatistas explains it, "We need not conquer the world. It is enough to make it anew" (2003, 34).

In David Graeber's description above, this functional discourse is expressed as *direct action*: ways of acting that "bypass parliamentary or bureaucratic channels to directly ameliorate or eliminate an injustice, or to slow down or obstruct regular operations of an unjust system or order" (Conway 2003, 508–9). The term emerged early in the twentieth century out of the Industrialized Workers of the World (IWW or "Wobblies") that "sought immediate redress for grievances at the point of production: the mines, mills, factories and fields" (Moynihan and Solnit 2002, 129). This is an expanded view of the Occupy do-it-yourself (DIY) culture (see Heath chapter 5 in this volume); not only is there a preference for getting things done first through volunteer efforts, it enacts the horizontalism as an economy of the present rather than of an ideal future. Sitrin (2006) describes this as *autogestión* in the Argentine revolt:

> We waited two months for the bosses to come back. We went to the unions, the Ministry of Work, all with the intention of getting the boss to come back and offer us a solution. He never came. So we decided to work. . . . We did it, and we paid the water bill and the gas bill—which is the most important—and that's how we worked. (Liliana, quoted in Sitrin 2006, 68)

The temporal dimension of direct action is, thus, rooted as well in the present, but as immediate action rather than as deliberation. This is a different sense of the present; it organizes for the immediate needs of a collective. Direct action is thus a discourse of power that does not attempt to oppose existing structures such as the state or capitalism; rather, it resolves differences through the immediacy of needs. It is an ideology that promotes action at the location of injustice and is thus a functional manifestation of power relationships.

"The Heavily Ritualized Nature of Modern Civil Disobedience:" Diversity of Tactics as Critical Discourse

While direct action is generally intended to be peaceful, it also faces a constant threat of violence from the police and military. Civil disobedience is a deliberate challenge to the perceived injustice of specific laws (Conway 2003). Direct action, then, also implies a discourse that critiques what Graeber (2006, 4) calls *structural violence*: "forms of pervasive social inequality that are ultimately backed up by the threat of physical harm." By that, he refers to those latent forms of violence that erupt only when authority is questioned but may otherwise go unrecognized. Institutions such as government are obvious targets of this label, but it also extends to institutions like banks who assume the power to determine what forms of debt default must be accompanied by court orders (with subsequent threats of police enforcement). What civil disobedience critiques is the use of implied threats of violence as a means of control. That is to ask, "Who gets to define what violence is?" when breaking specific laws.

Affinity groups within the movement, thus, express varying degrees of counterviolence as a challenge to structural violence. This discourse of critique in its various forms is often described in terms of a *diversity of tactics*: "an ethic of respect for, and acceptance of, the tactical choices of other activists" (Conway 2003, 511). Diversity of tactics is a critical discourse in Trujillo's (1992) sense—a reflexive quality of activism that seeks to understand a multiplicity of voices. Diversity of tactics consciously questions those who seek to control the tactics of others.

The discourse of diversity of tactics is expressed specifically when affinity groups tolerate deliberate acts of vandalism and property damage that is typical of Black Bloc tactics (Avery-Natale 2010; Conway 2003). In this sense, the need to maintain solidarity is thus a critical rather than a romantic or functional attitude. Black Bloc tactics serve to criticize the possibility of co-optation of activism by the corporate state, or as activist Harsha Walia (2010) expresses it, "one of the greatest utilities of the Black Bloc is that it serves to break the heavily ritualized nature of modern civil disobedience."[4] Walia is referring to the complacent sort of protest that long-time activists have established with the police, a relationship that Ehrenreich (2000, 29) describes as "the numbingly ritual quality of actions: Protesters sit down in a spot prearranged with the police and booked [*sic*], protesters get released."

The critical discourse of diversity of tactics questions the willingness of protests of the past to cooperate with global capitalism in rendering action as merely symbolic. It rejects the mild forms of "appropriate conflicts" (Deetz 1992, 254) that states and corporations use to present a semblance of democratic critique. This new activist discourse is an attempt to challenge corporate symbols directly, even to the extent of property damage, which often results in power ironies when such action is interpreted as violent:

> This situation often produces extraordinary ironies. In Seattle, the only incidents of actual physical assault by protestors on other individuals were not attacks on the police, since these did not occur at all, but attacks by "pacifists" on Black Bloc'ers engaged in acts of property damage. Since the Black Bloc'ers had collectively agreed on a strict policy of non-violence (which they defined as never doing anything to harm another living being), they uniformly refused to strike back. In many recent occupations, self-appointed "Peace Police" have manhandled activists who showed up to marches in black clothing and hoodies, ripped their masks off, shoved and kicked them: always, without the victims themselves having engaged in any act of violence, always, with the victims refusing, on moral grounds, to shove or kick back. (Graeber 2012, par. 19).

There is a subtle irony in the actions of property damage as a means of contesting capitalism when so-called pacifists express power in order to control other activists. Diversity of tactics is a discourse that attempts to wrestle how to oppose structural violence. It thus serves to critique both the capitalist state and those who are seen to cooperate with it even as they protest.

Expanding upon Graeber's earlier description of direct action—that action is brought directly to the point of contest (dig the well yourself) and defying state authority to stop it—diversity of tactics invokes a refusal to conform to ritual concepts of protest by exploring the limits of what violence means within the movement, and by respecting the actions of activists who choose to push the limits of nonviolent civil disobedience.

Thus diversity of tactics discourse validates horizontalism and direct action as critiques of corporate ideology and as explorative ways to oppose global capitalism. As mentioned earlier, the three discourses of the new activist ideology are mutually constitutive. They are romantic, functionalist, or critical points by which the ideology is expressed as discourse: as timeless attitude towards power as organizational emergence (romantic), as present need for action (functionalist), and a commentary on avoiding co-optation by structural violence (critical).

What I have attempted so far is a brief description of concepts expressed by the new activism in terms of what has occurred en route to the emergence of Occupy. These discourses provided resources for the constitution of globalization from below as a coherent set of practices that could replicate and coordinate global and local action (Graeber 2002). Occupy Portland serves as a case of how globalization from below works in practice and as expressed in a particular historical setting. In light of Ganesh, Zoller, and Cheney's call to "focus on the discursive process of organizing and power" (2005, 183), it is worth asking how ideological foundations of antiglobalization are expressed in local discourses. That is, what tensions and contradictions emerge from discourse on the ideology of antiglobalization? Specifically, how are tensions and contradictions among horizontalism, direct action, and diversity of tactics reflected in the discursive activity of Occupy Portland?

In response to these questions, I interweave narrative illustrations drawn from fieldnotes and various texts produced by Occupy Portland, as well as texts from the wider movement that directly influenced the discourse. My ethnographic methods involved being a full-participant as a member of the facilitation team in Occupy Portland. This also involved hermeneutic phenomenological analysis of texts I gathered both from ethnographic notes and the wider discourse surrounding my role as a consensus-process facilitator. (Please see Heath, Munoz, and Fletcher chapter 4 of this volume for a more extensive discussion on methods.)

My presentation strategy in the following sections is to explore the themes within the texts of Occupy using a sententious approach (Van Manen 1990) wherein I select a particular sentence or phrase that can stand to represent my understanding of the phenomenon being observed and apply these to the headings of each section. I then follow these with anecdotal vignettes drawn from fieldnotes that provide "a concrete counterweight to abstract theoretical thought" in order to allow the reader to sense the lived experience of participants grappling with the meanings of the ideology presented earlier (119).

DIALECTICAL TENSIONS IN THE DISCOURSE OF OCCUPY PORTLAND

In the previous chapter, Heath described the quandary of the facilitation team in having a leadership role thrust on them despite an ideological commitment to leaderlessness. That problem forms part of a greater dialectical tension that is revealed in local discourses surrounding the performance of activism in Occupy Portland. I highlight three manifestations of the most prominent dialectical tension—the dialectic of *appropriation* versus *distribution* of power that is inherent in the ideological discourses described earlier. In this sense, to appropriate is to take for oneself, supported largely by the values of autonomy and individualism, and to distribute is to share, requiring community decision-making and taking into account the diverse values of the community. This tension manifests in the discourse in at least three ways related to larger discursive ideologies of horizontalism, direct action, and diversity of tactics: (1) It calls into question *how* resources are distributed, established in the exemplars related to a gift economy of horizontalism. (2) It surfaces questions over *what* actions may be taken toggling with the decision to act independently or as a collective via deliberative sanctioning. And (3) the dialectic tension of appropriation versus distribution illuminates contradictions embedded in the act of defining, exemplified in the struggle to articulate what nonviolence means and *who* determines what counts as violence.

"Just Let Him Have the Table!": Ironies of a Horizontal Gift Economy

> Cigarette Guy tells me he'll start giving cigarettes away once he has a cup of coffee. He explains to me how difficult it is to get hot water in the camp since the donated generator was being used by the other camp groups for light and other power needs. Cigarettes are in short supply here in the camp. Whenever someone asks him for a cigarette he gives the same message, "if you give me some coffee, even a sip, I'll give you a cigarette." Or "if you give me a coin so I can buy coffee, I'll give you a cigarette. Then I'll give them all away." Most

people he says this to seem at a loss and reply with something like, "okay, I'll look for some coffee" to which Cigarette Guy would say, "sure, but it's really tough to find hot water around here." Even though I have cigarettes to offer those who ask, I don't since I want Cigarette Guy to get his coffee. I decide to help him out and "buy" a cigarette from him by donating a quarter into his bowl.

One fellow who passes by is different. After the usual message the new fellow says, "okay, I'll get you coffee." Cigarette Guy says to me, "he seems pretty confident; I bet he'll get some." Someone else buys a cigarette, so Cigarette Guy has enough money to buy some coffee and wanders away. I spend many minutes on the park bench just looking around. Eventually, Cigarette Guy returns with a cup of coffee from a nearby 7-Eleven. He offers me some but I don't have a container. He lends me a plastic shot glass that he wears around his neck and pours me some coffee from his own cup. While I am sipping the coffee, the confident fellow comes back with a french press full of coffee. "I told you he'd come through!" says Cigarette Guy; but he is out of cigarettes—he'd given them all away. Confident Guy looked disappointed so I tell him "I have one for you." His face lights up as I point my pack towards him. Confident Guy refills Cigarette Guy's coffee mug, then sits beside me as he refills my shot glass. Confident Guy is relatively well dressed in a vest and neat clothing; he has some theories about language and mathematics. We keep talking until someone comes along calling for him. It seems he is involved in kitchen duties and runs off with his french press. I learn later that both Cigarette Guy and Confident Guy are houseless; the camp is their home. (Fieldnotes October 29, 2011)

This vignette describes the *gift economy* (Graeber 2004) of the camp, where no money needs to be exchanged in order for resources to be available; social esteem is granted from the ability to gift the community. Yet, when resources are scarce (commodities such as cigarettes or hot water) capitalism intrudes, tensions emerge, and contradictions (exchange of commodities) become evident. This tension is seen in the DIY culture of the camp—action is always voluntary and based on the availability of bodies and resources, but once a scarce resource comes into play (i.e., money, coffee, and cigarettes), negotiation takes over.

The typical operation of the gift economy comes from the attitude of direct action—once resources are donated they are distributed as directly as possible. In practice, this often involves donations to an office rental fund, as well as donations of food or clothing for the houseless. In these cases, no one directs the disposition of resources and or the actions of people; *how* these are distributed depends more on the giver than the receiver. For example,

> Beatrice comes by with a large bag and sits beside me. She has a bag full of old clothes she is donating. This is her first time at any of the Occupy events so she asks me who to give donations to. I tell her I'm not sure so we approach the meeting facilitator, Kevin, who points to another person at a table nearby

> saying he's donating stuff and we could join him. I help Beatrice carry her bag over to the fellow at the nearby table. As Beatrice opens her bag, another activist comes by explaining that the houseless people are not here but elsewhere "digging in" for the night. He then begins to explain how these meetings are useless and not doing anything for the real houseless. We leave the bag on the table for whoever wants old clothes. I later see some of the houseless at the meeting looking over the bag and claiming various pieces of clothing. As the meeting is about to begin, I recognize someone from the now-evicted camp who I know to be one of the houseless. He shows me a scarf he claimed from the bag. (Fieldnotes November 25, 2011)

This episode, from an early spokescouncil held two weeks after the eviction, demonstrates the idea of Occupy as a means for distributing donations to the houseless seemed to be still at the forefront of people's minds. The vignette also reveals the normative operation of the Occupy Portland economy; no one takes charge over the distribution of resources. The facilitator's directions and the activist's gestures reveal this attitude; if resources are donated, they should go as directly as possible to where they are needed.

The direct distribution of resources becomes difficult when a resource is in short supply, which then also creates tensions when decisions have to be made over who gets to appropriate a resource. The typical manner of distributing resources is through deliberation, and the natural location for negotiating this is the spokescouncil. The original purpose of the spokescouncil was "dealing with the logistical needs of the camp and occupation, giving the meetings a clear focus, with opportunity for understanding and supporting the needs and aspirations of committees and caucuses" (*Portlandgeneralassembly.org* 2011). Following the horizontalist principles of Occupy, deliberation between committees is managed through facilitation. That facilitated meeting becomes a logical venue for negotiating the appropriation and distribution of resources and reveals contradictions of power embedded within the discourse of direct action:

> Vishnu explains again as he did during the Agenda Setting Meeting about theoretical matters on the need for maintaining an art space. During clarifying time it is revealed that this proposal involves who gets to determine the use of the large table in the Che Room. That room is Occupy's office space and is in a perpetual state of semiclutter, which large posters of Che Guevarra and Subcomandante Marcos observe with serious approval. The semiclutter includes a large meeting table that is now the object of deliberation. Some people raise concerns that this seems to be Vishnu's attempt to co-opt the table. But someone else remarks that no one is in charge of scheduling the use of the table and it might as well be Vishnu, who assures everyone that he won't prevent anyone from using it if necessary. He just wants to make sure that it remains available for artistic uses such as preparation of posters and such. The facilitator asks for amendments. Someone proposes that it's okay as long as meetings take priority. Another shouts, "Just let him have the table!"

> Someone else suggests that this be done on a trial basis and be up for discussion at the next spokescouncil. The facilitator then suggests that this will need more discussion in the future and asks if the amendment is okay. Everyone twinkles for this amendment. Vishnu gets his table, at least for the meantime. (Fieldnotes January 1, 2012)

Deliberation regarding the authority over the table reveals the difficulties when resources must be shared by the group at-large. As discussed earlier the more typical operation of resource sharing in the gift economy of Occupy is that donations are always welcome and are distributed as directly as possible among members, and as long as these resources go directly to where they are needed, there is little or no need for deliberation. An ironic element comes into the play of Occupy horizontalism when tensions over resources become apparent: horizontalism can manage resources easily when they are in support of direct action and not subject to distribution. But when resources are scarce, the need to distribute as directly as possible comes into tension with having to decide who gets to appropriate a resource, while still making it available for others. Thus, when an art table or a generator (for hot water as in the first vignette) becomes appropriated, suspicions rise, exchange becomes evident, and power relationships are re-arranged. "Let him have the table!" is an appeal to stop deliberation because the negotiations over power run counter to the core ideology.

"We're Going to Act it Out": Tensions with Process and Structure

> After all have spoken, the facilitator attempts to summarize the options spoken about. The facilitator puts forward the motions. "Option one: How many want to join Jameson Square?" Only a couple of hands are twinkling. "Option two: How many want the Jameson square people to come back here?" Only a few (but other) hands are twinkling. She mentions an option three but this is a compound option seeming to involve both, and one that no one seems to understand so no one twinkles. The Jameson Square representative shouts out, "Option four: How many want to move this GA over to Jameson Square?" Nearly everyone raises their hands, vigorously wriggling their fingers and showing agreement. It's certain that this is a consensus, and the facilitator can't help but show her delight saying, "Okay everyone; let's move this to Jameson Square! But don't forget to clean up as you go." (Fieldnotes October 29, 2011)

The above vignette describes a scene from an early general assembly, which describes a point when consensus towards action is achieved spontaneously without the need for facilitation to invoke a process. The Jameson Square representative's call for action was spontaneous and not emergent from earlier deliberation. Importantly, the facilitator also made no attempt to point out that the option was not even one of those discussed. Once the need for action is evident, process takes a back seat. Action is the ultimate point to the movement, with structure and process as only a means towards legitimizing action.

There was a great deal of horizontalist-style discussion going on within Occupy Portland that evolved from a need to coordinate and evaluate action. As illustrated earlier in this volume (see especially Heath), affinity groups often created their own meeting structures that acted independently of the decision making of the general assembly and the coordination of the spokescouncil. Spin-off groups like the Portland Action Lab invoked similar meeting processes that organized actions that were brought to the general assembly in order to legitimate and disseminate knowledge about particular actions. Other affinity groups ran small meetings, including those by the facilitation team, which planned around their own group structures and processes. These too would plan and coordinate action as well as contribute to the general understanding of meaning about particular actions. What developed was a rich repertoire of deliberative genres and practices that included town-hall methods (in a weekly movement-building forum) and a Feather Circle where the agency of the facilitator was replaced by an eagle feather. Each mode of meeting tended to engage in its own discovery process as well as invoke structures that participants were familiar with, such as the use of hand signals and the recognition that power had to be shared equally among all participants.

However, tension would arise when the romantic discourse of a horizontalist process had to allow for the functionalism of direct action in the day-to-day acts of organizing. Participants understood the need for creating processes and structures for coordination, but were often frustrated by the inability of deliberative processes to achieve anything more than a legitimation of action that had already been planned or executed by affinity groups. This tension is recognized and expressed as a guiding principle in the "Occupy Portland Facilitation User Manual":

> "Autonomous actions," taken in the name of the Occupy movement, can also be a confusing matter. Many people end up supporting autonomous actions *after the fact*, which may not have been supported in the GA/SC. At the same time, it is generally considered important that group consensus be sought on anything affecting the spirit, character, or vision of Occupy Portland. Many widely supported autonomous actions that markedly affected the character of OP in a significant way have taken place with little or no controversy (e.g., the lock-down at Terry Shrunk)—actions that may never have received GA/SC approval. Other autonomous actions have been widely condemned. There isn't a collective understanding on what autonomous groups can or cannot do without GA/SC endorsement, although there are many opinions. The somewhat liberating, invigorating, disconcerting, frustrating and even dangerous (depending on your perspective) reality is that sometimes *the only way to find out*

how people will feel about something is for someone to do it. (*PortlandGeneralAssembly.org* 2012, emphasis in original)

Although recognized in principle by facilitators, the tension between spontaneity of action as participants appropriate the meeting process, and the need to distribute decision-making power through deliberation, is ever present. What happens in practice is that action and coordination are done outside of process and structure, that experimentation is the rule, and that the primary meeting structures are used in order to legitimate, rather than coordinate action. The result is that consensus about the value of action cannot be fully resolved until the action has been taken.

The distribution of power through the meeting ultimately had to give way to direct action by allowing the legitimizing power of the general assembly and spokescouncil to be appropriated according to participants' needs. The need for the meeting evolved along with the needs of activists. In the early days, the day-to-day experience of organizing was much concerned with the minutiae of camp organizing, and participants often struggled to maintain the relevancy of the meetings as a representation of the movement as an organization. One facilitator said,

> I was there [at the camp], every day for many weeks but I wasn't living there and so I felt like it wasn't my responsibility to be a part of those conversations.... And then the conversation or the dynamic between people who are houseless and came to the camp to live, and people who are activists and came to camp to live, and [produced] the clash of class and privilege and everything else. There wasn't any kind of container that was created to hold that, to hold those issues. For anything, class and violence to who's going to pick up the garbage? And that became [a problem] over and over; violence in camp became a general assembly issue and [the GA] tried to be the violence peace committee.

The function of the early meetings to resolve issues over appropriation was inadequate for addressing the larger societal inequalities that were present in the camp, which were more easily resolved at the working-group level. As the meetings evolved into the more ordered weekly meeting schedule, after the eviction, the DIY feature of Occupy continued to be prominent as a means for creating action. Meetings would then be appropriated for action while ignoring process. Process was used for the distribution of decision-making power, but only up to the point where action, as needed by activists required it.

Thus, a contradiction embedded in the dialectic of appropriation/distribution is revealed when the process of discussion becomes secondary to the needs of action, and therefore, is simply bypassed as a model for distributing power. The meetings, though meant to distribute power in decision making, became appropriated by the day-to-day needs of direct action. Thus, the meeting process is a means to appropriate power by actors of direct action rather than a means of distributing power or resolving imbalances that are apparent within the organization.

"(When) is it Okay to Break a Window?" Definitions and Authorizations of Violence

> The fifth item was the emergency proposal to endorse a statement of solidarity with Occupy Oakland with regards to the recent police response there. Lucy read out the statement with much twinkling. . . . A final proposal was read out for a nonviolent march to be held the next day and details were given. No comments or concerns of importance were expressed when asked and this also passed unanimously. (Fieldnotes February 6, 2012)

> People spray-painted a passing car and broke a glass door at Genoa restaurant on Southeast Belmont with the end of a flagpole. Some protesters raided recycling bins and threw items into the street, while others in the crowd picked the trash back up. A demonstrator also broke a window of a car parked at Southeast Stark Street and 30th Avenue. . . . Some demonstrators advocated keeping the protest peaceful and others disagreed. (Mather 2012)

That brief vignette and the news story that follows it reveal part of a larger problem that is expressed and deliberated through a discourse on diversity of tactics. Although the general assembly was quick to issue support of the planned action, the events that happened the next day were unanticipated by many who originally granted legitimacy to the march. The property violence that accompanied the endorsed action was the result of Black Bloc tactics. The resulting discourse revealed dialectical tensions over how direct action should allow for the diversity of tactics—again direct action appropriates power, while "allowing" for diversity of tactics invokes a sanctioning conversation that requires the distribution of decision-making power to participants, even those who oppose Black Bloc tactics. The critical discourse of diversity of tactics surfaced two tensions related to the appropriation/distribution dialectic: (a) the struggle over appropriation/distribution to define violent/nonviolent action, and (b) the struggle over appropriation/distribution to express authority over whether or not to condemn violent action.

The attitude expressed by more traditional activism is that property damage is violent and, as a result, harmful to a movement operating on moral principles of nonviolence. As one Portland participant expressed in an interview: "The Occupy people that I know are nonviolent people, and in fact the Occupy people that I know tried to stop people that were doing property damage" (KATU.com 2012). Somewhat more pointed was the expression of journalist Chris Hedges who remarked how engaging in property violence was, in effect, engaging in a similar mode of violence as the police, thereby delegitimizing the movement's claims to nonviolent action:

> The Black Bloc anarchists, who have been active on the streets in Oakland and other cities, are the cancer of the Occupy movement. The presence of Black Bloc anarchists—so named because they dress in black, obscure their faces, move as a unified mass, seek physical confrontations with police and destroy property—is a gift from heaven to the security and surveillance state (Hedges 2012, par. 1)

Hedges comment about "the cancer" points to an ongoing dialectic about the definition of violence within the movement. During a press conference on the matter, Hedges related further:

> The power we have is our powerlessness, our transparency, and our honesty. If we can find the self-discipline, the moral courage, and the strength to hold fast to these values, and that will mean confronting and *expelling* those within the movement who refuse to accept those values, then I think we can bring them down. (Hedges 2012, emphasis mine)

More traditionally minded activists view nonviolent protest as a means towards bringing awareness and exposing the violence of the police. This view invokes nonviolence as a moral virtue whose transgression delegitimizes the movement. They therefore invoke deliberation as a means towards evaluating action in terms of their particular definitions of violence, and appropriate horizontalist processes in order to establish an authority to expel members.

The new activists acknowledge the moral dilemma, but contextualize it in terms of a larger structural violence already present in society. Proponents for a diversity of tactics see violence as a means towards exposing the nature of overwhelming police violence against protesters and larger society.

> Basically their point of view is that this argument of peaceful protest versus aggressive tactics that we're having here was had in Seattle recently etc., etc. Alright, the argument's already been settled. And the only people who hadn't heard the outcome are still arguing. And the outcome is that simply we can talk about for weeks about the moral question or questions of scope. Like how can you complain about breaking a window? They're killing people in Third World nations. So the argument of scope and morality . . . but when you think about it, you think about what our goal is . . . and so scope or morality are kinda meaningless. Tactics is really the only thing to decide on. Obviously we win the moral argument. Obviously we win the scope argument. So let's talk about what's effective and what's not. (Feather Circle participant)

One attempt to determine the value of violence is to reframe it as simply a matter of the efficacy of particular local tactics. A reflexive discussion about the nature of diversity of tactics was held that included relatively large meetings as well as small discussions wherein members shared their ideas on property violence as a tactic:

> We've talked about peaceful protest but we didn't talk about aggressive tactics. It's easy for everybody to bring an opinion that peaceful protest is best. We all have varying definitions about that. But I would like for us to be able to identify what are aggressive tactics. My thought is that it's not so much aggressive tactics that are the problem, as it is lack of clarity and lack of control and lack of direction with those tactics. (another Feather Circle participant)

The struggle over the meaning of what counts as violence is distributed through deliberation by framing it in terms of the local and emergent. Those who define Black Bloc tactics as violent reject the symbolization of the tactics and deliberate instead on the efficacy (functionality) of the tactics, in terms of how well they serve action. But the issue of defining violence in terms of functionalism cannot simply evade the moral issue; it has to consider both value and efficacy, and how this is done is left to discovery. In response to Hedges's remarks about "the cancer," David Graeber defines Black Bloc precisely as a tactic of particular forms of counterviolence rather than as an attempt to define the meaning of violence within the movement.

> These are not hypothetical questions. Every major movement of mass nonviolent civil disobedience has had to grapple with them in one form or another. How inclusive should you be with those who have different ideas about what tactics are appropriate? What do you do about those who go beyond what most people consider acceptable limits? What do you do when the government and its media allies hold up their actions as justification—even retroactive justification—for violent and repressive acts? (2012, par. 30)

Thus, violence is not simply a matter of definition within the movement; violence must be defined in terms of the structures of domination that the antiglobalization movement opposes. True to the horizontalist mode of deliberation, meanings are emergent and achieved through discovery. In order to do so, the ability to create that definition and determine its effects is highly contested. The meaning of violence, whether of moral value, efficacy, or as counterviolence towards capitalism, is never wholly resolved, but the struggle for meaning has implications for how power is negotiated among Occupy activists.

The appropriation/distribution dialectic is a tension that permeates the power relationships that the ideology of the new activism attempts to define. The interactions between participants on how resources are to be distributed, meetings are to be used, and struggles over definitions and authority of violence/nonviolence, reveal contradictions and ironies that emerge within the ideology of the new activism. These contradictions and ironies, in turn, illustrate how these negotiations of power constitute the organizational reality of the Occupy movement.

CONCLUSION

In an effort to understand the organization of Occupy through "tensions and contradictions that inhere in the dialectic [and] can create possibilities for organizational change and transformation" (Mumby 2005, 38), I reflect on how discourse within the dialectical tension of appropriation/distribution becomes a constitutive element in globalization from below. The play of dialectical tension creates new possibilities for the organizational efforts of local resistance to globalization, that is, as an answer to the earlier challenge to "examine connections between hegemony, counter-hegemony, and transformation" (Ganesh, Zoller, and Cheney 2005, 183). To demonstrate this play of local discourses, I return to Trujillo's (1992) romantic, functional, and critical lenses as they were expressed in the ideologies of Occupy.

The romantic/horizontalist attitude is one of "dreaming" in a timeless present. Action is not predetermined by abstract norms, but is enacted through deliberation based on needs. The appropriation/distribution dialectic becomes a problem for the horizontalist attitude to resolve once resources are scarce and deliberation becomes necessary in order to determine how distribution is to be accomplished. Deliberation that considers needs must choose between activists' biases for action over horizontalist deliberation and experiments in structure. The romanticism of the horizontalist discourse is thus tinged with irony. This irony devolves around how much authority a consensus process that distributes power can exert over tactics and whether or not such a thing as consensus is even desirable when such a consensus attempts to appropriate authority rather than to distribute it. Also riddled with contradiction, the functionalist discourse of direct action works as a preference for the immediacy of action over deliberation—it also appropriates rather than distributes power often bumping up against the horizontalist attitude in discursive negotiation.

Diversity of tactics is a critical discourse that demands reflection on the issue of violence, by reframing the argument in terms of morality, efficacy, and counterviolence. The need to establish meaning over this issue creates new deliberative spaces that would not otherwise have been engaged had issues of violent/nonviolent tactics not become apparent. The dialectic of appropriation/distribution needs the meeting space of diversity of tactics in order to functionally define action as a moral or effective means of critically challenging the violence of neoliberalism.

The discourses that express the ideology of Occupy are mutually constitutive even as they present struggles over meaning. Horizontalism, direct action, and the diversity of tactics are invoked at different times; but there is no action without deliberation, and no diversity without individuals choosing to directly act. The romantic, functional, and critical discourses of globalization from below are in constant negotiation. Meaning is negotiated through the interplay of discourses and shift interpretation according to the intentions, needs, and actions of activists. The dialectic of appropriation/distribution constitutes a discursive space for experimentation over power relations, both to contest oppressive societal structures as well as to determine the value of particular actions.

DISCUSSION QUESTIONS

1. How is Foucault's concept of discourse different from other understandings of the term?
2. How do the discourses of Occupy constitute an ideology? What would happen to our understanding this ideology if we were to ignore one of these discourses?
3. According to Mumby, dialectical tensions include discursive and nondiscursive practices. How do nondiscursive practices reflect tensions in the descriptions of activity within Occupy Portland?
4. Horizontalism is described as counterbureaucratic. How does it seem to differ from "traditional" organizing using bureaucracy? What aspects of bureaucracy does it consciously avoid?
5. Foucault describes power and knowledge as constituting each other. How is this seen in how Occupy Portland organizes?

NOTES

1. Sitrin's (2006) "Horizontalism" is a collection of interviews from Argentine collective workers after the Argentine revolt of 2001.

2. Hakim Bey's "Temporary Autonomous Zone, Ontological Anarchy, Poetic Terrorism," Chaos, can be freely accessed and used at hermetic.com/bey/taz_cont.html.

3. Della Porta (2005) refers to this as "horizontality," Sitrin (2012) as "*horizontalidad*," and others as horizontalism. The terms are considered equivalent.

4. Walia is alluding to Barbara Ehrenreich's "Anarkids and Hypocrites." See Ehrenreich 2000.

Chapter Seven

(De) Colonization and Collective Identity

Intersections and Negotiations of Gender, Race, and Class in Occupy

C. Vail Fletcher

Hi, my name is Jack. I don't live here in Portland. I live in Vancouver, Washington. The reason I am here today is the reason I have been coming here. This is my eleventh rally. Two and half months ago, before all of this started, I had been out of work for almost two years. I have a problem with depression and, uh, insomnia. I don't sleep good at all. All of this was starting to weigh me down. I started thinking about suicide, everyday. On a daily basis all I could think about was how worthless I was and I really felt like I had no reason to live. When this movement started, I started coming over here, talking to people, learning about what was going on, and, uh, I have heard so many great speeches from great speakers. Speeches of hope, unity, and now my frame of mind is a whole lot better. I don't think about suicide everyday anymore. I have a positive outlook on life now. And, uh, for me now, there is no direction but up. I just wanted to say that this movement, and specifically the Occupy Portland—you people here today—and all of the people that I have met and talked to over the last couple of months, are literally saving my life. And I just want to say thank you.—Paul, fifty-four-year-old, Waterfront Rally, Portland, Oregon, December 2011

The role of identity was and is paramount to the development, recruitment, retention, and in some instances alienation of participants in the Occupy movement from Wall Street to Oakland to Portland. How individuals came to be involved in the movement and why so many stayed involved was/is often in part due to the ways in which certain identities were/are allowed to be enacted and propagated—or not—within the social context of the movement.

In the opening narrative, Jack, a fifty-four-year-old Vancouver, Washington, resident and Occupy participant, was attending a December 2011 rally located on the Portland waterfront. His shared reflection offers a glimpse into the depth of connection many participants conveyed as part of their involvement with Occupy Portland. Jack is representative of many of the participants in the movement in the sense that he *wanted* to belong and in many ways *needed* to belong to something greater than his own immediate life—and Occupy provided him that opportunity in a meaningful way.

The Occupy movement seemed to tap into the very essence of what many individuals were missing or longing for in their lives (not to mention the precipitating master narratives and financial inequalities that they felt compelled to resist). From "soccer moms" to the "unhoused," the range of motivating factors for people joining the movement did not neatly encapsulate a specific goal, nor did it attract a singular type of person, rather a diaspora of personas rushed to get involved and reclaim their own place, space, and/or purpose in society—even if only for a limited period or season—of time. Furthermore Occupy was not a movement that could easily be captured by an outstanding or unifying label of identity, as "hippie" did for the 1960s peace and love movement; rather Occupy claimed a multitude of characters and identities. Perhaps this expansive collection of participants could initially be captured by the words of a male participant, Allen. He summarizes and perhaps simplifies how identity emerged in the movement, offering, ". . . it's very open, fluid thing . . . (laughter) and, I guess if . . . as soon as people identify themselves . . . then they are a part of it." Allen's follow-up comment hints at the complexities and potential for creating a tension between in-groups and out-groups that underlie the process of identity roles and group affiliation in the movement: "Yeah, you're in or you're out." In another interview held in December 2011 Thomas echoed the nuanced nature of identity claims in the movement when he proudly stated, "I am not an occupier, I am an occupant." He continued to elaborate on how the linguistic difference between these two identities was significant in terms of how society viewed him and how he viewed himself. "Occupier has a more negative connotation, while occupant implies the right to be there. Like, a tenant is an occupant of a space and has rights." This anecdote further illuminates the tip of the iceberg in terms of how significant identity and group affiliation was/is to participants in the Occupy Portland movement.

Still, there is a gap in the literature, even across multiple academic disciplines, regarding social movement identities. With increasing attention to identity issues by movement analysts (e.g., Polletta and Jasper 2001), several scholars distinguish among relevant types of identities. For example, Gamson (1995) identifies organizational, movement, and solidarity identities; Jasper (1997) delineates personal, movement, and collective identities; and Hunt, Benford, and Snow (1994) discuss protagonist, antagonist, and audience identity fields. Communication studies research has also demonstrated a dearth in its understanding and consideration for how identity and groups function in social movements (McCright and Dunlap 2008), while social anthropologists, sociologists, and political scientists have made the most headway in understanding the role of identity in social movements.

To help address this research deficiency, this chapter applies the project's overarching framework analyzing individual identity and group affiliation in Occupy Portland. Below, I will tackle the messy task of describing who participated/s in Occupy Portland, specifically focusing on: (a) naming the ways in which identity has functioned to provide—or block—voice, agency, and belonging; and (b) detailing how and why identity has become such a salient and contested part of the movement both locally and globally by deconstructing the romantic, functional, and critical narratives of the participants. Notably, in an effort to garner the most authentic knowledge, the voices of the participants will be the primary means of connecting conceptual ideas to the emergent understandings of the movement in the following analysis. Keeping in line with the spirit of the larger movement, I have made an intentional choice to allow participants to speak for themselves as much as possible. In addition, I want to be clear that I am analyzing the relationship(s) individuals are describing between themselves (i.e., participant) and the (metaphorical) movement—which was/is a very real relationship to all of the interviewees in the project. Participants connected deeply with the symbolic nature of the movement, and thus, their shared stories describing interactions between themselves and others in the context of Occupy sometimes revealed a blurring of lines between real and imagined—perhaps pointing out the very real but social constructive nature of our interconnected identities and experiences.

More specifically, this chapter will first outline key conceptual definitions that acted to strengthen or weaken identity formation and group affiliation in Occupy Portland, specifically intersectionality, colonization, and collective identity. These concepts contextualize the overarching macrolevel forces (e.g., sexism, racism) that act to affirm or challenge the individual's identity during the movement, but also situate and act as precursors to understanding who participants were before Occupy (i.e., the experiences that informed their positionality prior to the movement). Second, using the romantic, functional, and critical perspectives that frame this case study, I name and problematize how participants' understandings of identity emerged in the data to create tenuous values at the local microlevel, the often nuanced negotiations made between individuals in their everyday interpersonal interactions. Finally, I discuss what the movement suggests about the communicative practices of social identity and group affiliation in this particular case study, essentially answering the research question: How is identity both enabled and constrained in the Occupy Portland movement and what are the subsequent implications of that process(es)?

CONCEPTUAL DEFINITIONS OF IDENTITY FORMATION AND GROUP AFFILIATION

Several overarching concepts create the backbone of this exploration of identity by further clarifying the meaning and sense-making processes that informed participants' identities and roles in Occupy. Dissecting and overlaying these concepts also helps honor the first goal of this book, which is to examine social movement phenomena using various theoretical lenses. The movement as witnessed by me firsthand in Portland, and via the media in other locations domestically and abroad, was broadly described as being driven by individuals' desire for greater social justice and equity on a number of significant issues (see chapter 2 by Barnes for immediate background). Three conceptual ideas help lay groundwork, or act as precursors, revealing insight about the internal and external forces acting on and within participants and groups prior to and throughout Occupy Portland: intersectionality, colonization, and collective identity. In defining the nuanced nature of identity Hall (1996) shares the following:

> They [identities] arise from the narrativization of the self, but the necessarily fictional nature of this process in no way undermines its discursive, material or political effectivity, even if the belongingness, the "suturing into the story" through which identities arise is, partly, in the imaginary (as well as the symbolic) and therefore, always, partly constructed in fantasy, or at least within a fantasmatic field. (4)

Thus it is with this definition and/or understanding of identity that my contextualizing, problematizing, and rich(er) description of Occupy Portland's participants and their lived experience within the movement begins.

Intersectionality of Experience: "All these Problems are Interconnected"

Intersectionality (or intersectionalism), a feminist sociological theory first highlighted by Kimberlé Crenshaw (1989), is a conceptualization of the varying intersections between and among different groups of individuals and/or nonmajority groups. More specifically, it is an "analysis claiming that systems of race, social class, gender, sexuality, ethnicity, nation, and age form mutually constructing features of social organization" (Collins 2000, 299). The theory further suggests—and seeks to examine how—various social, cultural, and biological categories such as gender, race, class, ability, sexual orientation, and other aspects of identity interact on multiple and often simultaneous levels, contributing to systematic social inequality. Intersectionality suggests that the classical forms of oppression facing society such as racism, sexism, and classism do not act independently of one another; instead, these systems of oppression create a structure of oppression that reflects the "intersection" of various forms of discrimination.

Using this conceptual lens, I argue that in addition to the rhetoric of the economic inequality touted as the mantra of the Occupy movement during its initial few weeks of organizing, the intersections of oppression that many participants (and citizens) face in their daily lives in the form of classism, racism, sexism, and nationalism, were also a powerful motivator for involvement in the movement (and could be one explanation for why the "goals" of the movement appeared to be immeasurable and nonspecific). One participant, Mark, acknowledges the complexity of a social movement working against the various "-isms" that plague individuals in a society, while simultaneously sharing how Occupy is/was not necessarily different in its use of oppressive actions:

> There was a lot of stuff that was missed out in terms of addressing racism, things like sexism. . . . There were people that were trying to say that type of stuff and then other folks would say, "Well if we take care of the corporations, then we tax the banks properly, then magically racism will end. Magically sexism will end. Magically transphobia will end." No, all these problems are interconnected. The banks, and the corporations, and war, and nuclear energy, the corrupt electoral system, all those things is [sic] really hard to grasp it, but they are all interconnected. One thing that Occupy really missed out on, for me, is the reaching out to the indigenous communities and reaching out to people that [sic] have been fighting this fight way before Occupy was a meme or even an idea.

Mark points to a crucial barrier that the movement and perhaps society at large is often challenged by, which is the often imbalanced nature of trying to create a healthy experience for everyone in a society. So even in the process of very purposive and intentional action around building relationships, decision making, and organizing such as was claimed in Occupy Portland, even *confronting* and/or *resisting* systemic oppression might still further perpetuate injustices.

Intersectionality is an especially useful frame for unpacking how identity and group politics occurred within Occupy Portland. As individuals and groups struggled to unify and work together, in-groups and out-groups formed as tensions around decision making and political actions grew. For example, Occupy Portland was/is comprised of a predominantly white and a comparatively privileged class (e.g., college educated) of organizers and participants, yet the city also attracts and supports a relatively large unhoused (i.e., homeless) population, in large part because of its social service programs (Center for American Progress 2010), which is often disproportionately represented by the Lesbian Gay Bisexual Transgendered Queer (LGBTQ) community. According to the city of Portland, from 2009 to 2011, homelessness jumped 8 percent from 2,542 persons to 2,727. Using the broadest definition of the term, which includes all four categories (i.e., people who sleep: outside, in short-term shelters, transitional apartments, or on the couches of friends and relatives), the increase in houselessness increased from an estimated 14,451 to 15,563 (Kristina Smock Consulting 2011). Thus, when Occupy Portland overtook two downtown parks, Allen, a college graduate and male participant, shared his concerns with the literal intersections of varying classes in the camps by discussing how the unhoused gravitated to the Occupy encampment instead of shelters:

> I mean, partly also they got a little more freedom at the encampment so, you know ... shelters for example, are the services they [sic] apply strings to it. So you have be out by a certain time, you can't bring your girlfriend or whatever, you can't have guests, you can't bring drugs or alcohol. In the camp it was a lot more free [sic] to do that stuff.

These unhoused participants comprised a vulnerable population, often referred to as "the fringe," who gravitated to the movement naturally because of the considerable enough overlap with other Occupy participants in goals related to social justice. Still, this literal intersection between individuals from different classes, races, and gender groups highlighted—often subtly—nuanced forms of discrimination that occurred between individuals and groups in the movement. Mark reflected this tension between class and race using his own experience:

> I just, I don't know ... I'm not a fool, I let my voice be heard, I feel like I have to speak up because I'm a mixed guy. I'm a Chicano, I'm African American, part European. I have a very mixed background and come from a really poor background too so I just feel like that I had to let my voice be heard so ... and to dispel any myths of people [sic] you know what I mean? Because a lot of times I sound really angry and I am, and it's righteous indignation ...

There were some participants that reported deep awareness of society's discriminatory processes at work within the movement. Ivy, an intensive care unit (ICU) nurse and female participant, shared how her education empowered her with the knowledge to unpack and enact her own and others' experiences in the movement:

> ... solidarity group talking ... with the Women's Caucus, helping women understand why their experiences are the way it is [sic] and sort of diving into that. And then hopefully finding empowerment [for] them to find their voice

within their experience. So that's kinda [sic], yeah, I want to implement my Women's Studies degree . . . you know, Women's Studies is a lot more than you know . . . women's studies . . . it studies a lot of other, race, class, gender, environment, like intersectionality, interdisciplinary action.[1]

The personal experiences of various and often-simultaneous forms of oppression became an apparent and visible component of Occupy Portland. Spectators of the movement (and particularly of the encampment) often remarked that Occupy Portland was fraught with the unhoused, drug- and alcohol-addicted, and the mentally ill, essentially acknowledging (perhaps without empathy) some participants' very reason for wanting widespread systemic change. The intersections of the various forms of oppression many participants had endured over the course of their lifetimes seemed to provide a tipping point and motivation for wanting to change the very society that acted to oppress them. Yet it also served as an educational experience for participants around issues related to intersectionality. Elizabeth, a nineteen-year-old, female participant, now employed at a local homeless shelter, shared her newfound understanding of her privileged background discovered in part from her participation in Occupy:

> It [Occupy] taught me everything I know about activism. It taught me this understanding of privilege. This understanding that people are from different backgrounds and as a white person, and as a person of privilege, I need to acknowledge my own privilege in every situation. When I'm talking to a homeless person I need to acknowledge that we come from two very different spots and that changed my life. It has influenced the way I see the world and class and gender. I feel like I understand what it means to be an activist.

Ironically, and as Elizabeth illuminates, the intersections of participants' personal confrontation with their *own* gender, race, or class in combination with the confrontation with *other* participants' gender, race, and class appeared to help provoke a deeper understanding and gravitational pull to Occupy Portland for some. It became a place where participants could learn more about themselves and others, particularly in terms of mutual experiences of oppression. More clearly, if a participant was feeling disenfranchised in society because of her/his gender identity, that same participant was likely to find solace among other participants who were feeling that same sense of social isolation or struggle. Yet bringing similarly marginalized individuals together also seemed to be partly responsible for agitating and disintegrating the relationships and structures that occurred within the movement, as discussed more in the latter section of this chapter.

Colonization of Identity and Group Roles: "De-Colonize PDX"

Another key overarching and antecedent concept that helps explain how identity and group affiliation functioned in Occupy Portland was colonization, or the inhabitation of individuals by societal structures and systems. The process of socializing individuals in a society with a specific set of mainstream values, often introduced and projected by the media, governments, and institutions, (e.g., schools), and norms for what life should be like and how it should be lived (e.g., college degree, house, marriage, kids, vacations) seemed to have helped trigger a tipping point of action. More specifically, for some participants the message about what success and/or happiness *should* look like was often not their actual experience (e.g., graduating college with debt and no employment possibilities), creating a deep disconnect and sense of disenfranchisement, as these projected norms often appeared to be exclusive entities that only benefited certain members of society.

Habermas (1989) stated, "serious involvement with culture produces facility, while the consumption of mass culture leaves no lasting trace; it affords a kind of experience which is not cumulative but regressive" (166). Habermas eventually concludes that private enterprises and the nation-state do not treat people as citizens, but rather as consumers, and that the rationality of money and power colonize rational-critical thought. Ultimately, he detects a strategic colonization by the economic and bureaucratic means of the market and the nation-state of the lived experience—giving rise to structural violence exercised by the systemic restriction of communication (see Munoz chapter 6 for a discussion of violence/power). One female participant, Nelly, hinted at this disconnect between personal experience and mediated reality, ". . . you see the huge-ass disparity between reality and then what picture's being painted on television. . . ." This quote helps to further contextualize how participants felt an unfortunate disconnect between the life that was often being depicted in mediated contexts or by socializing institutions and the life they were actually able to afford and/or live. Basically, the "American Dream" is actually quite difficult to obtain in everyday life or as stated on several protesting posters in downtown Portland: "The American Dream is a Nightmare." If earning a college degree, owning your own home, getting married, and having two kids is supposed to equal success or happiness in the United States, what does not appear to be talked about with equal representation is how much these things cost and how these "achievements" may not be attainable for many individuals (e.g., gays and lesbians cannot legally marry in most states at the time of this book's publication). And not to mention the lack of dialogue around the relationship between these particular forms of success and personal well-being or fulfillment. Nonetheless, this lifestyle is continually shared and reified as being the ideal in our current culture (Cohen-Marks and Stout 2011).

The compounding nature of colonization may act as an invisible force in society leaving individuals feeling that they have personally failed despite following society's instructions for success. Deetz's (1992) analysis of corporate colonization processes focused on the connections among the ideology of managerialism and the linguistic construction of self and world, while Dahlberg (2005) aimed to reflect on the ways attention has been colonized via the Internet and how this process marginalizes critical communication. The eventual side effect of excessive colonization is that it can be inescapable, and it can function, quite detrimentally, without individuals' direct understanding or knowledge that it is at play (Valtysson 2012). Emma, a female participant and young mother, acknowledges the invisible and pervasive effects of colonization on individuals and society:

> The way I see it is that we're not just trying to change our world, there's a reason that the world is the way it is and I think that's through years and years of colonization but you have to remember that people have also been colonized. And the way that we behave and engage with each other and the way we interact, it's all been colonized. So when we get to those points we have to be willing and able to sit down and talk about this. And people have to have an understanding that maybe some of my behaviors, even though I have all these great intentions, I have to recognize the way that I might oppress others. Just because we're fighting for a really great cause doesn't mean that we don't have oppressive tendencies, oppressive behaviors and when we're called out on that, we really have to be open.

One of the ways Emma chose to contest colonization is that she shared her home with a deliberate and intentional community of activists (many of them former Occupy participants). One of her housemates was committed to trying to live without money, bartering and trading his skills and goods for the things he needed. This community deliberately rejects corporate colonization.

The colonization of citizens' lived experience created a rubber band-like experience, metaphorically speaking, for Occupy Portland participants, in which they often strived to stretch their identities and group memberships to include experiences outside of their home and work life to participate in the Occupy movement (e.g., joining caucuses, attending rallies, organizing actions). Yet participants often understood, even superficially, the tight rope they walked between the life they had been "sold" (via colonization) to live and wanting to resist some of the master narratives that ultimately left them unsatisfied, oppressed, and/or marginalized. For example, this tension between wanting to be involved and not wanting to disrupt everyday routines is expressed by Allen, who shared, ". . . people that were protesting out there in the streets and online and even people that were part of the peripheral, they were down [sic] for Occupy but they couldn't enlist that much time and energy." Alice, a female suburban mother and participant, similarly reflected the tension between wanting to be involved, yet feeling like she had responsibilities at home. Sometimes she could stretch her rubber band to make it possible for her to attend a rally or general assembly (GA) meeting, nevertheless she was quickly snapped back by the impending potentially colonized roles she played as mother and wife.

A multitude of individuals from different backgrounds could identify with the desire for upheaving the status quo, though just how far individuals were able to go in terms of giving time and energy seemed largely related to their tolerance for identity- and group ambiguity. Thus, the process of colonization works to simultaneously oppress individuals, internally and externally, often without their blatant knowledge that it is occurring. Still, other participants were more cognizant and aware that the "American Dream" was part of the colonization process of individuals' experiences and choices. Emma shares her frustration with the disconnect between society's message about the catch-22 between stability and wanting to enact change in society:

> The low for me . . . is that being a mother and being fully committed to this movement at the same time, has been very difficult and has not come without consequences to the structure of my life, the stable environment of my family. And the low point being that—being caught in-between trying to be a mother and as well as trying to fulfill this calling.

Marxist cultural studies have strongly informed research on colonization, which is influenced by the research of Althusser (1971) and Gramsci (1971). Similarly, Grossberg and Slack (1985) and Hall (1985) have articulated powerful critiques of the mass media as dominant contributors to identity formation. Mumby (1997) adds that there is still a strong focus on the media as instruments of "ideological subjugation that produce and reproduce capitalist relations of domination" (11). There is no hypodermic model of media influence operating here but rather a nuanced attempt to understand and critique the complex and contradictory ways in which systems of meaning and identity interact with mass communication practices. The media is a crucial part of the process of selling the dream that often leaves individuals feeling disconnected from society and its other members. A female participant, Lana, who attended classes at New York University without registering purely out of a desire to learn, reflected her struggles in trying to resist her colonized experience and the system:

> And really I have several anarchist friends that [sic] have bought houses and there's this fundamental dichotomy and divide that we're just born into in this day and age, in this country, and that is that in order to have something that I think is inherently mine, a piece of land, a spot to call my own, I have to buy into this horrible system. There are ways of avoiding that and getting around

them, but they're few and far between. And because of my lower socioeconomic status, those are largely inaccessible to me.

This quote helps to further illuminate how pervasive and invisible the process of colonization can be in society—and yet its potentially huge impact on how individuals seem to view what is in and out of their reach.

During data collection it became apparent that participants felt a push-pull tension between wanting to resist the narratives that had colonized their understandings of self (and others), and feeling powerless to enact change, thereby forcing individuals to work within the system. One Occupy Portland general assembly meeting resulted in a particularly heated debate when several participants suggested that "occupy" be replaced with "decolonize," further indicating the vast ideological knowledge participants had regarding their own oppression. While Occupy served the movement rhetorically, many expressed that colonization was the literal culprit of oppression.

Overall, and despite the critical connotation and global understanding of the word in its conceptual form, the process of colonization appeared to serve the movement and participants' identities by bringing individuals together and motivating them to want to act. They recognized that their identities and lived experiences were being colonized and once participants could name this often devaluing process it became something to rally against—and thus acted to coalesce participants in powerful and meaningful ways.

Collective Identity and "Shared Ethos"

Polletta and Jasper (2001), in their extensive review of collective identity and social movements, define collective identity as "an individual's cognitive, moral, and emotional connection with a broader community, category, practice, or institution. It is a perception of a shared status or relation, which may be imagined rather than experienced directly . . ." (285; see also Gamson 1991). In a similar vein to Benedict Anderson's (1983) notion of the imagined community, a sociological theory that argues the nation-state is a social construction, the collective identity of a social movement may be better understood as participants' shared sense of the movement as a collective actor. Basically, social movements act as a dynamic force for change that individuals identify with collectively and are inspired to support in their own actions. Occupy in general tapped into a ripe space for collective identity to bloom, and Occupy Portland was noted to have particularly active and motivated participants among the varying Occupy strongholds (e.g., New York, Boston, Washington D.C.). Emma shared her beliefs about the collective nature of the movement:

> I think that the movement was extremely effective in creating the platform, because, again, prior to Occupy there was no platform. I had all this knowl-

edge, all these ideas and all these grievances, but there was nowhere to voice them. You could stand on the rooftop and yell but nobody would listen to you. But for the very first time, there was a platform through which I could voice these things. And again it created the network necessary to go ahead and continue with these social justice issues. Change required collective action. Without collective action, nothing changes. And so using Occupy's network as a resource for that collective action to move forward—that's the biggest thing that it's provided.

Similarly, Elizabeth shared how the movement created a flurry of activity, saying, "but then Occupy plugs in, and I don't want to say that Occupy caused all those things at all, but I want to say that this new air of activism, this rejuvenation of people doing work created this ripple effect."

This new energy may be in large part due to the character of Portland, Oregon, being home to a large do-it-yourself (DIY), socially active crowd. Ethan, a twenty-six year-old male participant and community organizer, shared his desire for a new way of being: "A positive expression of something else that could be about community it's an alternative ways [sic] at looking at how societies work and community." Occupy Portland created an intense sense among its participants that they were part of a collective group, which informed their understandings of self in often important ways—still at points the "seasonal and high maintenance" nature of the movement made that same feeling of collective fade (Nunberg 2011). Lionel, a male participant and college graduate, echoed this tension between the known and the unknown collective and the power that this waxing and waning had on the movement:

> They had people who were staying in the encampment and then you had a number of people like me who were relatively engaged with that, came down to GA's, did some other things around the camp when we could, contributed when we could . . . And at the margins we kind of floated down into an even wider penumbra of people who they were the ones who came out to make 10,000 of us on October sixth. Or at the Pink Martini concert, which was the other biggest occasion. And a lot of them were really only connected electronically through the social media or e-mail . . . And so there was this underlying question of who is the real movement? That I don't think was ever entirely resolved.

It appeared that there was some momentum, empowerment, and discouragement gained from the surreptitious nature of individuals' involvement in the movement at any given time. This seemed to be part of the allure in that it was "anonymous" and therefore created the sense that the movement and its energy and organizing could be anywhere and everywhere (or nowhere) at the same time.

Holland, Fox, and Daro (2008) argued that collective identity is a dialogic process, echoing Polletta and Jasper's (2001) claim that collective identity subsumes two major dimensions: belonging and action. Common definitions of collective identity in the social sciences emphasize identity in relation to difference, often assuming that people who are considered culturally, racially, ethnically, nationally, or in some other way distinctive such that they warrant differential treatment, have a basis for individual belonging and group solidarity. A similar sense of collective identity worked to mediate participants' sense of belonging and action in Occupy Portland—and helped to determine who was included in a group (or caucus) and who was excluded.

Additionally, Occupy Portland struggled at various points with knowing who its participants' were exactly, though many felt this lack of clarity about who or how many were involved actually worked to the movement's benefit because it seemed that the collective nature of the movement signified that Occupy participants were everywhere, organizing actions under a variety of guises and in support of numerous causes (see chapter 5 by Heath for a leaderful versus leaderless discussion). Still, anyone could pronounce himself or herself a participant because the movement was so fluid and transient and wide reaching. The collective identity was, in its idealized form, very welcoming and inclusive. Chad, union activist and former Ph.D. student, reflected on the underlying appeal of the cooperative nature of the movement. He said:

> So there's this ethos and then a sort of looser . . . I call it a milieu . . . I have a friend that calls it Occupy Space, or something like that. There's a kind of social and political space that was created and relationships that were formed and created and built . . . I think that that ethos creates the basis for the *shared ethos*. (emphasis mine)

In many ways, collective identity and group affiliation were part of the charm and idealism inherent in Occupy, often leading to participants' stories of newly born perspectives and greater understandings of humanity. Collective identity and identification with the "other" served the movement and its participants in a idealistic way; the collective nature of Occupy allowed so many participants (and perhaps spectators) to envision a new, more equal society, if only for awhile. More clearly, many participants identified with a marginalized and/or silenced group in society and the collective momentum of the movement created an outlet for engaging in dialogue and action with each other in important and salient ways.

Overall, intersectionality, colonization, and collective identity helped to position participants' identities, personal motivations, and tensions, leading up to and during their engagement in the movement and offered additional context for understanding individuals' yearning to grapple with many of the forces at work in US American cities and communities. Next I will discuss how tensions emerged between the various romantic, functional, and critical lenses (Trujillo 1992) used to further unpack and frame the observation and interview data.

ROMANTIC, FUNCTIONAL, AND CRITICAL VALUES OF PARTICIPANTS' IDENTITIES

To honor the second goal of this edited book, which is to provide in-depth interpretive data that problematizes universal narratives of Occupy, this section will further contextualize how participants often found themselves negotiating the competing values of their romantic idyllic self, that of their functional roles, and the critical backlash of the power struggles and oppression that often comes with trying to resist identity norms. Trujillo (1992) states that the romantic lens serves as a way to understand the idealized experience(s) or understandings of individuals, the functional lens denotes the knowledge of a more instrumental experience, and the critical lens illuminates the role of power in individuals' interactions and experiences.

In Occupy Portland, identity and group affiliation were often spoken of or reflected upon in ways that allowed for varying interpretations of the romantic, functional, or critical nature of the participant's role and/or action(s) in the movement. As Occupy Portland evolved and moved from an encampment to a permanent and rented physical space, so did individuals' relationships to the movement and its changing values, goals, and ideals. This evolution or shift helped instigate some expressed values to come into tension with each other. For example, while it was expressed in interviews and field observations that participants valued inclusivity among all of its members, exclusivity was also being practiced in a variety of ways at meetings, rallies, and during actions (e.g., such as the dominating role of male voices). Whilst many contradictory tensions between participants' values and identities exist(ed) and surfaced in this year-long exploration, in this section, I will discuss only the most striking and contested values. Below I introduce a few of the emergent values, then I will demonstrate the saliency of the values using the participants' voices and words, and finally I situate the values and potential tensions surrounding them in the context of the movement.

Romantic Perspective: "Empowering People to have Agency"

Few observers and/or participants could deny that Occupy was driven by a highly romantic set of social ideals with appeals to many of the finest aspects of participants' personalities, desires, and values. Lionel captured the romantic ideal that underlies many individuals' motivations to be a part of Occupy:

> ... through education and community building, through getting to know our neighbors and trusting each other, sharing things with each other. And just getting outside our comfort zone and meeting people we wouldn't necessarily think to meet and showing up at events . . . just trying to build relationships. Pretty much, we are talking about in Occupy is an overall respect for life and each other. Because when you think about it, the 1 percent . . . all they want is safety and happiness for themselves and their children. But that's just a means for getting happiness only for their family. And the 99 percent is on the complete opposite side of the spectrum, but we still want the same thing. So if we can just understand that if we get to know each other, we could provide that for each other no matter what. I think a basic concept is that we can get freedom and we can get democracy and we can get all these things, we can continue to have a lot of the things that we have today. But there is [sic] in fact enough resources for us all. We just need to learn how to give.

As such, the romantic lens allows identity values such as inclusivity, solidarity, transformation, and agency to emerge in Occupy Portland, but for the purposes of this analysis I will focus on discussing only two: *solidarity* and *agency*. More clearly the following exemplars help to highlight the significance placed on each of the values expressed in this vein.

First, *solidarity* was a main value expounded on by participants involved in the movement and thus emerged as a defining identity construct. Participants reflected this important foundational component of group structure and affiliation as an integral part of Occupy Portland. Almost every participant interviewed used the word solidarity to explain their and others' actions. Participants overall expressed a deep affinity and connection for each other and the general belief that all of the participants were working together for a new world. Mark offered his perspective on the presence of solidarity in the movement and how it helped him feel more cohesion with others:

> I mean, just the people that have been holding space in front of City Hall. I've been living on the streets for a couple years and there's been folks like me who stay there occasionally to show solidarity and make sure things are safe. I mean I've had people tell me I was scared last night and I woke up for a second and saw you and I knew everything was cool. And even I've said that to people too because I've fallen asleep and been like, I'm on the street, this is crazy, you look over and see others.

The visual provided in this exemplar helps to paint a clearer picture of what unhoused participants may often experience living on the streets and the powerful sense of comfort that was created when a new community (i.e., Occupy) sprung up around them in solidarity.

The second salient emergent romantic value of identity was participants' newfound sense of agency and/or the power to resist oppressive structures in their lives. Lana shared, "People felt empowered for the first time at the beginning of Occupy and I think still to this day, in their entire lives and as result became so invested and were so afraid of losing their stake and their voice." A few participants expressed that their involvement with Occupy Portland allowed them to reclaim their identities and/or develop new sites of purpose and meaning in their lives perhaps through the process of being able to "give voice to the disenfranchised," while simultaneously "resisting traditional labels of identity." Jay, a male participant and service worker, reflected how certain occupiers resisted the mainstream culture and master narrative:

> And society takes away everyone's agency. Society built off fear, which takes away everyone's agency to have any kind of control over their life [sic] outside of the system. And Occupy is the exact opposite. It's empowering people to have agency. I can become this role; I don't need all these credentials, or a doctorate to do it. No, go talk on a panel, we will help you.

Lionel elaborated on the "empowering" aspects of helping others find their voice for the first time:

> I realized I had more of a personal passion for education and activist development and delivering information and empowering someone and those light bulbs going off and those stars in their eyes . . . the concept that they can do anything they want and to have these skills and these concepts and the ability to believe in themselves to do anything.

Overall, using Trujillo's (1992) romantic frame to unpack the voices of Occupy Portland allowed much depth and richness to emerge in terms of the absolute idealism that was the undercurrent of the movement.

Functional Perspective: "I Just Go to Wherever I See a Need for Something"

The second lens through which to view the data involves imploring a pragmatic and instrumental perspective. The Occupy Portland movement functioned in many participants' lives as a practical solution to wanting to do more "plugging in" to their daily experience, and in that process, helping to meet other identity needs. For some, the movement helped lapse time between jobs or employment (i.e., "Lost My job, Found an Occupation," slogan designed by NY Art Director, Jason Shelowitz).[2] Others found that the welcoming and inclusive nature of the movement helped fulfill (or find new) identity gaps and infused a new sense of purpose in their daily lived experience. The functional lens allowed several prominent identity values to arise, though I focus primarily on the emergent value identity role of *group affiliation*.

Desire and/or need for group affiliation and the process by which participants could become a part of a group (and there were many opportunities given the flurry of caucuses, rallies, and actions) acted as a practical foundation for many participants. For example, some of the thousands of citizens who sleep on the streets of Portland each night found that the Occupy movement could potentially offer additional comfort and community, and could definitely provide more supplies and/or survival essentials. Allen shared how this synergy between the movement and the unhoused occurred: "but yeah, then there's [sic] in camp . . . there were the people I guess, the homeless people, that just came for shelter and food." Still, others merely appeared to have found something greater than themselves to be a part of and/or were in search of a movement in which they could participate. Allen reflected, "This is exactly what I came here to look for," while Tally, a female participant, offered, "I just go to wherever I see a need for something." Similarly, in our interviews with several master's level librarians who were volunteering their weekends in the encampment, they said that they had "been waiting for something like this for a long time" and thus got involved in building a library in the camp as soon as the encampment started. Ultimately, it seems that Occupy help to fulfill a deeper need in many participants' identities and lives that functioned in powerful way to connect them to society.

Perhaps the functional aspects of Occupy were unintended and unforeseeable, as the organic nature of the movement could never predict from day to day what would happen to the movement or where things were headed. Displacement from city officials, resentment from the mainstream public, and the constant threat/surveillance from the police added to the sense of uncertainty. Yet the functional role the movement played in so many participants' lives may be immeasurable in terms of its impact. Many participants credited Occupy with fulfilling a foundational need in their lives beyond just the romantic ideals of the movement.

Critical Perspective: "Predominantly Made of Men"

The critical lens offers an alternative way of viewing Occupy Portland and its participants, specifically by deconstructing and peeling back some of the coexisting and idealistic layers claimed by the participants. Trujillo (1992) argued that the critical lens allows power struggles to be revealed in interactions and society structures and institutions. An early critique of Occupy Portland was related to how the participants appeared to be mainly comprised of the homeless and "druggies." This disconnect between the cause and frustrated participants often led to traditional types of interpersonal conflict such as arguing and loss of affinity, and fueled resentment, anger, and disenchantment with participants. Ironically, the fall-out within the movement between some participants often mimicked many of the forms of oppression, power, and control that many hoped to change in society. Lionel:

> The challenges we had at the camp. Like, not being a well-built society to deal with the drug addiction and mental illness and violence and gangs and sex trafficking, and we weren't the people to be able to handle that. So those meetings became a dialogue about the camps and the police had a laissez faire attitude about it. It was actually quoted that several police officials said that it was nice to see the camps sort of imploding on themselves. So we needed to clean that up, especially the public image.

This is not to say that the movement is/was less romantic in its essence, rather the critical lens allows the movement to be revealed as simultaneously ideal, pragmatic, and problematic in terms of how participants' identities were enacted, understood, and performed. Several significant values such as corruption, oppression, and silencing emerged in the data that helped to distinguish the need for the movement to critically reflect on its actions and processes. Still, marginalization acted as a main critical value that was expressed by the movement and thus is where I focus my analysis.

Marginalization occurred at a variety of identity and group levels. Issues of subjugation related to gender, race, and class were apparent during interviews and observational data collection. David Meyer, a professor of Sociology at the University of California Irvine, claimed that social movements often veil darker components of humanity: "These protests have a history of welcoming everyone and just assuming they're on your side" (Newcomb 2011). This tension that arose between the ranges of identities that joined the movement, often in solidarity, in many instances resulted in ill effects. Several specific forms of marginalization occurred that were related specifically to gender and race. For example, there were reports of sexual assaults at nationwide Occupy camps, and Portland was no exception. Several women reported having been sexually assaulted during the encampment, quickly forcing a "safe haven" tent to be erected for women's use only. Elizabeth recalled a group encounter with an accused rapist in the Portland encampment:

> Like one situation that I remember is this guy had supposedly raped someone in camp and so we wanted him to leave and I didn't know the whole situation so I didn't do the whole chanting thing since I didn't really know what happened. But this mob surrounds this person who doesn't understand what's going on yelling at him . . . I don't know.

This strategy of surrounding a suspected offender in an effort to shame him or her into leaving the encampment acted to marginalize specific participants. The desire to seemingly denounce the encampment's need for authority (in this case, police) to enforce and/or protect participants came into tension with the need to create a safe environment. Overall, it seems that in some participants' desire to create a society that lacked outside intervention, they failed to recognize the inherent danger in this resistance approach. Other issues of marginalization were related more clearly to perceptions of male domination in decision-making. Ivy shared her experience related to the clash between men and women in the movement:

> I don't know a lot of the people on Solutions [Committee] and it's just another meeting to go to and it's also predominantly made of men. When I look at a group of people and they say they're going to find the solution to the problem and it's a group of men there's nothing in me that wants to join the group. But, it's probably exactly the reason why I should be joining the group. But sometimes I can't muster up enough energy because I'm already doing enough work of my own. If that was [sic] the case of everything I would have to be on every fucking committee there is. Other than Women's Caucus. I just don't have the energy or the want.

The Occupy Portland movement was definitely infused with stories of gender disparities (see Lovejoy and Brynteson chapter 8 for gender representation by the media) and it certainly emerged as a salient theme for the female participants who were interviewed.

The marginalization of other participants' racial identities also played an unfortunate and powerful role in the movement. It emerged that certain types of participants were more valuable and useful to the movement (see Cameron Whitten's hunger strike controversy).[3] Again, it was this same process of marginalization that in many ways spurred the movement as a result of the intersections of some individuals' complex identities. Elizabeth shared how gender and race and class privileged some voices over others:

> I think that Occupy came to the table with this idea of starting a new culture, but wasn't willing to acknowledge that there was privilege dynamics or male/female intense dynamics that a lot of females felt like even me. I didn't feel like I had as valid of a voice as the men did in the movement. I felt it was harder for me to say something that was respected than it was for a man. And you'll see that the people who spoke the most and did the most and the people that were respected the most were able to create an action that had the most people coming were men. And were white. Or who had class privilege.

Similarly, Chad remarked on the hyper-masculine culture that often excluded women:

> There was this real macho edge . . . Partly militancy and are you ready to go out on the front line and get beat up by the cops and maced [participants] or whatever? And other parts of rugged individualism and camping and toughness, so . . . I stopped going to the GAs in the middle of the winter because I'm in my fifties and I can't actually think when I'm freezing. And that sometimes

came out in other discussions of gender dynamics within the movement and so there were some overlays of those kinds of issues.

In addition to sexual attacks and blatant racism, classism, and sexism within—and aimed at—the movement, the vulnerable nature of a large segment of the participants made other forms of marginalization such as manipulation, quite easy. Teresa, a female participant and therapist, shared the following sentiments of the defenseless nature of a movement that offered many participants newfound chances to enact power—it seemed that anyone could lasso the collective and manipulate the group:

> Anybody can get up and create an event and get support for it. In another words, I feel like we can very easily be manipulated. Because people feel that, people have access to a large number of people, they have access to good organizing tools and if emotions run high they can summon a lot of support for various things, which are not always, uh, perhaps in our own best interests even. But there's a little power you know, and anyone can step up.

This almost sheepish reflection about manipulation and power helps to illuminate the delicate nature of the organizing processes around people's identities and the potential of the collective to almost corrupt the movement from the inside.

Again, it becomes apparent how unprepared participants were for the perhaps inevitable nature of the camp—ultimately creating a ripe scenario for potential strife to occur. In the end, using a critical lens to unpack many of the participants' expressed values allows new ways of understanding the ways in which the movement failed, or at least struggled. Overall, the romantic, functional, and critical lenses reveal new ways of understanding a movement and its participants' nuanced identities that has been, by many, largely misunderstood.

CONCLUSION AND LESSONS

> There are people that are passionately [sic], despite the sedation and the apathy of the culture and the sort of drudgery and beating down that happens and the dehumanization of capitalism and the way so many of our institutions work, and how they're built on racism, I think that there's people that are awake and willing to fight for [justice] and I think that's a really important, and I don't think I knew that. I didn't think a lot of people were awake. And I thought I was walking around by myself and really isolated. And I think that's really what we are told for a reason. And not only are people awake, but we're willing to step into levels of connections that rehumanize ourselves and find a meaning and purpose for our generation. And also healing. I think a lot of us are healing a lot from what has been done. And a reconciliation of shattered relationships. Overcoming the huge borders that have been built to separate us

and to also make us think that we can't transcend those. But I really think there's a lot of people that are willing to give it all they've got and I think that's really powerful that we're not all apathetic. (Ivy)

This chapter applied the case study's framework to participants' individual identity and group affiliation by contextualizing the data with several key conceptual and theoretical definitions: intersectionality, colonization, and collective identity. I then analyzed participants' discourses and narratives using the romantic, functional, and critical perspectives as an entry point to illuminating some of the emergent identity and group-role values. This framework helped to capture individuals' and the collectives' value systems, while also illuminating participants' struggle for authenticity and agency through extrapolating data from interpretive interviews and fieldwork.

I began this project wanting to learn more about who the participants of Occupy Portland were before the movement and during the movement, and perhaps shed light on what some of the contributing and motivating factors for their involvement in Occupy may be. Through this year-long project, I gained interesting and nuanced knowledge about the participants both from observing them from afar and through interacting with them in a face-to-face interview(s) (or later reading the transcripts of their interviews). I feel two significant lessons related to participants' identities are worthy of highlighting. First, the movement had a profound impact on countless individuals' lives in very significant and powerful ways. Individuals connected with Occupy—and with each other (collective identity)—in a way that goes beyond real description other than to say that it was palpable and visceral and life changing for hundreds of participants directly (and surely thousands more who were engaging indirectly). The sense of belonging and purpose seemed to add a much-needed spark in many individuals' lives, especially those that had previously felt oppressed (and still do), but now perhaps feel less alone. The mutual knowledge that others were struggling too seemed to provide some comfort, albeit even if only temporarily. The agency and voice that was afforded to so many marginalized individuals had immeasurable effects on people's expressed sense of self.

A second important identity outcome was realizing how challenging it is for individuals to resist systems that oppress them in ways that are often invisible (colonization). And when those forms of oppression are made visible, they are still very difficult to undo and reset. Essentially, the impact of the intersecting forces of the systems of oppression that hinder individuals in society (e.g., racism, classism, sexism) in conjunction with the colonization effects of how life should look, ultimately have an enormous hold on individuals understandings of self and other. Participants ultimately shared how the system wants to repeat itself even when individuals are actively and aggressively attempting to deconstruct it—it sneaks back into the interaction before too long and begins to impede individuals' ability to resist or act against.

Overall, Occupy Portland and Occupy, generally, was a significant and noteworthy historical event that will hopefully be investigated for generations to come. I have no doubt that many of the participants' lives and identities were altered forever in small and large ways, particularly as a result of being a part of a collective—and that many of the narratives they shared with us will become folklore in their own families, and perhaps even helping to instigate shifts and/or changes to society each time a story of resistance, solidarity, and reclamation is shared.

DISCUSSION QUESTIONS

1. Why was identity such a salient yet contested part of the Occupy movement?
2. How were individuals' identities both enabled and constrained by the movement?
3. Imagine how the movement could have worked differently if there were more nonmajority identities at play. How could that have impacted the movement's progress or media coverage?
4. In theorizing, how does a social movement act upon an individual's identity and/or sense of purpose or self? How does it function?
5. If you were involved in the Occupy movement or another related social movement, can you reflect on how you noticed your identity shifting in the process of negotiating your identity with others?

NOTES

1. Interview printed with consent of participant.
2. Jason Shelowitz, the New York art director and designed some of the most ubiquitous protest signs for Occupy Wall Street (e.g., "Lost My Job, Found An Occupation #occupywallstreet"). Shelowitz also designed the signs "Less Employment = More Occupations" and "The 99 Percent Are 100 Percent Fed Up." Read more: articles.businessinsider.com/2011-10-18/strategy/30292579_1_sign-project-yard-signs-pdf-files#xzz2Q4c9I1hY
3. Another striking example of marginalization involved Cameron Whitten, an Occupy Portland participant who staged a hunger strike by sleeping on the steps of Portland City Hall for fifty-five days (beginning June 2, 2012) to support his call for housing justice. This act ended when City Council announced that it would "enthusiastically" attend and participate in a local Summit on Housing and Homelessness in response to Whitten's protest. Still, a slightly closer look at the discourses aimed at him from outside the movement about his strike demonstrated widespread racism and dismissal of Cameron's motivations and critique of his lack of alignment with the movement. Local news articles that covered the event are ridden with hundreds of comments that attack Cameron's race and class and show enormous disdain for his actions. Two website respondents (among hundreds in the same vein) shared disdain for Whitten: "A hunger strike? Hay [sic] Cameron, since you are not using your food stamp card anyway, can I have my money back?" And another comment, "This dingbat would walk around

downtown during the mayoral campaign shirtless and wearing a giant 'vote for me' sign . . . this is what happens when you have too much time on your hands and probably too much exposure to weed!" (Oregonlive.com 2012).

III

Re(presentations) and Revelations: Occupy Mediated

One other thing that was most important to me as an activist was getting a full blast of, uh, the reality of the mainstream media. And a full blast of the weaselings of government and the police department in terms of their behavior and what they insinuate, and just how disingenuous they can be about so many different things, and about how personally hard it was to drive mainstream media to . . . to be true to their word.—Mac, Occupy Portland Participant, November 2011

Chapter Eight

Violence, Bias, or Fair Journalism?

Understanding Portland Media Coverage of an Episodic Protest

Jennette Lovejoy and Keeler Brynteson

Media coverage of an event is paramount to the public's understanding of the event. Of particular importance are events in which the public is directly involved, such as social movements. Not only may media coverage influence the amount of public participation or time volunteered and money donated, but it may also affect public officials' understanding and subsequent policy making that seeks to embrace and promote, or at times control or mitigate the social movement at hand. We understood and continue to understand the Occupy movement, and local Occupy Portland movement, through the media.[1] We know that we are not alone. Many of our coworkers, neighbors, and friends also turned to media to understand the tenor, pace, and status of the Occupy protests and encampment in downtown Portland.

Our media landscape has exploded in the last decade with the use of social media and citizen journalism to complement our more traditional means of gathering news—print newspapers, television, online news, radio, and magazines. When media consumers think about media content they often think about the front page, the cover, the sound bites or clips of the news hour, and the online homepage. This content, usually in color and accompanied by pictures, big headings, and pull quotes, gets the most visibility. It can be read without necessarily buying the full issue (or getting through the online pay wall) or paying attention to the whole publication. This is the valuable real estate for news. The content that accompanies these highly visible articles are carefully chosen, written, presented, and edited. In the news industry, article selection, positioning and framing are very deliberate and purposeful and can be very influential on how the news information is interpreted and understood (Tewksbury and Scheufele 2009).

However, there are factors beyond article prominence and framing that can affect the reach and influence of a news story. Saliency of an issue can also drive interest in an article and readers may seek out headlines that, in turn, assign special importance (and attention) to those issues made easily accessible (Iyengar 1990, 1993; McCombs and Shaw 1972). The Occupy movement that spread across the country and world in early October of 2011 was (and still is) presented and framed as salient to many individuals (i.e., "We are the 99 percent"). Occupy news also gained prominent status early on, arguably due to the media quickly sensationalizing the Occupy movement (Stelter 2011). This sensationalization, which happened in part through the publication of news headlines, photos, and videos that highlighted the conflict and potential for violence of the movement; and, in part, also due to citizens feverishly posting graphic, violent videos and photos online, contributed to a widespread and devoted following of Occupy news coverage. The often controversy-laden and attention-grabbing Occupy news was placed in visible and accessible news space; thus, interest and attention to how typical news outlets treated the movement were heightened.

The Pew Project for Excellence in Journalism (PEJ) reported that Occupy news coverage accounted for somewhere between 5 and 13 percent of the overall news hole during some of the greatest activity—October and November of 2011. The PEJ also reported that the US economy dominated news coverage during these same months, largely due to "increasing attention to Occupy Wall Street protests" and "coverage that focused on the confrontations between protesters, law enforcement, and the city governments that preside over the public spaces that have become encampments" (PEJ News Coverage Index, par. 2). While one might argue that media coverage of the Occupy movement was a core responsibility of the press to report on issues of public interest, the sensationalization of the coverage may have been driven by the pressure to draw large readership.

News about protests and social movements can potentially be reported on at all hours of the day and further disseminated beyond the daily news with online updates and social media to promote articles and cultivate an online discourse. Perhaps with the ability to constantly disseminate information, the public has in turn come to expect and hunger for more news. In fact, coverage of these current events has changed in recent decades. According to Di Cicco (2010), news increasingly contains what he termed "nuisance coverage" of social movements and protests, with a 13 percent overall increase since the mid-1960s (141). In addition, Di Cicco reported that "critical characterizations" or those that "characterized a particular protest as being ineffective, unpatriotic, or bothersome" (142) increased two-fold during the same time period and constituted almost 60 percent of all news segments analyzed.

This illustrates, perhaps, a shift toward more coverage in a tightly corporate-controlled media world where "individuals exposed to such coverage were less likely to support protesters or protests in general," (146) resulting in challenges to democratic ideals. The authors suggest the protests in the 1960s (antiwar, antisegregation) were much more inflammatory and dividing than the protests of the 1990s (i.e., World Trade Organization, antiwar). Thus, the finding that the negative media coverage of protests had increased dramatically since the 1960s (i.e., more antiprotest news) comes as a surprise. The potential for news coverage to shape the effectiveness (or ineffectiveness) of a social movement highlights the importance of investigating the landscape of media coverage surrounding such an event.

Not unlike national and global markets, local media outlets feverishly covered the Occupy Portland movement. The purpose of the current study is to examine how two major newspapers in Portland, Oregon, treated one of the largest social movements since the 1960s: the Occupy movement. In particular, we employed a news content analysis to better understand the landscape of media coverage surrounding the Occupy Portland movement. This chapter builds on existing literature that examines protest in the media and further complicates the findings by considering how Trujillo's (1992) romantic, functional, and critical lenses provide a unique interpretation of the Occupy Portland media coverage.

LITERATURE REVIEW

With a documented increase in the amount of coverage social movements and protests receive, scholars focused on how the media portrayed the people involved with the movements or protests. In the United States, "protestors are generally portrayed as lacking in political efficacy" (Wittebols 1996, 354). Also, the way the protest is shown in television news "relegates it to amusement or ridicule" (356). This shows how the (US) news outlets are using the social movements or protests more as a spectacle, and something not to be taken seriously when shown on the news. Boyle and Armstrong (2009) performed a study that examined the tactics that abortion protest groups used and the coverage they received in the media. The authors found that the tactics that a certain protest group used in their movement were the strongest predictor in how they would be covered by the media. According to the authors, groups that used "more extreme methods were treated more critically with little influence of either legal position or public support" (166). As an example of extreme methods used by protestors, the authors cited the World Trade Organization (WTO) protests in Seattle in the late 1990s. This group of demonstrators was treated very negatively by the news media, perhaps due to the protestors' use of violence and disruptive tactics.

The authors' findings further suggested that protest groups should take note because "more modest and nonthreatening tactics may be ultimately more effective because they will lead to more favorable news coverage, which is key for raising awareness of issues and events while maintaining public support" (179).

Other researchers have found that news outlets are primarily interested in broadcasting attention-grabbing news. For example, Smith et al. (2001) found "the presence of counter demonstrators, arrests, and/or violence produced more reporting on the demonstration event itself and less attention to the issues at stake" (1404). The authors posited that news outlets attempted to attract viewers by showing the protests through the most exciting angle, essentially minimizing the actual reasons for the movement that the viewer may find uninteresting. Besides trying to attract viewers with the interesting parts of the protest, research has also shown that news outlets give more attention to groups who have money and resources (Ryan, Carragee, and Meinhofer 2001). In contrast to those who hold the institutional power in the United States, the marginalized groups—traditionally those who are experiencing inequalities and who may be more motivated to protest an enduring problem—are likely to lack significant resources. As a result, when a movement is trying to gain legitimate attention from news outlets, protestors are unlikely to have the financial resources or political clout that will give them the media's attention (Ryan, Carragee, and Meinhofer 2001).

The media have also been shown to frame protest in certain ways in order to elicit specific responses from the viewers. One study looked at the network news branding of the major television news stations. The authors found Fox News to be the most conservative, NBC was roughly in the middle of the continuum, and CNN, ABC, and CBS were found to be the most liberal in their television news content (Chan-Olmsted and Cha 2007). If news outlets are seen as having a certain political slant in how they cover current events, the people watching different news stations are likely to be shown varied interpretations of the events at social movements and protests. The more conservative news outlets will portray the protest and protestors in a light that is more in line with conservative views whereas more liberal news outlets are likely to portray the protest and protestors from a liberal viewpoint. Thus, given many choices of news, media consumers are able to watch, read, etc., media coverage that most closely aligns with their own values.

However, even with an increased potential for media consumers to select their news to match specific viewpoints, one study showed that the framing of protests has remained constant over time, making an increased ability to select news a moot point. Boyle et al. (2005) examined newspaper articles between 1960 and 1999. The authors found that protest-coverage headlines and articles were basically neutral toward the protests. This was despite the fact that the coverage, in general, was also shown to be less radical as time wore on, perhaps either (or both) reflecting a shift away from covering more deviant protests in an "attempt to retain their [newspaper] audience" (646), or noting that fewer radical protests were occurring in the first place. Although protests were found to be less deviant over time, they were "treated much the same way as their 'deviant' predecessors were" (647). Thus, the authors suggested, "newspapers have become more likely to perform the function of social control for protests that would barely have registered as problematic just a couple of decades ago" (647).

A similar superficiality of coverage was found in a study analyzing how ten different print and television news outlets covered the anarchist protests in Minnesota during the 1980s. In this study, Hertog and McLeod (1995) found that "most mainstream stories de-emphasized or ignored the social critique advanced by the protestors" (11). In addition, the authors posited that "deeper political discussion and emphasis on enlightening the audience is a common feature of alternative accounts," (12) suggesting that mainstream news coverage focused more on the physical conflicts of individuals involved in the protest, whereas alternative media coverage narrowed in on the social or political debate behind the protest (Hertog and McLeod 1995).

In another study, McLeod and Detenber showed participants one of three different television stories about a particular protest. Viewers who saw the segment in which the media gave the most amount of status quo support (pro-authority, pro-government) were more likely to be "more critical of, and less likely to identify with the protesters; less critical of the police; and less likely to support the protesters' expressive rights" (1999, 1). In a similar study, viewers were shown either a one-sided story supportive of police and critical of protestors or a story more "balanced and empathic to the protesters" (McLeod 1995, par. 33). Those who saw the very one-sided story were less critical and more defensive of the police and their actions. One of the authors' major conclusions was that "even subtle differences in tone of protest coverage can have a large impact on the audience's perceptions of protest groups" (McLeod 1995, par. 66). People can be greatly influenced by the way a certain news outlet reports on a demonstration or protest.

More research on the effect of television news coverage demonstrates how the amount of information and knowledge a television viewer has about a particular protest can have a large influence over how the viewer is likely to be affected by the television news story. Detenber, et al. (2007) found that if a person has a good working knowledge of a particular political movement they are less swayed by a biased television news broadcast of the movement than if they know very little or nothing about a movement. This suggests that those with higher levels of education and those who pay more attention to current events will be less affected by slanted news broadcasts. Other research has looked at the importance of visual stimuli as well as previous knowledge in news coverage of social movements and protests. Arpan, et al. (2006) showed participants video clips of high and low levels of conflict in a certain protest. Those who saw the high levels of conflict had more negative feelings about the protest as well as the protestors than people who saw the low levels of conflict. Additionally, participants who started the study with higher pre-existing and positive attitudes toward protesting were "more likely to identify with the protestors . . . and to perceive that the protest was more effective than were those with more negative prior attitudes" (16). This study demonstrated that visual stimuli do have an effect on peoples' perceptions of the news story and that levels of previous knowledge on the topic change how viewers react to the news clip.

However, news reports are not as biased or spun as people may think. Smith et al. (2001) found only 27 percent of all the television stories coded had "any discernible bias and the bulk of those stories favored demonstrators rather than government authorities" (1416). The caveat in these findings is that the news outlet was more likely to favor authorities when coverage included "counterdemonstrators, arrests, and/or violence" and focused on the attention-grabbing episodes of the movement rather than "the issues at stake" (1416). Thus, if a story covered the overall themes of the protest and did not focus on the actual events, the story was more likely to favor the protest. On the other hand, if the story was more focused on the actual events of the protest (a more episodic look at the protest), then the story was less likely to favor the protest.

Research about protest and social movement news coverage has shown television networks to be politically biased (Chan-Olmsted and Cha 2007), to consistently report on protests in a negative light (Di Cicco 2010), and to frame stories in a way that aligns with institutional interests (Wittebols 1996) or highlights conflict at the expense of providing a deeper political discourse (Hertog and McLeod 1995). However, other research has found news outlets to be less biased than people believe (Boyle and Armstrong 2009) and stories are presented neutrally (Boyle et al. 2005) or given less spin than what is assumed (Ryan, Carragee, and Meinhofer 2001).

Clearly it is difficult to articulate in a general way how media outlets have covered and reported on political protests and social movements. In addition, a single theory of the effect of news outlets and news coverage on media consumers is hard to prove. Instead, it is important to understand that various parts of the country consume their news differently and that each social protest has unique characteristics that may affect subsequent media coverage. Some segments of the population have differing levels of education and information regarding social movements and protests, and news outlets may give differing interpretations of a social movement/protest, perhaps depending on the current political climate. It is thus necessary to analyze specific protests/movements in specific geographic regions in order to further elucidate what effect news coverage had on, for example, public perception, funding (whether people donated money or not to the cause), and reactions or involvement from public officials and political organizations. Although elucidating potential effects of media coverage should be considered tenuous extrapolation at best, it is one place to possibly further understanding of the aftermath or continuation of a particular protest/social movement.

Arguably, the national Occupy movement as a whole was branded and understood by the news coverage of the many local movements in cities across the country. For example, one widely circulated belief was that *Adbusters.org*, an anticonsumerism magazine, gave language and inspiration to the movement with a published blog post on September 17, 2011, calling for an "'occupation of Wall Street" (Kaste 2011, par. 4). Further, *Adbusters.org* was credited with the first use of the Occupy hashtag (#OccupyWallStreet) on a blog post in mid-July of 2011 (Lotan 2011). The Occupy movement began in the fall of 2011 and continues to make an impact on social and political thought in the United States.

The purpose of the current study is to provide an initial understanding of the media coverage of the Occupy movement by offering a unique look at how local print publications covered, framed, and reported the events of Occupy Portland during the peak of protest and encampment in downtown. By looking at newspaper theme, bias, and sourcing, we describe the landscape of news coverage in the two main newspapers of the city, and also point to differences in how each newspaper covered this political and social movement. We further contextualize and complicate these findings by applying Trujillo's (1992) romantic, functional, and critical lenses.

The following research question guided this work: What are the differences in theme, bias, and sourcing for the *Oregonian* and *Willamette Week* when covering the Occupy Portland movement?

METHOD

The current study employed a content analysis to compare the coverage of the Occupy Portland movement in two local news media publications—the *Oregonian* and *Willamette Week*. Newspapers are often one of the most trusted sources of news, particularly when it comes to breaking news or news that is most salient. Both of these newspapers boast wide readership to a general audience, thus, selective exposure and attention may not be as much of a factor in selective readership compared to blogs and other media.

The *Oregonian* is the major daily in Portland, Oregon, and in September of 2012 was the twenty-fourth largest daily newspaper in the United States, according to the Audit Bureau of Circulations (Auditedmedia.com). Although the *Oregonian* is not owned by one of the known corporate media companies (i.e., the Big Six: Time Warner, Disney, Viacom, News Corporation, CBS, and NBC Universal), it has been owned by the corporation Advance Publications since 1950, a company that also owns as many as thirty-seven other newspapers along with various other media outlets across platforms. In the last decade, the *Oregonian* has produced award-winning journalism covering a wide range of social issues—from exposing official agencies in a 1999 Oregon Coast oil spill, to investigating problems with the immigration and naturalization service systems in the United States, to stories that highlighted the failure of a federal program designed to assist people with disabilities find employment. The *Oregonian*, like most newspapers, has undergone significant changes in the last three years—a new publisher and editor took over at the end of 2009. In 2010, the paper employed approximately two hundred news reporters, but in mid-2012 there was rumor that the paper may no longer be a daily paper in years to come (Mesh 2012). The *Oregonian* boasts that 78 percent of Portland residents read their paper or their website. Indeed, it is Portlanders' and many Oregon residents' main source of local news.

There is a known rivalry between the *Oregonian* and *Willamette Week*, Portland's widely known "alternative" weekly. The daily paper has been criticized for its conservative bias and *Willamette Week* has been criticized for its liberal bias. Although competition between a daily and a weekly is less common due to different production, and therefore news-gathering schedules, *Willamette Week* made headlines when it scooped the *Oregonian* most notably with the 2004 scandal involving Oregon's former governor Neil Goldschmidt, which has subsequently allowed them to claim the title of "the only alternative weekly ever to win the Pulitzer Prize for investigative reporting" (Wweek.com). *Willamette Week* was founded in 1974 and claims that "readers count on us to be independent, thought-provoking and in-depth," (par. 1) disseminating roughly seventy-five thousand papers per week in the Portland area and another ten thousand to the surrounding communities. In 1984, the paper went from being a paid publication to being distributed for free and reliant on advertising for its sole revenue.

The sample for the current study was drawn from the *Oregonian* and *Willamette Week* newspapers. The most significant period of protest and encampment of the Occupy Portland movement was from October 4, 2011, until November 17, 2011, so only published articles between those dates were used. October 4, 2011, was the first day Occupy Portland had a protest and rally in downtown Portland, and thus the first local news stories about Occupy Portland came out that day. Although the encampment was officially disbanded on November 13, 2011, the last major protest aligned with this time period was on November 17, 2011. In the *Oregonian*, there were eighty-one articles about the Occupy Portland movement between those dates. In *Willamette Week*, there were fifty-four articles about the Occupy Portland movement between those dates. All articles published during that time frame were accessed and coded from both sources. The articles from the *Oregonian* were accessed via LexisNexis and the articles from *Willamette Week* were accessed via the online search tool from their website.

The unit of analysis was each individual article. For each article, identifying information was recorded—the newspaper title, date of publication, and word count. Each article was next examined for mention of violence from Occupy protesters as well as violence against the protesters.

Violence *from* protesters was coded if there was a mention of any crimes, fights, physical retaliation, or violence in any form that originated from the protestors.[2] Violence against protesters was coded if there was mention of any arrests, riot control, release of pepper spray or similar substance, or any police brutality against protesters.

We determined if each article was episodic, meaning it was more focused on the actual events or timeline of Occupy Portland, or thematic, meaning the article was focused on the reasons *why* the protesters were protesting or the underlying issues of the Occupy movement. Then, each article was subsequently coded for a specific theme.

For the different thematic categories, Hertog and McLeod's (1995) themes were used to categorize the articles under five different categories: circus/carnival, riot, confrontation, protest, and debate. Circus/carnival "[f]rame focuses on [protestors'] actions rather than their political views . . . Oddity and peculiarity are emphasized and the symbolic meaning of protestors' gestures is de-emphasized or completely ignored . . . bystanders are shocked, confused, or amused, but never enlightened" (19). Riot was used ". . . when an emphasis on the unusual turns to emphasis on public disorder and the element of implied danger rises . . . the protesters become a menace to the public order and even to citizen health and well-being, . . . and are no longer simply odd balls, [but] have become criminals. They lash out indiscriminately, equally endangering all members of society" (20). Confrontation "treated the anarchists [protesters] and the police as combatants, much like a sporting event" and "confrontation stories focused on the tactics and actions of the groups involved. Deeper political and economic discussions were usually left out of stories employing this frame" (21). Protest "acknowledged the [protesters] as a legitimate political voice. The conferral of legitimacy does not necessarily imply supportive or positive portrayal, but treats the [protesters] as a group presenting a political viewpoint that deserves attention. Protest stories presented [protesters] as committed and thoughtful, and their actions were taken as an expression of their political views" (21). Finally, debate ". . . de-emphasized physical actions involved in the conference and marches. The marches and meetings acted as a springboard for discussion of philosophical conflicts and contradictions" (22).

After the theme was identified, gender and type of sources were compiled for each article. A source was identified as a unique individual anytime he or she was quoted or paraphrased in an article. All sources within an article were categorized as a protestor, bystander, or authority label, and the specific gender of each source was coded. Finally, articles were coded as biased or unbiased based on a weighing of three different factors: (1) how the article was phrased (i.e., analyzing headlines and/or article content that insinuated fault or blame toward one side or the other); (2) which sources were used (e.g., if the majority of the sources were from authority, the article was considered biased toward authority); and (3) whether the article was considered thematic (i.e., addressing deeper issues the movement was calling for) or episodic (i.e., addressing the topical events or timeline). If it was unbiased, the coding was complete. For biased articles, the direction of bias was coded: (1) in favor of protestors, (2) in favor of authority, or (3) a neutral bias—meaning it had elements of bias for both sides.

The intercoder reliability was calculated for ten articles from each of the two newspapers used (n = 20). The coders had an overall simple agreement (Holsti 1969) among coders of 87 percent. This level was deemed sufficient for coding purposes and the 135 articles were divided amongst three coders.

RESULTS

Landscape of Coverage

The final set of articles that were coded included 81 from the *Oregonian* and 54 from *Willamette Week* for a total of 135. Relatively few of the articles were longer, investigative pieces, indicated by the average article length being approximately 500 words (mean word count = 508). Over 80 percent of articles were episodic, meaning that the article focused on the actual events of Occupy Portland, and slightly less than 20 percent were considered thematic, which were articles that focused on *why* the protesters were protesting and the deeper issues raised by the Occupy movement. In all coverage, just under half (46 percent) of the news coverage contained mentions of violence. A third (30 percent) of those articles contained mention(s) of violence from only one side, while fewer articles (16 percent) contained mention(s) of violence from both sides. More of the articles focused on violence from the protestors (37 percent), while the remaining 23 percent focused on violence against the protestors (e.g., violence by law enforcement against the protestors). Forty-five percent of the total articles were biased. When looking at the biased coverage broken down by newspapers, just over half of the *Oregonian's* coverage (52 percent) was biased, while 35 percent of *Willamette Week's* coverage was biased. Thematically, the preponderance of Occupy Portland coverage was considered a protest (58 percent). Over a quarter of the demonstration coverage was considered a confrontation (29 percent), and a few articles were themed a circus/carnival (7.4 percent) or a debate (6 percent). No articles were riot themed.

In general, both newspapers used protestors as sources in the articles more than establishment and bystander sources. Seventy percent of the articles contained no female sources quoted. The highest number of females quoted in a single article, four, appeared only once, whereas the highest number of male sources quoted in an article at one time was fifteen. The use of female sources did not differ depending on the type of coverage (episodic or thematic); however, the sourcing in both newspapers was overwhelmingly male when violence was mentioned in the article (mean = 2.5 male sources/article), while articles that did not mention violence sourced fewer males (mean = 1.3 male sources/article), $t(133) = 3.547, p < 0.001$.

Research Question

To answer the research question, the data analysis focused on the differences of the *Oregonian* and the *Willamette Week* in the type of article, the bias, and the sourcing types. We first conducted a Chi-Square test of association to determine if there was a difference between the two publications for news article type (episodic or thematic). Results indicated that the *Oregonian* published more episodic news coverage than expected, while *Willamette Week* had more thematic news coverage than expected ($M^2(1) = 13.09, p < 0.001$). To illustrate the differences, descriptive statistics show that just over a third (33 percent) of *Willamette Week's* Occupy articles were labeled thematic and 91 percent of the *Oregonian's* articles were labeled as episodic coverage.

A second chi-square test of association compared direction of article bias (whether the article favored the protestors or authority) between the two newspapers. Slightly under half (45 percent) of the total news coverage was identified as biased, and the *Oregonian* news coverage tended to favor authority, while the *Willamette Week* coverage tended to favor protestors ($M^2(1) = 14.88, p < 0.001$). Of the biased articles (45 percent of total coverage), the *Oregonian* had approximately one third (31 percent) biased toward the protestors. On the other hand, 84 percent of *Willamette Week's* coverage was biased toward the protestors.

Finally, three independent samples t-tests examined the differences in the number of protestor, bystander, and establishment sources used in the articles of the two publications. The *Oregonian* had an average of roughly one (mean = 1.07) protestor source per article, whereas *Willamette Week* used protestor sources more, with an average of 1.63 sources per article. Both newspapers used quotes from less than one bystander source per article (both means = 0.29). Finally, similar to the amount of protestor sources quoted, the *Oregonian* averaged approximately one (mean = 1.01) establishment source per article, while *Willamette Week* utilized less than one establishment source per article (mean = 0.72). No differences reached statistical significance.

CONCLUSION

This content analysis set out to understand how Portland's major daily newspaper, the *Oregonian,* and prominent weekly newspaper, *Willamette Week,* covered the Occupy social movement and protests from the birth of the movement on October 4, 2011 to November 17, 2011, four days after the downtown encampment disbanded. We identified 135 articles as containing Occupy Portland news coverage, with 81 from the *Oregonian* and 54 from *Willamette Week.* The analysis focused on the differences in type of news article, evidence of bias, and the number and type of sources between the two newspapers.

Descriptive findings indicate that the landscape of coverage focused on Occupy Portland with episodic event-coverage rather than addressing the why or deeper thematic issues of the movement. Mentions of violence were in almost half of the total coverage and tended to be about the violence by protestors, rather than against protestors.

Similar to Hertog and McLeod's (1995) finding that protest coverage was often dominated by conflict and in particular, physical confrontation, our study found that articles framed Occupy Portland to be primarily about a protest and confrontation, relegating other themes to a few minor articles. We found none of the articles to fall under the riot theme, reflecting that coverage did not overly emphasize extreme chaos and criminalize the protesters. Rather, when violence was a focus, it tended to focus on how each side was dealing with the confrontation and how further violence was being avoided. For example, a headline[3] in the *Oregonian* read, "'We are concerned this is moving toward a confrontation,' police say" (November 13, 2011). Another headline was, "Protesters allege police brutality; mayor says eviction was 'about as peaceful as one could hope'" (*Oregonian* November 15, 2011). *Willamette Week* also demonstrated the focus on both sides with the headline: "Chaos to checkmate – Mayor Adams and Occupy Portland played a game in city parks. Police Chief Reese won" (November 16, 2011).

While both newspapers published more news on the logistics and events of Occupy Portland rather than the larger and deeper issues upon which the Occupy movement was founded, it was interesting that a much greater proportion of articles published by *Willamette Week*, relative to the proportion published by the *Oregonian*, employed more thematic coverage—addressing Occupy Portland's main themes and issues of social inequality, homelessness, and power. An article in *Willamette Week,* "Homeless, not faceless," focused on how the Occupy Portland movement potentially served to expose the larger issues of homelessness in Portland and how homeless "contributed to what did work in the camp" through working in the camp kitchen and security services (November 16, 2011).

The *Oregonian*, on the other hand, primarily utilized episodic coverage—publishing articles about Occupy event highlights, encampment logistics, or demonstration timelines. For example, an article in the *Oregonian* (October 18, 2011) titled, "As Occupy Portland reaches its second week, calls surface from Commissioner Nick Fish for a 'peaceful conclusion,'" focused on the cost of damage to city parks due to the encampment and reported that Commissioner Fish called "for protestors to channel their energy elsewhere, saying the parks should not be 'sacrificed' to the cause." The article goes on to quote an Occupy protestor, Ethan Edwards, responding to Fish by saying "To me, this park is more beautiful than before because it's providing people a place to live." This article demonstrates a focus on each side's logistical position. Two more *Oregonian* headlines, "Occupy Portland rally planned for Thursday; Portland police encouraging permit for event" (October 4, 2011), and "Police close steel bridge citing concerns about protestors" (November 17, 2011), again show the focus on logistics and event details. Political news coverage often falls under the same sort of critique when articles tend to emphasize which candidate is ahead or behind in a race (i.e., horse-race coverage), rather than focusing on the larger issues and campaign platform of each candidate.

With episodic news coverage, readers may tend to receive a more topical understanding of Occupy Portland that highlights effects of the encampment on the city parks, a confrontation during a protest, closures, an upcoming protest event, or action taken by authorities. This is important information that keeps the public informed and, perhaps, involved with the social movement. In the news industry, it is the "hard" news of the day, or the "need-to-know" information that the public must have to stay informed about an event. It is information that would allow someone to go and take part in a protest or learn how the two sides in the protest were dealing with each other. It is not information that explores the larger issues of inequality or the political/business systems under fire.

Some researchers have shown that episodic news articles focusing on the events and the attention-grabbing parts of the movement favor authority figures, while the thematic articles that focus on the actual causes favor the protestors (Smith et al. 2001). Our findings are consistent with prior research. Relative to *Willamette Week*, the *Oregonian* had a greater proportion of articles that favored the authority. Limitations of our data did not allow us to ascertain the extent to which publication ownership played a part in how news articles were written and edited. However, it is noteworthy that we found the *Oregonian*, which is not locally owned and perhaps susceptible to more corporate interests, to provide slightly more coverage of the authority or establishment figures associated with Occupy Portland—for example, one article in the *Oregonian* titled, "Occupy Portland: Mayor Sam Adams watches, waits and exhales as downtown squares are cleared" (November 13, 2011). In the article, Mayor Adams is quoted as saying, "I think the fact that things have gone better here than they've gone in other cities is a tribute to great professionalism on the part of the police . . . and a good working relationship with Occupy Portland coordinators." Giving authority figures more "voice" in a news article can create the feeling of bias toward the authority.

To add dimensionality to our data, we chose to utilize Trujillo's (1992) romantic, functional, and critical lenses to further interpret our findings. In short, Trujillo's romantic lens focused on the pure, idealistic aspects; the functional lens focused on the realities of a system embedded in a social culture; and the critical lens centered on how a phenomenon served to commercialize, marginalize, or control certain aspects in society. We applied these three lenses to the media or news system, in general, and to our newspaper content analysis findings, in particular.

Trujillo's *romantic* lens would remind us that media professionals are concerned with providing us with both sides of the issue and work hard to provide fair, balanced, and objective news. Romantics want to believe the press is without an agenda and thus interested in telling stories the public needs or wants to know because news is instrumental in our shared understanding and knowledge of social issues, including social movements/protests. Romantics recognize that news articles must give timely information that directly affects the public (i.e., business closures due to demonstrations, downtown traffic affected by protests, etc.). And from this lens we recognize that the *Oregonian's* focus on episodic coverage was a choice to get the daily "play-by-play" Occupy Portland information to the public. This is commendable. In the same vein, from the romantic lens, we salute *Willamette Week* for providing a little more thematic coverage and acknowledge that their publication cycle (weekly versus daily) most likely allowed journalists to dig into the deeper questions the Occupy Portland movement was raising.

Christians, Ferre, and Fackler (1993) argued that the press, in particular, is central to facilitating an understanding of social problems that may lead to possible solutions. Using Trujillo's romantic lens, we see the press as interested in bringing communities together, uniting us during good and hard times, bridging divides among individuals and our communities, and exposing social inequalities. The press upholds our First Amendment freedoms and exhibits freedom of speech to keep us fully informed. Because we know that media coverage forms the debate and narrative of a social movement, the romantic in us wants to believe that the press provides accurate and truthful accounts of an event.

Further, media romantics are bound by the belief that media coverage often serves as a catalyst for continued interpersonal conversation and may motivate information seeking from other information sources such as blogs, official websites, and social media. Thus, it is imperative, from a romantic view, that the press acts and serves in the best interest of the public and moves beyond social, economic, and political lines. This idea, termed social responsibility theory, was born out of the 1947 findings of the Hutchins Commission on the Freedom of the Press. The report implored the press to exercise its constitutional freedoms by (1) providing a "full, truthful, comprehensive and intelligent account of the day's events in a context which gives them meaning"; (2) "serving as a forum for the exchange of comment and criticism"; and (3) "giving a representative picture of constituent groups in society and clarify[ing] the goals and values of society" (McQuail 1994, 124).

Thus, Trujillo's romantic lens lauds the reporters (who wrote the stories analyzed in this study) for reporting from within and telling the hard stories that distill the complexity of the protestors' movement into news stories that allow us to understand the protestors and bridge the divide between those involved with the movement and those who were not. From a romantic view, the embedded reporting style found in some of *Willamette Week* articles may also be helpful in a journalist's quest to provide the most accurate and truthful account of an Occupy Portland event. This view rests on the assumption that there is such a "truth." When, in fact, it is easy to imagine how two different stories can emerge from the same news event. News is a human production. It is not mechanically created or produced; it is steeped in human interpretation and inherently bound to the system in which it is produced.

In fact, Trujillo's *functional* lens reminds us that the majority of US media companies are independently owned and separated from government ownership in order to preserve our value of freedom of expression. Yet this view also highlights the limits of working within a capitalistic society where advertising dollars support news and deregulation policy that favor business is often developed by elected public officials. In addition, each city across the country sought to give "24/7" news coverage of their local Occupy movement. From a functionalist point of view, the press is a machine that cranks out event coverage and packages complex stories into easily digestible quotes, headlines, and simple narratives. This does not mean that the functional perspective fails to acknowledge that our news processes are inherently speckled with human subjectivity. Rather, this view highlights that journalists are bound by the most effective and efficient way to produce news. Consequently, the *Oregonian*, as a daily newspaper, was subject to different news-gathering techniques and writing deadlines than *Willamette Week* was on a weekly publication cycle.

Clearly, tighter story turnaround times inherent in a daily newspaper plays a role in forcing journalists to rely more on convenient and typical sourcing patterns and news-gathering techniques that facilitate quick story production. Reporters rely on these typical routines, and social movements may have an "uphill battle in attempting to change the way media cover them" (Barakso and Schaffner 2006, 39). However, for any type of media publication the ubiquitous nature of information forces institutions and journalists to routinize the way news is gathered and written. In order to compete for readers, news coverage must have an incredibly quick turnaround time and therefore be efficiently produced.

Tuchman's (1973) notion of typification created a certain journalistic routine that allocated specific amounts of time, depth of coverage, and sourcing techniques, depending on the type of event. Typifying events gave journalists permission to gloss, predict, summarize, or throw out information in order to fit the newsworthy event into a particular category. For example, Occupy news stories may be typified as conflict news and journalists may focus on telling the "he said, she said" story rather than focusing on some of the deeper, more complex issues the Occupy movement posed. The way events are routinized and practically managed has created a system that allows newspeople to "construct or reconstruct social realities by establishing the context in which social phenomena are perceived and defined" (Tuchman 1973, 188). For example, Fishman (1982) found that beat reporters relied on making a routine check of activities through a small number of governmental organizations (i.e., following limited, focal points of information such as meetings and officials). Tuchman suggested a newsmaking system that relied on routinization defined not only what happened but also the *way* it happened. Using Trujillo's functional lens we can argue that Occupy Portland coverage, although unique in nature, made "news" by utilizing the same template that has been used to cover countless other events and issues.

Lastly, Trujillo's functional lens reminds us that journalists are emblematic of the American hard work ethic as they incessantly labor to tell important and investigative stories. News is valued in our society and the current move toward online pay-walls and subscription rate hikes reinforces the notion that information is not free and if we want good, important news at our fingertips, we must pay for it.

However, through Trujillo's *critical* lens, we could argue that news publications take advantage of their position of power and make money by telling the stories they want to tell. News critics argue that highlighting the protestors' agenda could be a form of news commodification in that emphasizing, and perhaps sensationalizing, the protestor perspective helps sell news. Critics view news storytelling decisions as all leading back to a means to gain readership and sell news in order to support the publication or parent company.

Media business generally relies on advertising dollars to be successful and stay in production. The more readers, viewers, and subscribers a news outlet can garner, the more appealing they are for advertisers' dollars. The fact that the majority of articles were framed as a protest suggests controversy was at the heart of Occupy Portland coverage. Focusing on the tactics participants and police were each employing to achieve their goals illustrates game-like coverage that sells news well. The commodification of news is well established (e.g., Jackson 2009) and the consolidation of media ownership in recent decades is often blamed for a corporate/bottom-line approach that threatens democracy (Cohen 2005). In fact, by employing a critical lens, we would ascertain how Occupy Portland media coverage served to ignore the poor or the powerless. Critics may analyze: whether news coverage enforced or reaffirmed our societal hierarchies, whether the press worked to overly promote conflict or the negative aspects of the movement, the possibility that news coverage served as a tool for social control, or whether it revealed problems of our culture that the Occupy movement tried to expose. In order to understand the pushes and pulls on mass media, economists have studied elite control of economic institutions.

When looking at the media as part of the economic system, economic constraints or pressures have been found to limit or bias "the forms of mass culture that are produced and distributed through the media" (Baran and Davis 2003, 234). Schudson (1989) argued that media content ends up reinforcing or coinciding with the culture associated with the dominant economic institutions and social classes and that news may primarily serve established power. The resulting consequences are a "reduction of independent media sources, concentration on the largest markets, avoidance of risks, reduced investment in less profitable media tasks (such as investigative reporting and documentary film-making), neglect of smaller and poorer sectors of the potential audience and often a politically unbalanced range of news media" (McQuail 1994, 82). In other words, critics assert the business models of media may covertly influence news coverage in ways that favor the supporting of economic institutions or people of power.

Trujillo's critical lens asks us to consider whether Occupy Portland's news coverage reaffirmed social hierarchies and power structures or whether it challenged or exposed social problems of our culture. Our analyses suggests that coverage did highlight messages from authority figures, giving them more quotes and space, which may inherently reaffirm our current social structures. According to McLeod and Detenber (1999), support in the media for the status quo, or authority figures, produces a "framing effect" in which media consumers may believe that there is less public support for the protestors, which "might in turn reduce viewers' willingness to speak out or take actions on behalf of the protestors and their issues" (17). Because we found the *Oregonian's* Occupy Portland coverage more biased in favor of the authority, the readers of this newspaper may have become less connected to the protestors and perhaps gave less support to them.

On the other hand, *Willamette Week* had the opposite bias compared to the *Oregonian*. The *Willamette Week* coverage showed more support of the protestors and their ideas, lending support to previous research done in the field showing that protest coverage focused on protestors (Detenber et al. 2007; McLeod and Detenber 1999; McLeod 1995). *Willamette Week* also devoted news space for a regular article titled "Occupier of the day" where a journalist chose a protestor to interview for an in-depth question-and-answer article. Thirteen of these special articles, accompanied by a picture of the protestor, were published during the timeframe of our analysis of coverage. In addition, *Willamette Week* had two embedded reporters, Aaron Mesh and Matthew Korfhage. Journalist Korfhage wrote articles with the tagline "notes from a protest," as he became part of the protest in order to write about it, and Mesh spent forty-eight straight hours inside Occupy Portland's encampment as the basis for one of his longer, investigative articles. Both journalists wrote these articles with first person voice, which may have contributed to a tone of favor toward the protestors. In short, they were a part of the protestors and their perspective, rather than embedding themselves in the police force or local politician groups. Clearly, this would affect their reporting and reporting style. Critics of media publications and the production of news may laud these instances of coverage that demonstrated a commitment to represent those claiming powerlessness and, at the same time, point fingers at news coverage that failed to take into account the marginalized perspectives from within the Occupy movement.

To further support our findings regarding mixed biases in the news, a survey conducted by researchers at Portland State University's Survey Research Lab on November 13, 2011, of participants from within the Occupy Portland encampment found the majority (64 percent) of them felt that the local media coverage was not accurate, 28 percent felt that coverage was "somewhat" accurate, and 7 percent felt that local media coverage was accurate. The rest did not know or respond (Charles 2011). It is worth noting that it may be convenient to be critical of any company, regardless of performance, when the individual that is polled is involved in a broader protest against such power.

In the end, because news is necessarily a product of production, each news organization in this study may ultimately be seen as operating from Trujillo's functional lens—delegating as much, or as little, resources that they have to cover Occupy Portland. In a wake of newsroom staff cuts due to declining newspaper subscriptions and print advertisers, and uncertainty about how to make a profit off online news, there may have been fewer resources to devote to Occupy Portland coverage. In addition, covering Occupy Portland most likely meant devoting time and energy away from other news events and stories. It is important to consider what other "newsworthy" stories did not make the news during this time due to an emphasis on the Occupy movement. This frequently happens when an event or issue dominates a community. The template for deciding what is news becomes unbalanced. However, news-gathering, interviewing, and story-writing processes of Occupy coverage must operate under the same constraints and freedoms other types of stories are afforded. From a functional perspective, although Occupy coverage is not routine news, it must be *routinized* and conveyed in the same way all news becomes news: utilizing the same method of gathering sources from "both sides" and highlighting information that fits in with the established news values of conflict, emotion, prominence, proximity, timeliness, and novelty.

DISCUSSION QUESTIONS

1. The authors suggest that media content studies are important, for one reason, because the public's understanding of an event can be influenced by the media. Do you think this is true? Why or why not?
2. The authors found bias in about half of the news coverage on Occupy Portland. Regardless of which direction the news was biased, what are the pros and cons of having biased news?
3. Why would media outlets tend to favor the status quo instead of the views of the protestors?
4. Of the three lenses identified by Trujillo, which did each newspaper primarily employ in covering the Occupy Portland movement?
5. The authors maintain that "it is imperative, from a romantic view, that the press acts and serves in the best interest of the public and moves beyond social, economic, and political lines." Did the newspapers studied in the article follow this imperative? Why or why not?
6. Explain the justification the authors provide for why daily newspapers like the *Oregonian* are forced to provide more episodic articles and the *Willamette Week* is able to provide more thematic articles.

NOTES

1. The authors would like to thank graduate students Keith Foster, Kate Gilronan, and Marit Tegelaar for their work in article gathering and coding for this project.

2. This chapter refers to the participants of Occupy Portland as protestors due to the fact that the media coverage consistently referred to individuals involved in the movement as protestors. Further, using the term protestors follows the pattern in similar media content studies.

3. Although this is a quantitative study and we did not do a qualitative analysis, we use examples in our conclusion in order to highlight and illustrate more tangibly some of the

differences in coverage. Because the function of news headlines is to focus the story and frame the information that follows in text, we primarily use headlines as exemplars.

Chapter Nine

An "Official" Account

Delivering Occupy Portland's Eviction Notice

erin daina mcclellan

> All kinds of crime happens [*sic*] in downtown Portland every single day. Hundreds of people are homeless out in the street every single night, regardless of whether Occupy exists or not. And it seems to only be a crisis when it's actually at City Hall's doorstep. The existence of our movement has cast light on the plight of economic refugees whose lives have been endangered and are forced to sleep on the street, thanks to the policies of the 1 percent.—James Oliver, Occupy Portland Participant, November 2011
>
> A mature understanding of movement rhetoric must take into account the nature and persuasive powers of its vernacular rhetoric.—Hauser and mcclellan 2009, 25

So what if it doesn't? Hauser's theory of vernacular rhetoric (1998, 1999, 2001, 2006) claims that the everyday ways people coordinate their action rely on unique communication practices and strategies that are grounded in specific symbolic understandings of daily life. Such a theoretical lens helps to see how "rank and file members" of a social movement inevitably make sense of their participation in the movement differently than their leaders and those against whom they are protesting. Even though he makes a compelling case, our everyday accounts of social movements, like Occupy Portland (Oregon), continue to either tokenize the individuals participating (or linked by proximity) or sympathize with (or demonize) the institutional leaders against whom the protesters have gathered. Much of the mainstream media coverage of Occupy Portland appears to meet this prescriptive way of "reporting" on the people, events, and purposes of social movements. In particular, the voices of the people on the ground protesting have been edited, decontextualized, and otherwise collectively attributed to one particular person or persons. Other chapters in this book will appropriately and complexly bring our attention to how this collective of voices is worthy of being comprehensively represented, heavily contextualized, and otherwise diversified beyond a single voice closest to the proverbial microphone. It is my aim in this chapter, however, to focus on how the absence of focus on vernacular rhetoric reveals a singular narrative about Occupy Portland that fails to take into account (on the surface) many of the complexities that coming to understand this social movement necessitates. By focusing on a singular narrative told in one particular "official" voice—that of Portland Mayor Sam Adams, Occupy Portland as a movement is presented as advocating on behalf of a worthy cause but derelict in its duty to create a "better" city of Portland. The overt functional language utilized by Adams to (successfully) justify the need to end the Occupy Portland encampments will be further discussed through a critical lens, which reveals not only the romantic nature of much of Occupy Portland's oppositional rhetoric, but also how particular power relations emerge in the production and consumption of rhetoric as public discourse.

As a democratically elected citizen representative and oft-turned-to "expert" about what is best for Portland and its citizens, Mayor Adams explains the consequences of Occupy Portland in particular ways that provide a specific understanding of social movements while offering advice about the most appropriate ways in which social movements more generally should be engaged. A rhetorical analysis of how Mayor Adams evicted Occupiers in the city of Portland from their 2011 encampments presents Occupy as a specific social movement that conflicts with the mayor's determination of what is "best" for the people of Portland. This particular focus on eviction garnered both national interest and a highly engaged local response. The specific texts produced by Mayor Adams (and other identified official voices) in relation to this event reveal a particular way of understanding Occupy Portland that is both limited in scope and fails to account for alternate possibilities of sense-making about the movement. The "right" way to think about the evictions of the Occupy Portland encampments is inherently presented in Mayor Adams's formal statements to the press, which are significant for understanding (1) how romantically social movements are understood as inherently good or bad for the larger society they are purporting to change, (2) how functionally such language is used to achieve persuasive ends, and (3) how a critical read of these texts identifies salient absences that result in singular understandings of Occupy Portland that disassociate it with particular power relations, contexts of importance, and possibilities of future consequences for effecting change.[1]

Mayor Adams's argument that the Occupy Portland encampments were "necessary" to evict produces a compelling call for response that addresses the (lack of) ways that such necessity is defined, addressed, and discussed. I argue here that Adams's approach to narrating the need for the encampments' eviction simultaneously disempowers Occupy Portland as a social movement able of creating effectual change, and logically constructs a way of thinking about social movements more generally as problematically disruptive of "life as usual" rather than purposefully disruptive of life as usual.

MAYOR ADAMS: OFFICIAL VOICE OF PORTLAND'S PEOPLE

The mayor's office requires taking an oath to solemnly swear to "faithfully, honestly and ethically perform . . . duties" with no "undisclosed financial interest in any business located in Portland or . . . contracts with the City," to "hold no other office or position of profit," and to remain apart from "any partisan political committee" (*Portlandonline.com* Auditor's Office 1995). The FY2012-13 Requested Budget from the office of the mayor begins with a statement that "The Mayor's Office is the central hub for all City business and affairs" (Portlandonline.com Office of the Mayor 2012). It would suffice to say that the mayor's obligations are generally complex and require a variety of efforts to continually attempt to uphold all parts of his mayoral oath of office. However, it is difficult to envision how each of these tenets of the mayor's oath can be upheld at any one time, particularly in times of complex political strife, like that which occurred in the fall of 2011 when Mayor Sam Adams chose to announce that the Occupy Portland encampments required eviction.

On November 10, 2011, Mayor Sam Adams held a press conference and announced that the Occupy Portland camps were officially deemed "unsafe," "unsustainable," unable to "evolve," and therefore necessitated "evicting" those people physically gathered—and their belongings—in the name of protecting the city of Portland and its people. By analyzing Mayor Adams's public statements between November 7, 2011, and November 11, 2011, I aim to better understand the way that the city of Portland's official voice argues for dismantling the Occupy Portland encampments in an effort to make life better for the people of Portland. Analysis of this functional narrative of Occupy Portland (1) reveals the possibility for a romantic resistance to emerge, and (2) critically fails to take into account ways that the social movement is understood and experienced beyond what Mayor Adams decrees.

A "TRADITION"AL READ

Four specific texts were identified as directly relevant to the creation of Mayor Adams's narrative explaining the need for Occupy Portland's eviction. These texts provide an opportunity to read (both in terms of linguistic choices and in terms of interpretive, value-laden consequences associated with such choices) this narrative as a consistent and unified accounting of events that positions certain people, behavior, and values in particular ways. Thus, the average audience member of this media coverage is guided to understand this official account as equivalent to the larger public discourse about Occupy Portland and the "best" way to make sense of Occupy Portland as an (un)successful social movement.

The tradition of rhetorical analysis is embedded in the neoclassical roots of Aristotelian criticism. In other words, a "traditional" analysis of these texts may focus solely on the ways in which Mayor Adams's rhetoric was (un)successfully persuasive in achieving his stated end goal of evicting the Occupy Portland encampments. While my aim, here, is *not* to focus on the end state of persuasion that was or was not achieved, I *do* focus on the official perspective provided about the eviction rather than the varied accounts provided about the eviction from other vernacular voices. This analysis will demonstrate that neither a traditional read, nor a focus solely on official accounts, are alone sufficient to understand a complex social movement.

Within this official narrative, my analysis focuses on identifying and discussing Mayor Adams's position in relation to (1) Occupy Portland as a social movement seeking to alter existing cultural norms and values, (2) the city of Portland as an entity in need of protecting, and (3) the people and places in need of management and control. In all four texts, these three aspects produce a unified and consistent explanation of Occupy Portland as a social movement that is advocating for large-scale systemic change while treating it as separate from day-to-day (vernacular) life in Portland. Thus, the mayor's authorization of the eviction of the encampments "on behalf of" the city of Portland simultaneously prioritizes some (people's) values over others in the quest to bring about change.

This official narrative of eviction began in an open letter to the Occupy Portland encampments released on November 7, 2011, in which Mayor Adams first warned movement participants that "something" needed to be done to change the conditions he deemed to be "urgently" in need of address (Theriault 2011). Three days following this open letter, on November 10, 2011, Mayor Adams made a formal statement at a press conference, where he was accompanied by Portland Chief of Police, Mike Reese, and City Commissioner-in-Charge of the Portland Housing Bureau and Portland Parks & Recreation, Nick Fish, to announce a three-day eviction notice (Adams 2011). That same day, Adams also participated in a *National Public Radio,* "All Things Considered," interview hosted by Guy Raz further explaining his decision and position (Raz 2011), and the following day, on November 11, 2011, a *PBS* "NewsHour" story aired with Jeffrey Brown hosting an interview with Mayor Adams and Occupy Portland liaison, James Oliver, about the eviction notice and its consequences (Brown 2011). The resulting narrative, after it is told, can be further made sense of as romantically resisted, functionally consequential (as [un]successfully persuasive), and critically interrogated. But before such a narrative can be consequential, it first must be told.

An Open Letter to the Occupy Portland Encampments

In the first text, in an open letter to the Occupy Portland encampments, Mayor Adams is reported to be "urging occupiers to do more, and do it faster, to deal with problems involving violence and drug use and mental illness" (Theriault 2011). His view of Occupy Portland as a movement devoid of humans can be seen immediately in how he chooses to address the letter: "To the Occupy Portland Encampment." By addressing the encampment rather than the campers, Mayor Adams both avoids having to distinguish between those who are part of the movement and those who are simply temporarily living in the camp. He similarly, by employing such a greeting, addresses a nonhuman entity (the place) rather than a collective of people (Occupy Portland as an "uninstitutionalized collectivity").[2] He begins his letter with a statement of solidarity while still clearly differentiating himself from them: "I know that you agree."

In the first paragraph of his letter he further collectivizes both Occupy's and the city's need to "immediately address" the "illicit" activity that is happening in these encampments because they are (1) on public land, and (2) a threat to public safety. The focus on public both warrants the mayor's involvement and creates a need for him to justify acting in direct opposition to the US Constitutional First Amendment protections that implore Congress to "make no law respecting an establishment of religion, or prohibiting the free exercise thereof; or abridging the freedom of speech, or of the press; or the right of the people peaceably to assemble, and to petition the Government for a redress of grievances." Mayor Adams claims that "the way things are operating now is not sustainable," implying that First Amendment protections must be *sustainable* in order to override his obligation to put *public* good over *individual* rights. In order for Occupy Portland participants to be protected in their practices of free speech, peaceable assembly, and petitioning the government for a redress of grievances, they must be seen to be exempt from the time, place, and manner restrictions[3] established by the US Supreme Court that allow Mayor Adams to override such individual rights for the public good of the people. These formal restrictions dictate that "free speech zones" for protesting (i.e., exercising one's right to free speech and peaceful assembly in particularly designated places and spaces) are appropriate when conflicts challenge a "significant government interest" (*The Free*

Dictionary). Thus, Mayor Adams's focus on *urgency* and *immediate action* upholds the focus on *time* that the eviction notice is eventually predicated on.

Adams goes on to say "I know there is a nationwide Occupy process for working through those things . . . but we cannot wait long," revealing not only a focus on time but also on *place*. Since Mayor Adams reflects (ever so briefly) a relationship between Occupy Portland specifically and Occupy as a broader and far-reaching social movement advocating for change generally, the negative experiences of Occupy encampments in Vancouver, B.C. (one suspected drug overdose death) and Washington D.C. (two reported hit-and-run incidents) produces an impetus for place restrictions that override Occupy Portland's existence as constitutionally protected. In other words, Adams's address of these specific other places foreshadows an "or else" looming in the not-so-distant future.

The last paragraph of Adams's letter begins with an implication that he is making good on a threat he articulated previously: "I have said from the beginning that I believe the Occupy movement would have to evolve in order to realize its full potential." He then recounts how Occupy protesters in Bend, Oregon, have left their encampment but still "meet regularly," implying that this is a suitable *manner* into which Occupy Portland could *evolve*. This focus on manner of protest also follows the pattern of arguing that there is ample evidence from other places in previous times and instantiations of Occupy protests to advocate for systemic change in ways that implore an end to the individual protections that have allowed Occupy Portland to exist in the time, place, and manner it has at the time of this letter.

Adams ends his letter with an invitation to move forward together. However, his invitation is not focused toward the Occupy Portland social movement participants, but to their *supporters*, saying "We've got work to do . . . I look forward to finding solutions in the coming days." His letter reveals a clear address of time, place, and manner. This focus "*others*" Occupy participants from both himself and the typical citizen. This provides an opening for Occupy Portland participants to be reprimanded or otherwise sanctioned by the government if something is not done to address the problems the protest presents to the typical Portland citizen. These vague articulations of the problems specific to Occupy Portland make it difficult—if not impossible—to address appropriately the problems Mayor Adams identifies. His content focus on the time, place, and manner restrictions of the First Amendment further sets up future articulations of Occupy Portland to be deferential to the needs of the Portland public. Thus, the inability for Occupy Portland participants to address the threats posed by Mayor Adams in this letter leads to an inevitable and conclusive future: eviction.

The Eviction Notice

In the second text Mayor Adams prepared a statement he read at a press conference held on November 10, 2011 (*Oregonian* 2011). He appeared with two other city government employees—one he identified to be responsible for dealing with enforcement of the eviction (Police Chief Reese), and one he identified to be responsible for dealing with the "fallout" of the eviction, namely to help with issues of homelessness and affordable housing (City Commissioner Fish). His statement was direct and succinct, and very clearly foreshadowed in his previous open letter. He begins with an historical attempt to characterize his relationship to the movement as consistent and clear: "Since Occupy Portland began five weeks ago, I have been very clear in my objective: We must balance people's rights to free speech, with keeping the city safe and moving. From the beginning, behavior has mattered." He begins his statement claiming both a respect for rights to free speech and an official priority to keep Portland safe and moving. The next statement is more interesting: behavior matters. It seems that his setup for delivering the eviction is premised on the logic that actions speak louder than words.

After bringing attention to what was being *done* in—rather than what was being *said* about—Occupy Portland, Mayor Adams delivered an account of specific events leading up to his announcement: "While the Constitution requires city governments to facilitate speech by citizens, city governments also have the authority and responsibility to regulate associated behaviors on behalf of the general public." In other words, the time, place, and manner restriction logic that guided the organization of his open letter released three days earlier appears again. The concerns Mayor Adams expressed in the first text are now deemed to be warrantable grounds for restricting the free speech rights that are otherwise protected by the First Amendment. He asserts that as mayor of Portland he has both the authority and, as he will explain, the responsibility, to shut down the camps.

Adams went on to identify four specific "problems" that justify the need for his intervention: two drug overdoses that required medical intervention, the use of a homemade incendiary device nearby the camps, an increase in assaults "in and around the area of the camps," and "health and sanitation issues" encountered while gathering a "collective" of people in public for a prolonged length of time." Interestingly enough, his account of the problematic *behavior* of people perceived to be associated with the Occupy encampments does not directly reflect participation of the Occupiers themselves other than the final reason given in regards to health and sanitation issues. Three of the four problems Adams named indicate that the behavior of people "in and around the area of the camps" was more problematic than the behavior of the people protesting. In other words, the central problem does not appear to be primarily with the Occupy Portland movement or its participants but with the way that the larger population is (re)acting (in relation) to the choice of the participants to appear as a physically visible collective on public land.

Adams explanation goes on to reveal what he deems to be Occupy Portland's downfall: "Occupy has had considerable time to share its movement's messages with the public, but has lost control of the camps it created." In other words, Occupy Portland has been understood as an appropriate and acceptable voice in the city of Portland until it was seen to exist for too long and otherwise failed to control its public display of protest. Adams justifies this by claiming that "the cost to the larger community is rapidly increasing." According to Adams, the economic burden of dealing with the movement's attempt to advocate for change outweighed the movement's right to advocate for change by collectively gathering in two of the city's public squares:

> The City will soon temporarily close Lownsdale and Chapman Squares to the public, to put an end to safety, health and crime problems, and to repair the park land. When the City re-opens the parks, the City will enforce all park and criminal laws in the Squares and the sidewalks, and the park land will be available for large, organized speech events by permit.

Halfway through his statement, time, place, and manner restrictions appear again—in this part of the narrative to warrant his authority to resume business as usual, claiming city interests trump individual citizen interests within the limits of the law. In other words (1) the protest has gone on for too long and is now deemed disruptive to city life more broadly conceived (falling within the time restriction exception for protecting First Amendment rights); (2) the public squares are no longer good for the public-at-large because they are neither safe nor sanitary (warranting place restriction exceptions for protecting First Amendment rights); and (3) the physical collective gathering on *city* property is no longer deemed an *appropriate* way to petition the government for a redress of grievances (imploring manner restriction exceptions for protecting First Amendment rights).

After making good on his foreshadowed justifications of time, place, and manner restrictions for overriding individual First Amendment protections, Adams's statement begins to reveal a series of ways in which Occupy Portland has failed. He began by referencing the specific legal statutes that prevent people from being in a public park past the hour of midnight and building any structures in a public park. This was followed by announcement of the full closure of both public squares hosting the Occupy Portland encampments in the name of the city's obligation to "repair and to remediate any remaining safety, health and crime problems." His orders for the police to engage in an "orderly and peaceful closure to the camps" were explained as "not an action against the Occupy Portland movement"; yet he did not explain how these orders were not against the movement.

Instead, while commending Occupy Portland for drawing attention to "the challenges our community, like many across the country, are facing with homelessness," Adams focused in detail on the ways that the city of Portland was prepared to provide both resources and support systems for participants seeking housing and health care. In this topical shift, Adams seems to indicate that the primary focus of Occupy is to address issues of homelessness, even though the larger Occupy characterization of its goals does not claim this as a primary focus.[4] Adams's depiction of Occupy Portland as specifically focusing on issues of homelessness aligns with only a small part of the Occupy movement that claims to be advocating for systemic change of a banking system that has already evicted its own tenants for being unable to pay a mortgage that the Occupy movement claims the banks themselves were also unable to pay.

This focus on a very specific part of the Occupy movement was then further connected to a focus on the inevitability of the order to evict: "I have said from the beginning that I believe the Occupy movement would have to evolve in order to realize its full potential." Adams's dismissal of the movement's current state of affairs is reflected in his optimism that Occupy Portland can "flourish in its next phase—a phase where we can focus all of our energies on economic and social justice, not on porta-potties and tents." In other words, the mundane logistics of protest like those involved in ensuring public sanitation should not be the focus of such an "important" social movement; instead, its visibility should be addressing, according to Adams, "widespread economic inequity" in *other* ways. This assessment of Occupy Portland's failures and necessary adjustments for its future direction did not appear as a friendly suggestion but as an authoritative decree. Although many Occupy Portland participants did not outwardly resist the mayor's decree, the formal thanks directed to the "broader community" for being "understanding and support[ive] of the approach . . . taken to balancing the right to free speech, with the need to keep our city safe and moving" implies a clear follow-up to the legal mandates for delivering the eviction notice that he foreshadowed in the beginning of his narrative. The end of his formal statement began much in the same way as he began—by characterizing Occupy Portland as a movement ready to change its active relationship with the city in the name of ensuring a better city of Portland.

Talking to the Press: NPR "All Things Considered" and PBS "NewsHour" Interviews

The final two texts reveal a less formally prepared and scripted Mayor Adams as he responded to interview questions about his decision to evict the

Occupy Portland encampments. Although he briefly answered questions from the press immediately following the eviction notice delivered on November 10, 2011, his interview with Guy Raz from *National Public Radio* (Raz 2011) was one of the first times Mayor Adams began discussing Occupy Portland and its challenges beyond the formal statements he had been releasing in primarily written form. These two texts focus on expanding the narrative that Adams so carefully constructed in the first two texts—this time revealing particular discursive closures that present his vision of what is best for Portland as the inevitable and conclusive end to what he deemed a long and complicated matter.

Raz began the interview by asking, "Why draw a line in the sand now?" His question about timing is answered by Adams: "Our job was to both protect free speech but that was balanced against keeping the city moving and keeping the city safe. And in the last week, things have just gotten so unbalanced that it is time to end the encampments." Adams's answer corroborates his formal statement to the press that the primary problem of Occupy Portland resides its inability to allow the city to *move* and its inability to keep Portland citizens *safe* in its current state. He further upholds his previous characterization of the camps as protecting individual rights to free speech but not at the expense of public safety. The same three problems addressed in his formal press statement explaining how the encampments failed to be safe and instead appeared to be disruptive to the city as a whole appeared for the second time: drug use and overdoses, the use of an incendiary device nearby, and an increase in local area crime reported to police.

Next, Adams is asked to elaborate on his claim that the encampments were unsustainable. Adams explained further about the challenges he identified in his formal eviction notice:

> Well, the unsustainable aspects of the camp that I'm most worried about are the drug overdoses . . . And, you know, at open-air camp like this is no place for folks that are facing, you know, illness, mental illness, or drug addiction to be [*sic*]. And the concentration of all that is, you know, just beyond the ability of folks, with the best of intentions who put the camp together and are trying to maintain it, it's just beyond their own ability to handle.

In his attempt to further explain unsustainable, Adams expands upon the need to end the camps—death is an end, treating illness is a solution (and thus an end to a problem), and evicting tenants from their living quarters effectively ends their ability to be a physically proximate community. In other words, to sustain seems to mean to continue in some manner; Occupy Portland is seen to be unsustainable because Adams does not portray the possibility of a version of continuing the encampments as they are, so thus, they must end. His answer reflects a preference to discuss what *is* happening in the encampments and how that aligns with his decision to evict rather than what *could* happen if particular changes were made to address his stated concerns of keeping the city moving and safe.

Raz continued the interview by asking Adams about his purported sympathy with the larger Occupy movement. Adams, for the first time in the interview, revealed information not previously articulated in his formal statements:

> I have mixed feelings. You know, I come from a hardscrabble background, and what the Occupy movement is calling for in terms of better, smarter financial global and national regulatory policies, you know, bringing people to justice that [*sic*] drove this global economy into the ground and we're still suffering from, you know, more equal access to opportunities. I got into government in part, you know, to work on those issues.

His response for the first time both revealed his perception of what Occupy is advocating for in terms of large-scale systemic change apart from his position as mayor of Portland, and further characterized the movement as attempting to bring justice to those who caused the current economic hardships faced by so many people worldwide. But this fleeting revelation quickly became buried in his mayoral tone, which connected this personal insight back to his role as a politician: "In my role as a mayor, I have to treat everybody the same . . . I have to both guard free speech and balance that against keeping the city moving, and keeping the city safe." Although he explicitly identified his aim as attempting to be equally fair to everyone, it is clear that such a lofty goal cannot possibly be achieved. Inevitably, in attempting to balance interests, some interests will necessarily be privileged over others. This is revealed in his previous articulations about the tensions between protecting individual First Amendment rights and eliciting time, place, and manner restrictions as the law allows. What is best for Portland may not be what is best for each of the individuals in Portland.

Adams then continued to justify his claim that Occupy Portland's evolution should be aligned with moving away from managing the physical resources associated with the encampments and toward the discussion of ideas. Raz responded by asking Adams, "What if it is about those things, about being visible, about being outside and with those tarps and under tents and with the porta-potties? What if that is a big part of why it's getting so much attention?" Adams appeared wholly unsure of how to respond as he quickly shifted the topic of conversation towards the federal government's inability to "bring to justice folks . . . that drove the global economy into the ground." After his uncomfortable stammer, Adams returned to his original central message: "Visibility is important. But every movement to continue their success, the full potential of their success has to evolve."

A similar opportunity to discuss the decision to evict the Occupy Portland encampments beyond the formally prepared statements delivered in the press conference was provided in a *PBS* "NewsHour" interview with Mayor Adams and James Oliver, an Occupy Portland liaison, that aired on November 11, 2011, one day after the formal eviction notice was delivered by Mayor Adams (Brown 2011). In this interview, Mayor Adams appeared sitting shoulder-to-shoulder with James Oliver, in some senses physically being held accountable for his explanations and decision to evict—quite different from the manner in which his *NPR* interview the day before was engaged. Host Jeffrey Brown began by asking Adams, "Why have you given an ultimatum to clear the parks?" Adams responded:

> Well, our concerns have not been with the Occupy Portland organizers or facilitators . . . It has been to the other folks that have also gathered at the encampment, and our concern is with a growing 20 percent increase in crime around occupations. It's the concern about two nearly-fatal drug overdoses in the camp. It's concern with someone who . . . ignited a Molotov cocktail in a building nearby . . . [he] used the camp as sort of camouflage for his activities. Those are our concerns, that . . . the camp is out of balance and is unsafe.

This response seems to diverge from Adams's previous statements in a significant way: he clearly cites impetus for the eviction notice as coming not from Occupy Portland participants or organizers but from citizens associated with the public-at-large who are engaging in illicit, potentially harmful activities *nearby* the encampments. These same examples that originated in the open letter and have persisted throughout Adams's narrative about the need for an eviction notice—this time, however, are used to support a new claim: Occupy Portland's encampments are out of balance and unsafe because these other activities nearby them are making them such.

Brown picked up this focus, asking Oliver to comment on whether or not he sees these incidents as isolated. Oliver's response was brief: "Absolutely they're isolated incidents." After time spent articulating Occupy Portland's central messages advocating for change around identifying and "calling attention to the real criminals in . . . our society," Oliver concluded his explanation about the movement more generally with, "We, as Occupy Portland, will continue to stand strong." However, whether this was meant to refer to the physical or organizational strength of the movement is not clear. Brown seemed to interpret this statement as an indication of the movement's refusal to leave on their own and proceeded to ask Adams, "What are you planning to do?" Adams's response reflects his previous narrative construction of Occupy Portland as a social movement disempowered to effect change in its attempts to disrupt everyday public life (because of legally imposed time, place, and manner restrictions) in the context of individual First Amendment protections: "I have talked about the need to balance free speech with the need to keep a city moving, and to do all of that in a peaceful manner." He included a more nuanced recollection of prior incidents in which case police were involved in clearing, preventing further expansion of, and assisting the federal government to remain safe from Occupy Portland encampments in some manner.

Adams followed this recollection with a return to personal empathy for the larger cause for which Occupy Portland appears to advocate:

> The important part of the Occupy Wall Street movement, the founding reason that the Occupy Wall Street movement took place, you know, I agree with a lot of the—economic justice, the bringing to account a lot of folks that have driven our global economy into the ditch. And I think Occupy Wall Street has done a lot to raise those issues.

Interestingly, Adams does not discuss these founding reasons to be associated with Occupy Portland—only with the original Occupy encampment, Occupy Wall Street. Additionally, Adams talks about Occupy as a social movement in the past tense. He says Occupy *took* place, and has *done* a lot, implying that the social movement is not evolving, as he often explained in his narrative previously. Instead, his references in this last text treat Occupy Portland as a failed movement unable to evolve and thus pronounced dead.

Such a pronunciation of death seems to inevitably justify the eviction of a now deemed useless physical protest: "I have to balance . . . that freedom of speech and the desire to [protect] . . . people's lives. I can't—I'm not going to wait until somebody dies of a drug overdose and I'm not going to wait until someone is seriously hurt." What Brown asks next, is not only warranted, but perhaps even begged in Adams's depiction of the encampments as overwhelmingly responsible for the impending death of individuals within it: "Well, Mayor, I mean, one of the questions people would have [is, wouldn't these things] happen in a city in any case . . . are these things enough to shut down the whole demonstration?" A more candid and direct reply from Adams emerged:

> In the end . . . my judgment was the camp itself is inherently unsafe, and the folks that have added themselves in to the original organizers of Occupy Portland . . . I think events have conspired to get away from them, and us to a degree, and that's why the notice, the three-day notice to evict came about.

Adams explicitly and clearly—for the first time since issuing the open letter to the Occupy Portland encampments—explained his decision to authorize an eviction notice to be *because* "the camp itself is inherently unsafe." Oliver's description of the camps in the same interview, however, departed from Adams's account:

> We are petitioning our government for a redress of grievances. . . . The goal of the Occupy movement is to make systemic changes to the economic and

political systems in this country that are failing the 99 percent of Americans who see our wealth decreasing, as the wealth of the .01 percent of Americans who control policy in this country increases.

Oliver's reference to the First Amendment mirrors Adams's organizing narrative logic but advances an opposing claim that Occupy Portland has a primary right to occupy these two public squares rather than functioning as subservient to city interest as Adams advances in his time, place, and manner restriction justification. Brown responded to this dueling logic by asking Adams, "Are you worried about the reputation of your city at this point if things do get violent?" Adams responded timidly this time: "Our goal moving forward [is] to enforce the notice of eviction. You know, those people that want to get arrested for civil disobedience purposes, we have facilitated that before." The ending of Adams's narrative reveals a bit of defensiveness: "It's not just about the fact that it's on the doorstep of City Hall. We take these kinds of enforcement actions all over the city, you know, all the time as the need arises."

With these two statements, Adams effectively ends his high profile discussion of a need to evict occupiers from their encampments in Portland with a dismissive air; the city has the ability to enforce, occupiers of public property do not, and the city can—and does—enforce its will "all over the city . . . all the time." Adams's narrative may address a variety of complex issues, relations, and contexts, but it does so portraying Occupy Portland in a particular way: as unsafe, unsustainable, inherently detrimental to the city of Portland, and impossible to balance movement participants' right to free speech with the ability of the city to move. The consequences of understanding Occupy Portland as *conclusively* in those terms are many, but a primary effect of understanding Mayor Adams's narrative as a functional account is that alternative sense-making about this particular social movement—and I would argue about social movements more generally—is precluded from emerging altogether.

Similarly, a romantic narrative of resistance to the larger system (run by "the man") often claims legitimation only in relation to the claims of illegitimation put forth by those in positions of influence within that system. This narrative also fails to account for alternatives apart from the arguments put forth in official rhetorics that precede them. As the next section of the chapter addresses, both functional and romantic narratives of Occupy Portland fail to account for the emergence of alternative sense-making opportunities that can potentially shift its justification and purpose for effecting change.

OCCUPY PORTLAND AS FUNCTIONAL OR ROMANTIC RESISTANCE?

Mayor Adams's rhetoric about Occupy Portland encampments portrays them as inevitably ineffectual. Thus, the romantic notion of Occupy Portland as a social movement functioning "in an ideal, even idyllic, way" (Trujillo 1992, 364) to bring about large-scale systemic change is dismissed as useless. Instead, Adams's functionalist narrative focuses on "reinforc[ing] important values that must be learned in order to be a working (and playing) member of American society" (Trujillo 1992, 366). In other words, individual freedoms are important but not as important as the government's ability to get things done (Portland's ability to move, as Adams says many times in this narrative). Determining morality and appropriateness is an individual endeavor unless it jeopardizes the safety and well-being of those trying to get things done. Safety is a concern only when one's own liberties are not in danger of being violated. A social movement challenges each of these functionalist understandings. When government's interests are put before its individual citizens, there is no room for individuals to collaborate to make social change. When activities like illicit drug use or health concerns like mental illness are associated with a social movement protest, then government resources are not deemed appropriate because the protest is advocating for changing the government; their support and aid in bettering the lives of the protesters is not justified as appropriate. The safety of the people trying to support the government (helping the city to move) is privileged over the people trying to advocate for changing the government; the obstacles people face trying to get to City Hall's doorstep must be removed lest they make it too difficult for said people to participate in the existing governmental structure. In these ways, Adams successfully spins a tale of triumph for Portland and its people; however, as I would like to expound upon, a critical read of this same narrative enables questioning the absence or dismissal of alternatively deemed important parts of Adams's story.

A CRITICAL NARRATIVE OF OCCUPY PORTLAND

These four texts together tell a rich narrative that reveals (in)consistency in the coverage of events, particular relations of power, and specific discursive closures that present Occupy Portland as a weak social movement failing in its mission to advocate for the social change for which it purports to stand. In other words, although Mayor Adams made it clear in his press conference statement that, "this is not an action against the Occupy Portland movement," A. F. Litt on his blog, "Democracy in Distress," comments, "This is exactly when these movements get interesting. This is when they start accomplishing things. Camping out for a month, getting bored, drifting off. . . . That is what those in power always expect to happen. It throws them for a loop when people actually turn out to be serious about their causes" (Litt 2011).

A critical narrative of Occupy Portland has the potential to bring to the surface the very insight that Litt articulated. But rather than relying on outside responses to the public discourse being created in the moment, a critical lens asks us, as average citizens, to engage our public discourse in attempt to understand critical narratives for ourselves. Perhaps it is less useful to understand the narrative that Mayor Adams told as a functional narrative told to persuade us of a particular message (e.g., "Occupy Portland encampments are unsafe, unsustainable, and therefore bad for the city of Portland and its citizenry"), or as a narrative to which a romantic resistance can be formed (e.g., "Occupy Portland is capable of thwarting the legal sanctions and government attempts to enforce its eviction because it is a collection of Portland citizens"). Perhaps, instead, we can think of this narrative as a critical narrative capable of interrogating the taken-for-granted in a way that helps us to see what is under the surface of the logics, language choices, and contextual elements like associations with other official voices. By looking beyond what is taken for granted to be an objective accounting of events, perhaps it is more useful to treat any account of events as a reflection of already embedded values, power relations, and connected (inter)actions. Treating Mayor Adams's rhetoric in these four texts as a critical narrative rather than a functional narrative provides a different understanding of what Occupy Portland is and has the potential to become.

There are three tensions that emerge in Adams's narrative that, if interrogated further, have the ability to reveal positions and meanings that may not otherwise be considered if we treat his narrative in primarily functional terms. First, according to Mayor Adams, Occupy Portland is a social movement characterized as devoid of both embodied and local consequence. Second, Mayor Adams depicts the city of Portland as in need of protecting. His narrative associates the illicit use of drugs, nearby illegal activities, increases in crimes in the area of the encampments, and identified individuals with mental health issues and/or the homeless with Occupy Portland. By associating the Occupy movement with larger societal debates like what to do about the homeless or the mentally ill, Adams successfully shifts the concern with the Occupy encampments away from its stated objectives and toward their lack of direct care for the health and well-being of those who support their cause. Third, Mayor Adams's narrative explains that the people in and around the camps need to be controlled. Particularly, his narrative explains that the movement fails to regulate how its participants do (and do not) engage in activities related to health and sanitation. Nor does the movement account for the adverse impact (both financial and symbolic) on the physical places in which their encampments exist (Chapman and Lownsdale Squares).

His narrative positions Occupy participants as imposing on the rights of *all* of Portland's public citizenry to use these public squares in ways that provide a multitude of protections of use. In other words, if the squares are not safe and hygienic, then those making them unsafe and unhygienic must be removed.

Treating his narrative with a critical frame, however, requires discussing how such a narrative "affirm[s] the status quo" (Trujillo 1992, 365) rather than does or does not advocate (or support those who are advocating) for its change. In other words, Mayor Adams's narrative fails to identify and discuss several other aspects of Occupy Portland that are still revealed in his narrative but not developed as significant to understanding and making decisions about Occupy as a social movement or about what is best for Portland as a city. As Trujillo reminds us, interpretive research exposes "multiple senses of reality (including power and ideology) . . . [that necessarily] reveal the multiple (not just managerial) voices which assign meaning to these senses of reality" (Trujillo 1992, 366). Across these four texts, these three distinct tensions seem to indicate a fracture in the link between Adams's conceptual explanations of Occupy Portland *as a social movement* and his articulations of Occupy Portland *as a place or group of people in need of management*.

Moving versus Stopping

Mayor Adams consistently and frequently referred to his primary interest as keeping the city moving. He effectively explained that this governmental interest overrides an individual's (or collective's) right to free speech. By discussing the need to balance these two, always conflicting interests, Adams further characterized a successful city as being *able to* move. What he did not explain is *how* it should be able to move. In other words, if one can still access the city, albeit, through a less efficient or effective route, should one be able to claim that his or her right to access the city is being fundamentally constrained? Further, if the purpose of a social movement is to disrupt business as usual, then it seems as if a disruption of (city) movement as usual should be allowed unless it somehow bars movement altogether for anyone who is not participating. In other words, Mayor Adams's argument that a city's movement is somehow fundamentally disabled because one part of it requires a detour seems problematic. Similarly, Adams's claim that stopping movement is detrimental to a city's interests seems equally weak, as cities are designed to be stopped in, and a public square would serve as a distinct and specific stopping point within any city. In some senses, Occupy Portland's choice to camp within the confines of its public squares does little to disrupt business as usual because people should be legally allowed to occupy such places and spaces with little to no restriction. However, the choice to select the public squares as host to the Occupy encampments made it equally difficult for Mayor Adams to evict them legally. By choosing such a visible, democratic, and seemingly legally protected location in which to create the encampments, Occupy Portland effectively enabled a lengthier stay that required more planning and forethought by city government than if they had insisted on a different location.

Safe versus Empty

Another consistent theme of Mayor Adams, when explaining the impetus for his eviction notice, was that he had a responsibility to keep the city of Portland and its citizens safe. Each time he referred to issues of safety, he simultaneously referred to three specific, not necessarily connected incidents: one around the issue of drug overdoses, one around the use of a Molotov cocktail weapon nearby to the encampments, and one around the increase of crime more generally in the area of the encampments. As James Oliver pointed out in the *PBS* "NewsHour" interview:

> All kinds of crime happens in downtown Portland every single day. Hundreds of people are homeless out in the street every single night, regardless of whether Occupy exists or not. And it seems to only be a crisis when it's actually at City Hall's doorstep. The existence of our movement has cast light on the plight of economic refugees whose lives have been endangered and are forced to sleep on the street, thanks to the policies of the 1 percent (Brown 2011).

Adams's argument about the threats to safety of the average Portland citizen, again, seems weak. As Oliver quite competently points out, a city does deal with crime, as its inevitable status of high density living among a diverse population with various backgrounds, experiences, interests, and access to resources and opportunities often results in conflict, illicit activity, and what in legal terms amounts to crime. Some of these crimes are economically driven and some socially driven; both lend themselves to assessments of a city (or parts of a city) being deemed unsafe.

In the case of this particular narrative, Adams defines safety in terms of the *inability* of social movement organizers to ensure their own safety as well as the safety of others who have physically aligned themselves in close proximity to the movement's participants. In this way, Adams is able to argue that ensuring safety in the camps *is* a fundamental problem; however, as one blogger's response (paraphrased here) to Mayor Adams's eviction notice reflected (Adams 2011), why can't the police regularly patrol and enforce laws inside of the camps? Why do they only respond to calls of distress from outside of it? Although there is a compelling argument about the distribution of resources, this question is a good one, and perhaps, one that should be considered by city government officials as they attempt to continue to justify their attempts to keep *all* Portland citizens safe. The only way that *all* Portland citizens can be kept safe from each other is for them to avoid going into public. In other words, Adams's argument relies on the fundamental logic that in order to keep people safe, he must empty the squares of the people occupying them. Emptying them to where, however, is not part of this narrative.

Sustainable versus Evolving

The last major tension that appears is between the conceptual framing of the terms (un)sustainable and evolving. Adams uses both of these terms in each of the four texts analyzed here. The terms themselves prove to be curious choices as they do not necessarily go together, although they appear to be connected inherently based on the manner in which Adams uses them. The term sustainable most generally refers to the ability for something to subsist or be maintained over time. More recently, this definition has been extended to refer specifically to environmental approaches to maintaining balance—whose balance, however, is not explicitly clear. Evolve, on the other hand, refers most generically to the ability for something to improve over time, especially generation to generation and from simple to complex in form. In this way, Adams's use of the terms seems counterintuitive. Adams clearly claims to be seeking some sort of balance between protecting individual free speech and protecting citizens-at-large as a larger collective constituency. If he simultaneously believes that (a lack of) sustainability practices are the answer to allowing—or impeding—Occupy Portland's success as a social movement, then Mayor Adams, as a city government official, must make a case beyond a reasonable doubt that the rights of a few actually impede the safety of the many. In other words, if Adams's claim that Occupy Portland is unsustainable in its current form is to hold water, he must clearly show that it is *unable* to maintain its commitment to occupy the public squares in accordance with its stated purpose to petition the government for a redress of grievances. This is certainly absent in Adams's reasoning expressed in these four texts.

Similarly—and contradictorily—Adams uses the term evolve as an ideal state that Occupy Portland has been unable to achieve. This, too, proves somewhat problematic for Adams because the explanation that the movement should be adapting and changing both over time and from simple to complex in form would require making more permanent, expanding, and/or creating more institutional support around the existing encampments—not dismantling them. In other words, the definition of evolving seems to indicate that the camps should be attempting to become more complex and better functioning, not absent and moot. In these ways, Adams has attempted to consistently make sense of Occupy Portland as a social movement worthy of its associative connection to advocating on behalf of social change at the level of federal and global policy. But it is not depicted as a useful way to sway local policy or attempt to disrupt city government, because as one blogger put it, "This isn't cute anymore!" (Litt 2011).

IN ABSTENIA, WHAT VERNACULAR VOICES CAN PROVIDE TO THIS OFFICIAL ACCOUNT

In the end, even this critical read of Mayor Adams's narrative fails to consider alternative sense-making about Occupy Portland that does exist alongside, in conversation with, or in rejection of, this existing way of sense-making about Occupy Portland as a social movement. In other words, although a critical lens provides the impetus to question power relations that inevitably influence any singular way of making sense of a social movement, without a narrative that comprehensively includes various and diverse voices that may not tell the same story about the same social movement, a limited understanding of that social movement remains. This is not to say that inclusion of vernacular voices will *necessarily* produce a persuasive justification of Occupy Portland as a worthwhile social movement, for example, but it does indicate a compelling *need to include* such voices in attempts to understand that a social movement does exist beyond its official liaisons, beyond its characterization by elected officials who have the ability to call formal press conferences, and beyond the explanations provided in official press coverage. It is these contested narratives together that provide an altogether new understanding of what has been, what continues to be, and what is possible in the future: "These portrayals of the contest between society's 'ins' and 'outs' find their most evident manifestation in social movements that seek control of society's resources" (Hauser and mcclellan 2009, 24). In other words, in the process of contestation amongst vernacular and official voices emerges the potential to both understand and embody the possibilities to engender change in the world[5]—in both policy and in practice. The implications of engaging in only traditional rhetorical analyses of texts such as those complex narratives told by government officials during times of strife involving social movements is not only one sided but detrimental in our quest for attempting to both understand a social movement in its present form *and* as having potential for future success or failure in engendering the change it seeks.

Thus, the inclusion of on-the-ground voices—not just the official (reporting of these) voices—is not only useful for coming to understand large-scale social movements like Occupy, but also for coming to understand how local sense-making of such large-scale advocacy for change (like that represented by Occupy Portland) inevitably affects how we come to know what any social movement is, and can become. The ability to (en)vision diverse resistors as simultaneously existing *in relation to* what they are resisting in diverse ways requires first recognizing that studying a social movement requires an approach that is as complex, multifarious, and as specific as its participants, critics, and reporters. What is best for a public at large is at stake not just because Occupy Portland should serve as a model of organizing, persuading, or leading a charge of resistance, but because discussing Occupy Portland in this way provides a rich opportunity to re-assess how we come to know a social movement as necessary and worthy of our support in advocating for large-scale systemic change.

DISCUSSION QUESTIONS

1. This chapter begins with a reflection: "A mature understanding of movement rhetoric must take into account the nature and persuasive powers of its vernacular rhetoric"—Gerard Hauser and erin daina mcclellan. What do you think—must it? Explain your answer.
2. Based on the functional frame of Mayor Adams's official rhetoric, what do you see him to be missing in his discussion of Occupy Portland? How would a romantic frame require him to discuss something differently?
3. What are the benefits of someone like Mayor Adams using a critical frame to engage in announcing the encampment's eviction notice? What would it include that the actual eviction notice rhetoric did not? What are the drawbacks of using a critical frame to engage in announcing the eviction notice? What particular constraints or obstacles might he face in attempting to use a critical frame as the Mayor of Portland?

NOTES

1. See Trujillo (1992) for a detailed discussion of three particular frames of meaning-making (romantic, functional, and critical) and their consequences.
2. See Herb Simons (1970) for a more comprehensive definition and discussion of what counts as a social movement.
3. TPM restrictions "must be content-neutral, be narrowly drawn, serve a significant government interest, and leave open alternative channels of communication" (Time, Place, and Manner Restrictions).
4. Occupy Wall Street (2012) characterizes itself as, "A people-powered movement . . . fighting back against the corrosive power of major banks and multinational corporations over the democratic process, and the role of Wall Street in creating an economic collapse that has caused the greatest recession in generations."
5. According to Hauser and mcclellan (2009), failing to include vernacular voices in attempts to understand and (re)act in relation to social movements is consequential in four central ways: (1) It provides a skewed picture of the public sphere because central sense-making processes are articulated only by privileged voices, and public attention is not focused on

resistance as it is experienced in everyday exchanges. (2) It misses mundane ways of expressing resistance (e.g., practices of politeness or civility that are demeaning but often unrecognized by those in positions of influence or power). (3) It ignores exchanges between those in positions of institutional influence and those resisting it that create entirely new ways of knowing. (4) By focusing on leader statements, bodily displays of resistance are often dismissed as supplemental to a movement's larger cause rather than constitutive of it. And (5) it fails to account for the possibility that "hidden transcripts of resistance" can exist and emerge at later, more appropriate times as ways to bring about change that would otherwise not be possible (25).

Chapter Ten

Interconnected Discontent

Social Media and Social Capital in the Occupy Movement

Doug Tewksbury

> The term Occupy isn't necessarily needed to be an activist anymore. It connected all these people that [*sic*] are activists. People found affinity for different groups and they plugged in and a lot of them don't need the term Occupy anymore so they kind of disassociate. So now we're trying to support communities.—Hey Zeuss, Occupy Portland Participant, January 2013

It was clear from the very onset that the global Occupy movement was a different kind of political movement than those of the past. Inspired by the recent Arab Spring and Spanish anti-austerity movements, Occupy started as a physical encampment in Zuccotti Park in New York City, in September 2011, employing a generalized critique of corporatism and economic inequality (Schwartz 2011). The encampment quickly expanded, becoming a long-term occupation of the park that drew thousands of participants, and soon spread to a worldwide phenomenon. Its sheer scale is worth noting: Within a month, there were Occupy-influenced demonstrations planned or underway for 951 cities in 82 countries (Tedmanson and Byers 2011). It was the largest global resistance movement since the late 1960s, and between the sister movements of Occupy, the Arab Spring, and a number of other anti-austerity participatory movements in Europe, Canada, and Central and South America, tens of millions of people around the world exercised their right to have their voices heard in the space of a year. It was remarkable in its scope, and it was unprecedented in its range of practices.

The Occupy movement used as its central tactic a populist strategy of nonviolent resistance through the occupation of space. It was a strategy that was noteworthy in its ability to resonate with a number of constituencies around the globe. Many of these participants' lived experiences may have been dramatically different from one another, but their collective pains were shared by an increasing economic inequality and the questionable practices of the global banking and finance systems (see Barnes chapter 2; Nadesan chapter 3 in this volume). The fundamentals of a participatory democratic movement were there; however, in allowing for a decentralized network power matrix, one horizontally structured that afforded collective empowerment and action, group decision-making, and community agency. This flexibility, in turn, allowed for activists to develop their practice around whatever specific issue that was meaningful to each collective, and to take steps to offer correctives for their local or national community.

Stated simply, the Occupy movement showed that if any cracks were to be found in the highly structured organizations of the political, economic, and disciplinary institutions in many states, they were going to be found only through the dispatching of a decentralized, network-structured, globalized resistance that transcended nation-state boundaries. Fighting organized and mobilized capital (particularly capital protected through legal, institutional, and security apparatuses) would require a new approach to organizing and mobilizing constituencies for social change, both offline and online.

The New York City encampment, the spiritual center of the Occupy movement, would thrive for just under two months until the New York City Police Department would forcibly evict the inhabitants of Zuccotti Park on November 15, 2011 (Barron and Moynihan 2011). Most other Occupy encampments around the globe would either disband or be evicted in the upcoming months. And while a number of critics have more recently dismissed the Occupy movement as over, its legacy exists not as a static, historical moment but more as an enabling catalyst, as dozens of individual movements have emerged following the end of Occupy encampments, organized by smaller collectives and interest groups focused on more narrowly defined goals such as debt, banking reform, community service, or hurricane relief. It is perhaps as Schneider (2012) suggests, that Occupy has become a "productively subdivided movement of movements" (par. 19). Though at the time of this writing, it is still too soon to be able to evaluate the long-term impact of the movement, it remains clear that the momentum of this, the largest political protest of recent decades, continues to affect activists, advocacy organizations, and political discourse more than one year later.

What is less well known, however, is the way in which Occupy built social capital by bridging its online-offline communities. While the concept is often alluded to in cultural studies literature, the question of addressing the concept of *community* in terms of the global, decentralized Occupy movement has been notably absent from much scholarly work on the movement thus far, primarily in terms of the discourse-facilitating uses of social media and user-generated content within these groups. Yet such an analysis is important if we are to formally examine the way in which communities (especially politically active ones) navigate the relationship between online-offline knowledge generation and practice (Sheller and Urry 2006).

One of the primary reasons that scholars—particularly cultural studies researchers—have found Occupy to be such an interesting case study is the fact that this movement was unlike the vast majority of protests in the later twentieth and early twenty-first centuries that were hierarchically structured, vertically oriented organizations that had leaders, and then had followers. Rather, Occupy was network-centric, decentralized, horizontally oriented, leaderless (see Heath's chapter 5 in this volume). Like many paradigm-shifting movements, it was difficult to pin down and not easily summarized through a quick, one-sentence description, yet firmly represented a leftist reformist/revolutionary model for rethinking a number of progressive issues. It also worked to reify the political and economic critiques of academics who had long argued that the forty-year rise of neoliberalism was firmly rooted in establishing an ideology where inequality was a necessity, whether economic, political, or social (Agamben 2005; Hardt and Negri 2000, 2004, 2009; Harvey 2005; Klein 2007).

The press, though, focused much attention on the question of what this movement wanted, looking for concrete terms and goals that could be met. It was clear that the movement was important; *Time Magazine*, for example, declared its 2011 Person of the Year to be "The Protester" (Andersen 2011). But one thing that set Occupy apart from protests of the past was that there was no one demand to be met other than the abstract, no one issue to be tied down to, no one goal that could be judged based on its fulfillment or nonfulfillment, no quantification of agenda to be argued about in terms of proper magnitude, and no finishing point at which the work would be done. It was this novel approach to large-scale political activism that was a sound response to the empirical powers to which Occupy was opposed, as capital (at least in the neoliberal sense) sets no final goals or endpoints in its attempts to marketize every corner of modern life (Hardt and Negri 2000, 2004, 2009; Harvey 2005). In a sense, if the media's central focus appeared to be on the why of the moment rather than the so what of the movement, the question seemed to ignore one of the central aspects of Occupy's practice: The interconnectedness of its participants.

COMMUNITY BUILDING IN THE OCCUPY MOVEMENT

This chapter argues that the practices of these collectivities represent a new way of thinking about grassroots participatory democracy in the interactive media age, and it explores the way that these communities built social capital through social media and user-generated content to foster an interconnectedness of community constituencies. Grossberg (2010) argues the usefulness of applying the case study methodology to the examination of cultural artifacts in order to problematize cultural conjunctures, and as such, this chapter offers a critical discourse analysis of the discursive uses of web 2.0/social media through a close analysis of several modes of online discourse from one notably vibrant case study: The Alternative Banking Working Group of the New York General Assembly.

Critical discourse analysis (CDA) is a strategy of bringing social theory into the study of media texts by looking at the way that social relationships are built, maintained, and transformed through what Van Dijk (1993) notes are the discursive "practices of production" that explore the "role of discourse in the (re)production and challenge of dominance" (249). CDA explores social phenomena and links the production and practice of these phenomena to a theoretical construct, tying social theory to discursive texts through spatial and temporal locations, material resources, particular experiences, and semiotic and linguistic resources (Fairclough 2000).

One of the advantages of using CDA methodology in analyzing this case study is that the working group and its affiliated and spun-off projects have continued to maintain their relevancy with vigorous deliberative platforms of interactive mediated communication, long after the disbandment of most of the Occupy encampments in late 2011 and early 2012. These efforts, spawned from online-offline discourse, organization, and action, have resulted in post-encampment branches addressing the issue of debt (e.g., Strike Debt and the Rolling Jubilee debt-abolishment campaign launched in late 2012), bank and finance reform (e.g., Occupy the SEC, Occupy the Banks, the Occupy Bank), and other movements focused on advocating justice in a variety of fields. Given Occupy's roots as a protest against economic inequality and the banking and finance industries, it is not overly surprising that many of this working group's efforts have managed to harness the trajectory of the Occupy moment into "next-step" action.

Furthermore, in determining the way in which this group constructed what Carey (1989) defines as "representation of shared beliefs" (18), Trujillo (1992) provides a useful framework for deconstructing an organization such as this in terms of a tri-part interpretational lens, using romantic, functional, and critical approaches to the study of culture that works particularly well for navigating the online-offline community of this group through a variety of vantage points on one singular organization.

Using these theoretical and methodological tools, this study deconstructs the online discourse of one particular wing of the Occupy movement: the Alternative Banking Working Group of the New York General Assembly. I explore approximately sixteen months worth of group online deliberations and dialogue, the sources of which include the groups' forum page in the

General Assembly's Working Groups headquarters,[1] its ongoing blog at the NYC General Assembly,[2] its Twitter feed,[3] the Occupy Bank,[4] and a number of related spun-off initiatives.

In particular, I am interested in connecting the way that these communities used web 2.0/user-generated content platforms to form what Lave and Wenger (1991) call communities of practice collectives that share and deliberate knowledge and information with the goal of belongingness, identity, solidarity, and action. Social capital is always built through interaction and connection between community members, and while the recent rise of social media has introduced a rupture in traditional understandings of community building and community participation (especially following the mobility turn of the past decade) (Cresswell 2010), these media also represent a materially different way of conceptualizing both the dynamism of community practices and—notably useful for this case study—the vibrancy of community knowledge-sharing. Furthermore, I use Trujillo's (1992) three-part interpretive framework to explore the romantic, functionalist, and critical readings of this movement, its social-capital building strategies, and its community's social and user-generated media uses. In sum, this study looks at the ways in which these online, mediated, discursive strategies have established new forms of communication that help us to problematize the notion of community belongingness across space, but also provide a window into the different forms of political, economic, and social activism that have sprung forth in recent years.

BUILDING SOCIAL CAPITAL THROUGH COMMUNITIES OF PRACTICE

Lave and Wenger (1991) developed the concept of the community of practice in order to describe the way in which discursive strategies and interpersonal interaction allow for communities to work together in order to share and generate knowledge. Different from simply the idea of *community*, a community of practice requires a collective of individuals to not only belong to a group unified by some common interest, but must also allow for that group to learn from each other through discourse in order to foster both its group identity and its individual members' skills, knowledge, and practices. Wenger (1998; 2006) describes the concept:

> Communities of practice are formed by people who engage in a process of collective learning in a shared domain of human endeavor: a tribe learning to survive, a band of artists seeking new forms of expression, a group of engineers working on similar problems, a clique of pupils defining their identity in the school, a network of surgeons exploring novel techniques, a gathering of first-time managers helping each other cope. (par. 1)

A community of practice forms a collective bond around some value, belief, or interest, shares knowledge through interaction and discourse, and develops a domain of practice that is dynamic; changing with group membership, different collective articulations on group identity, and knowledge-sharing structures. As communities of practice develop their domain, their community structure and organization, and—in this case, most importantly—their practice, they become stronger and more skilled at using cultural practices to further their interest (Lave and Wenger 1991; Wenger 1998, 2006). That is to say, a community of practice is a collective formed around doing some common thing, and learns how to do that thing better through sharing and community building.

Furthermore, communities of practice are fundamental to the building of social capital, a concept that Putnam (1995) defines as the "features of social life—networks, norms, and trust—that enable participants to act together more effectively to pursue shared objectives . . . [the] social connections and attendant norms and trust" (664–65). Social capital, in essence, is built through the establishment of networks of interaction and cooperation that strengthen the ties of a given body of people that have something in common. Lave and Wenger's work resonates well within this framework, but argues that a community of practice is fundamentally defined around its notion of working together to solidify its identity and practices through *discursive knowledge sharing*. Media studies researchers were quick to utilize these theories in cultural analysis following the emergence of the web 2.0 era in the mid-2000s, a movement that O'Reilly (2005) defines as a shift in the nature of the web from being primarily a source of information retrieval to instead a participatory and collaborative platform. When the web overwhelmingly became a place of individuals interacting with each other through interactive technologies rather than simply consuming content, communities began to develop as individuals built ties with one another through these new communicative platforms.

However, some have argued that this vision of a connected-but-isolated online community leads to social fragmentation, individualization, and separation of individuals to each other, particularly in terms of online-offline social integration (Turkle 2010; Van Dijk 2006). All new technologies have their advantages and disadvantages, but it is noteworthy that the space-spanning capabilities of social media have created new places for online discourse to foster communities that either would not be able to exist in the first place, or would not have had a forum for the quantity or quality of rich, deliberative, knowledge-sharing dialogue to establish community ties. As Putnam (1995) states, "social capital presumes that, generally speaking, the more we connect with other people, the more we trust them, and vice versa. At least in the contexts I have so far explored, this presumption generally turns out to be true: social trust and civic engagement are strongly correlated" (665).

As a related theory, Trujillo's (1992) ethnographic study of the American narrative of baseball as a cultural institution provides a theoretical frame to deconstruct a complex cultural institution such as Occupy. Through a detailed ethnography of baseball fans, employees, and players, Trujillo distinguishes three perspectives: The principled, community-based, rooted-in-tradition *romantic* frame; the approach centered on the complex and interwoven socializing forces of the institution in the *functionalist* frame; and the *critical* frame, which explores the way in which an institution encourages the reproduction of unjust structures through the processes and practices of the institution itself. These three frames allow for a number of perspectives that often overlap, but at times come into conflict with each other, though the object of study is the same. In the end, the usefulness of the framework that Trujillo provides allows a close examination of the role that the participants of a community play in reinforcing certain meaning structures within a given culture. This framework opens up the Occupy movement's community-based deliberative strategies by exploring the *values* that the group holds, as well as the internal/external critique of those values that takes place through mediated discourse.

WEB 2.0: USER-GENERATED CONTENT AND SOCIAL MEDIA PARTICIPATORY PLATFORMS

As a theory, the community of practice works well in providing a practical and conceptual framework to explain the way in which organizations organize, maintain and transform, learn from each other, and communicate both theoretical and practical knowledge (Wenger, White, and Smith 2009). In terms of building knowledge-sharing resources and communities of practice, though, the success of the movement lay in the means of communication—the interconnectedness of its constituencies. Occupy Wall Street's online presence was felt immediately following the establishment of the encampment at Zuccotti Park, but it did not happen by accident. As a movement comprised of a number of technologically savvy constituencies, Occupy's online presence was woven into its practice from the very beginning through formal means—a media working group that established a foundational involvement in social and nonsocial media—as well as through informal means through the individual uses of these technologies by the protest's participants. News of the movement indeed did spread quickly through traditional media outlets–television, newspapers, radio, and such—but the sharing and resharing of information through personal, online social networks was essential to the protest's effectiveness and ability to send its message virally (Byrne and Wells 2012; Kellner 2012).

As such, social media quickly became a hot topic of the press coverage of the Occupy movement, perhaps due to the social-media aided Arab Spring that had occurred several months prior. But while politicians and media pundits around the globe weighed in on the Occupy movement's efficacy, purpose, tactics, and legitimacy, it became immediately clear that it represented a new kind of political community that used these media differently than their more common usage as tools of participatory democracy. As Castells (2012) states, the Occupy movement was "born on the Internet, diffused by the Internet" (168).

However, the Occupy movement wasn't exclusively a social media movement, a spectator sport of protest lived through friends' link-sharing or "slacktivist" outrage, but rather, it was that the movement's dynamic structure was mediated *through* these technologies. Media narratives tended to overplay the role of social media in these movements, often offering a narrative that privileged the technological means of communication over the meaning-based discourse of the constituencies using these media as a community-building platform. Hardt and Negri (2011) counter this somewhat lazy narrative, writing that, "The prevalence in the [Arab Spring] revolts of social network tools, such as Facebook, YouTube, and Twitter, are symptoms, not causes, of this organizational structure. These are the modes of expression of an intelligent population capable of using the instruments at hand to organize autonomously" (par. 4).

In other words, these technologies are not magic bullets, but instead tools with advantages and disadvantages that are to be harnessed as supplementary tools for community building. This was not simply the "plug-and-play" of a technology such as social media into a politically dissatisfied polity that created this social movement. Rather, it was the *community-forming interconnectedness of constituents, the building of online-offline social capital,* that allowed for a dynamic aggregated body politic to take emerge. These movements were social-media aided, not social-media determined outcomes of some larger social structure.

There is, however, no denying that online technologies were important, and the numbers are telling: A study by Milkman, Luce, and Lewis (2013) surveyed 729 Occupy Wall Street participants at a 2012 Occupy event on their sources of information about the Occupy movement, the top three being reliance on the Internet (35 percent), interpersonal connections (24 percent), and social media such as Facebook, Twitter, and YouTube (14 percent). While 60 percent of respondents noted that they monitored Occupy events online via live-streaming sites such as uStream or Livestream, only 11 percent stated that television or radio was their main source of Occupy information, and 8 percent was attributed to newspapers. Clearly, in a horizontally organized, network-centric organization, there was a demand amongst those involved to be active participants and to make connections with others both online and offline.

OCCUPY WORKING GROUP SOCIAL MEDIA AND DISCURSIVE COMMUNITIES OF PRACTICE

If there was one element that best exemplified the open-access, consensus-building, deliberative approach to the Occupy movement, it was the establishment of the working-group model of the general assembly. These assemblages, designed to be "autonomous collections of people (just like you) who work on a wide range of projects and topics" (Nycga.net 2013, under "Working Groups"), functioned as a communicative center for an organization that had a decentralized structure. Though it might seem at odds in an organization dedicated to diversifying its power structure, the diffuse power of Occupy was actually strengthened through the centralization of the assembly's discursive platform. The discussion forums for the working groups on the Occupy General Assembly website functioned as an environment for the collective exercise of individual voices in order to introduce ideas, build relationships, and to debate organization identity and practice—a public sphere of sorts with few barriers to entry and a relatively open participatory platform. And while the scope of this paper examines only the discursive forums and social media recognized as part of the New York General Assembly, it is important to note that there existed hundreds of other online forums elsewhere on the web where similar sorts of dialogue and deliberation took place, in addition to countless Occupy participants' (and Occupy critics') Facebook pages, Twitter feeds, and YouTube channels.

Inviting involvement from individuals around the globe to participate, the General Assembly Working Groups Forum's home page (Nycga.net 2013) solicited participation from the very start: "Occupy Wall Street is powered by people. Do you see a way to make a positive difference? Are you fed up with the current system and want to make your voice heard? Have a good idea about how we can do something better? We want you to join us, we want you to be one of our many leaders" (Nycga.net Groups, under "About"). As of early 2013, there were ninety-one working groups with forums on the site. Most were quite vibrant spaces of online discussion during the 2011–2012 occupation of Zuccotti Park, although a number of these working groups' forums have fallen into relative disuse in the ensuing months.

Among the most effective (and still vibrant) is the Alternative Banking Working Group. This multifaceted group was formed in the early days of the Occupy Wall Street encampment and is still vibrant today through its working group and through its spun-off initiatives that began from the communities established in online and offline networks. Some of these include the Strike Debt resistance action group, its affiliated project, the Rolling Jubilee, which raised over a half-million dollars in late 2012–2013 to purchase debt at a steep discount from creditors and forgive it,[5] as well as the initiative to establish a bank or credit union founded on the principles of the Occupy movement, which appears as of this writing to be facing considerable organizational and practical challenges to achieve viability. Each of these efforts are part of the common organizational structure utilized by the Occupy approach, whereby multiple, concurrent efforts act independently through a decentralized network of issue-based movements.

In deconstructing the content of these platforms in terms of actionable building of social capital and communities of practice, the social media/user-generated content platforms of the working groups can be categorized into three analytical frameworks: horizontalism and consensus building, deliberation over the establishment of a common narrative of community values and beliefs, and the translation of organizational and deliberative conversations to both knowledge-sharing and applied practices.

Horizontalism and Consensus Building

Though the approach of establishing a horizontally organized political movement has been used in the past through a number of revolutions and civil rights movements—Iran in 1978, many of the 1988/1989 revolutions against Soviet rule in Europe, civil rights or feminist movements of the twentieth century, the 1999 Seattle protests, and others—the leaderless, nonhierarchical organization of Occupy operated without a firmly defined central command of individuals. While most political protests of the past worked in a top-down organizational structure with a power disparity between those deciding the direction and practices of an organization and those participating as group members (Tufecki 2011), Occupy's culture of horizontalism proved to be one of the essential strategies for building a vibrant community of practice, as the principle facilitated a strong degree of online-offline relationship building, community voice, and consensus-derived decision-making (see Munoz chapter 6 in this volume for a discussion of horizontalism).

The movement advocated this principle directly in its "Statement of Autonomy"[6] that firmly establishes this principle as central to the movement's philosophy:

> Occupy Wall Street is a people's movement. It is party-less, leaderless, by the people and for the people. . . . We welcome all, who, in good faith, petition for a redress of grievances through non-violence. We provide a forum for peaceful assembly of individuals to engage in participatory democracy. We welcome dissent. . . . The people who are working together to create this movement are

its sole and mutual caretakers. If you have chosen to devote resources to building this movement, especially your time and labor, then it is yours. Any organization is welcome to support us with the knowledge that doing so will mean questioning your own institutional frameworks of work and hierarchy and integrating our principles into your modes of action. (Nycga.net "Statement of Autonomy," par. 1–6).

Decentralization, however, does not necessarily mean disorganization. Occupy did indeed have structure, but rather than being a vertical, top-down approach to the development of organizational practices and the articulation of community values, the movement used consensus building through a working group model, alongside the larger general assembly. In this approach to organizational management, each chapter could establish any number of working groups around any number of issues, with voluntary participation of any interested community member. In a site visit to the Zuccotti Park chapter of the Occupy movement in October 2011, I observed both the general assembly and several working groups addressing the needs of the organization, including groups on direct action, coordination, public relations, education and empowerment, media, medical, and legal, amongst two dozen or so others. These working groups allowed for decisions to be made through consensus rather than dictate in order to address both short-term issues and long-term goals of the encampment, as a whole, and its constituents.

Post-Zuccotti Park, the working groups have become among the most vibrant spaces for discourse translating to direct action as the Occupy movement has evolved since its de-encampment, and as such, they have also become the central online space for the continued maintenance and transformation of the Occupy community. Notwithstanding the flexibility that the horizontally organized, working group model afforded in allowing for the development of Rawls's (1987) concept of an overlapping consensus, whereby individuals with differing interests can cooperate on common goals, the group's overarching philosophy that the public good is served through the diffusion of power allowed for a break from the twentieth-century industrialized thinking of institutional organization around a firmly established leaders-and-followers hierarchical relationship. The network society has shifted societal consciousness increasingly away from top-down institutional structures and more toward lateral relationships in most parts of postindustrial society through technological means (Castells 1996), an approach that has both its strengths and weaknesses for any organization. However, the benefits of a social, lateral interconnectedness between group members not only affords more agency and inclusiveness for group members, it also allows for a collective approach to the articulation of group identity and the establishment of a community of practice through the building of consensus and autonomy.

Establishing a Common Narrative:
Articulating Community Values and Beliefs

Wenger (1998; 2006) states that through community praxis, members of a community of practice "engage in joint activities and discussions, help each other and share information. They build relationships that enable them to learn from each other" (par. 2). And as many scholars have noted, when it works ideally, social media allows for the creation of relationships and communication in ways that could not exist through other communicative forms.

The Alternative Banking Working Group's postings function as an open space for deliberation and debate over the values and beliefs of the community, and from a wide variety of perspectives and personal narratives. For example, the meeting minutes from February 5, 2012, posted online to document the working group's offline discussion, included a long list of topics centered around existential questions over the working group's trajectory, including an extensive working list of demands that had been decided through offline consensus, and would later be discussed in a number of forums, including comments to this posting. User Mosheh responds, stating, "I, instead, realize that Bankers are not the problem, and that it is the structure of our banking system, and that one of the solutions to our nations and world's problems is to redesign that banking system nation wide, and even world wide, and provide it with the clear benefits and means to do much more than it presently can do, under the misguided present methods" (Nycga.net).

These narratives often took their form through the sharing of personal experiences alongside practical strategies and practices. Communities of practice work to learn how to do a thing from other group members, and with that knowledge, to understand how to do that thing better, and through this discourse, build a commons of knowledge sharing as an interactive space for deliberation. Yet it is also important that a community of practice works through cooperation as a community. This is especially relevant with a decentralized organization such as Occupy, as the organization has articulated its principle of horizontalism and consensus building. These appeals to community values reflect Trujillo's (1992) notion of the functionalist frame, distinguished as a values-based assessment of the way that certain practices build common identities, collective identities and solidarity, as well as the way that these community practices weave individuals into the fabric of the collective through socialization.

During the Occupy encampment in Zuccotti Park, there was certainly much deliberation and debate occurring in offline circles during working group meetings, but these conversations worked in tandem with online communication in a number of forums. For example, one of the primary ways that this group used user-generated content to open the floor to online-offline consensus building was through the posting of the minutes from physical meetings of the Alternative Banking Working Group in a common, shared document for feedback, as well as soliciting discussion topics and project initiatives online to be taken up in offline discussion. The group had a number of discussion postings reflective of forum organizer Cathy's October 2011 post, "What's Wrong with the Current Banking System?" where she stated, "Let's start a discussion on basic issues that we feel are corrupt, important, and actionable. I'd like to put some ideas as well as references for discussion at our Sunday meetings here" (par. 1).

The suggestions would often extend to the development of not only offline strategies of community action, as shown by the meeting minutes in the following weeks, but also for online strategies to extend the reach of both awareness and activism, particularly through the use of social media and user-generated content. The sharing of knowledge in the collective is especially useful in maintaining a successful movement, and the employment of user-generated content allows for the transference of individual knowledge and experience into a community forum to be adopted, transformed, embraced, or rejected. This sharing was also beneficial in that it allowed new members to have an entry point into the organization, but also encouraged those with a level of expertise on these matters to bring this experience to the table, contributing their individual knowledge to the collective knowledge of the group. For example, a number of collectively constructed documents (using the Google Docs collaborative platform) resulted in several proposals during late 2011 and early 2012, from a mission statement for the People's Treasury Global Banking Network, to a number of proposals to the general assembly for the endorsement of a new banking system (which would later become the now-stalled efforts to begin an Occupy Credit Union). There existed collaborative and consensus-built reports and white papers on such topics as usury laws and the nature of money in a capitalistic system. Most notably, there evolved a public document that would advocate for debt forgiveness, which would a year later evolve into the quite successful Rolling Jubilee debt abolishment program through Strike Debt.

For a new and decentralized organization, it immediately became important to these communities to be able to effectively share their resources with one another. These discursive strategies allow for the creation of a community of practice in which the sharing of knowledge influences group decision-making and identity. One of the strengths of the movement's constant and evolving existential narratives was that the overarching value structure of Occupy was a relatively loose one, focused around a broad philosophy that united community members as an overlapping consensus rather than on specifics or targeted achievements. This philosophy of increased equality in economic opportunity was established as an overarching value for all of the Occupy movement, but through the working group model, a more consensus-based approach of specific, practice-able action could be decided upon by the group, with real effects on the lived experience of those on whose behalf Occupy was fighting.

Practical Knowledge-Sharing Practices

In the end, though, Occupy was an actionable movement. The protest had as one of its goals to raise awareness of the issue of wealth inequality and financial/banking malpractice, and did so quite effectively, as media references to the phrase "wealth inequality" jumped by over 400 percent from August 2011 to October 2011 (Milkman, Luce, and Lewis 2013). However, awareness-raising was not its primary objective, but one secondary to Occupy's central goal: to serve as a forum for social change through action. The working-group model allowed for a number of initiatives to develop organically through the participation of group members, but perhaps none was more interesting than the Alternative Banking Working Group, an effort focused on developing alternative economic and banking models and initiatives. Wenger (2006) notes that communities of practice are defined by the collaborative approach to developing group action and problem-solving practices through interconnectedness and discourse, establishing a "shared repertoire of resources: Experiences, stories, tools, ways of addressing recurring problems" (par. 2). Indeed, through the establishment of the best principles of a healthy public sphere of a free, diverse, and open forum of communication, innovative and wide-ranging approaches to problem solving are often achieved. As a centralized platform of open communication for a decentralized movement, the working group for Alternative Banking allowed its users and communities to discuss the problems with the current banking and financial system, to educate each other through link or video-sharing, to write short essays or offer generalized comments, and—most importantly—to postulate new, actionable ideas and tactics.

One of the earliest proposals for the Alternative Banking Working Group's discussion board was to start a new bank or credit union, or to purchase an already existing one and change its practices to more adequately align with Occupy's. This online conversation began in October 2011 with the forum topic, "OWS Credit Union," from username Jason Nichols:

> I would like to establish an OWS credit union. The first step to accomplish that, in my mind, would be to establish a NFP organization to meet the membership requirements as set forth by the NCUA (i.e., this credit union would be available to all members of XYZ a Not For Profit) . . . I understand that OWS has no formal hierarchy, but if we could find a group of like minded individu-

als who would like to start this process, I volunteer to to [sic] the leg work. I have the experience in forming corporations, and have already contacted the NCUA to begin filings for a separate credit union. . . . I'm open to suggestions here, and I'm looking for support, so if anybody wants to have a hand in this, let's get together (par. 1–6).

This workshopping of ideas would continue through a number of comments in the posting on the feasibility of this project, but more interestingly, would spawn a great number of other postings to the website. The topic was continually revisited in a number of forum topics, blog postings, collaborative-created resolutions and working papers, but perhaps most notably in a December 2011 topic, "New Form of Banking Institution," that began a vibrant discussion. Username 4thVoice followed up, "I believe the co-op bank (and other industries) is the way to go in the future. For customers of the bank to have ownership instead of profits going to shareholders without the customer being first priority" (par. 1–2). The conversation would evolve in ideas, many users commenting on the need for a community bank, with some degree of dissent, as well. Username Enrico, however, took the conversation in a different direction, "Would anyone like to add to the ideas on forming a Social Enterprise bank? Ideas with regard to structure, the creation process, operations, rules/ethos (not exhaustive) are all welcome. I would like to compile all the possible details in this thread. I will post more myself yet I feel it is very important that my views are not the main views about a bank for the people and by the people" (par. 1).

However, when battling such a firmly entrenched institution (and one with strong state political ties) as the banking and financial sectors, it is clearly important to ensure that there is a well-thought-through approach to problem solving, and to start any new project, it would have to harness the collective knowledge of group members in order to workshop ideas, drawing on a diverse skill set and range of experiences within the community of practice.

Sometimes, this deliberation would lead to dead ends, but productive ones. The community constituency of this working group was quite diverse, and the expertise of the individual members of the group would often result in a pre-emptive negating of proposals due to feasibility, scale, or a number of other factors. Furthermore, there was an open welcoming of dissent and disagreement, both on fundamental terms and approaches, as well as on practical approaches to problem solving in these forums. The Occupy Alternative Banking Working Group discussions would often lead to a challenging of ideas in this open forum, and it is worthwhile to note that unlike in many other Occupy-based discussion groups, I rarely encountered any comments that were disrespectful or dismissive; quite a feat when considering the usual viciousness that disagreement can take in many online discussion forums. Often times, these would be in terms of practicality or over the best utilization of the organization's resources, such as this October 2011 posting in the "OWS Credit Union" discussion thread by username Iden over the need for an Occupy Bank, "If you wouldn't mind my asking how would creating another credit union in addition to the existing many credit unions serve a use? What does creating an OWS credit union do?" (par. 1).

The conversation over the creation of an Occupy Bank would continue through dozens of posts, new forum topics, and onward as deliberation continued. The discussion would be fruitful, and in October 2011, this conversation would grow in magnitude, eventually resulting in a new working group to explore the possibility of creating a new financial institution (Ross 2011).

However, the case of the for-now stalled attempt to create an Occupy Bank also highlights some of the difficulties in effective community building: Maintenance and continued forward trajectory during a difference of opinions and working within an overarching framework of organizational politics, particularly one that requires the principle of inclusion and open-access. The New York General Assembly voted on December 20, 2011, that in order to be recognized as a working group, chapters must have a mission statement, a working e-mail or phone number, a publicly announced weekly open meeting with more than five people in attendance, and to publicly post the minutes from these meetings, per a forum post, "Groups Policy Implementation" on Jan. 25, 2012.[7] The Occupy Bank project, which had started strong by coming from a bridging of online and offline discourse, began to falter. Michele, one of the organizers of this working group, recounts the brief history of this working group's demise on the Wordpress site for the Occupy Bank:

> Even though the group often had several dozen attendees and met weekly, the meeting time, location and minutes were not posted on the NYCGA.net site in conflict with OWS policy. Operating as a subgroup allowed The Occupy Bank Working Group to fly beneath the OWS radar. The group voted to become an official, separate OWS-NYC Working Group but they never took action to make sure the new Occupy Bank Working Group was established through NYCGA and added to NYCGA.net web site . . . I am now hearing The Occupy Bank Working Group has reverted to its previous subgroup status, below the radar and off the screen. This is very sad because the concept has tremendous potential. It will need people who have the focus, experience, energy and expertise to make it happen. (Moore 2012, par. 3–9).

The creation of an Occupy Bank has now been taken up by a number of individuals, working individually or in small collectives to overcome the great organizational, legal, regulatory, and indeed personal hurdles to establish this project, and as of this writing the results remain to be seen.

The lessons from the faltering of the Occupy Bank Working Group show the difficulty of building consensus amongst a diverse group of individuals with differing visions for an organizational structure (as developed in Heath chapter 5 in this volume). Wenger (1998) notes that communities of practice often develop through a shared interest, but can at times gain or lose members based on the fulfillment of personal needs and vision of individuals within the group. When members are unable to come to consensus, or are not feeling as though their vision is shared by other group members (or indeed, if personality problems emerge within a group), the long-term sustainability of the group can be at risk.

Furthermore, this failure reflects Trujillo's (1992) critical interpretive lens, an approach that complicated the deconstruction of a cultural phenomenon in terms of the contradictions, ironies, and tensions within a given organization. Occupy had no shortage of critics, and a common (if not overly easy) critique of the movement was that its inclusiveness and willingness to come to consensus was lip service. It is true that many of the general assembly meetings, as well as working group meetings, were messy, disorganized, or prone to infighting. Trujillo's critical lens highlights the fact that when dealing with a principle such as horizontal leadership and working group initiatives, the goals of the movement might be hindered through the very principles that the group espouses as core beliefs. In the case of the creation of the Occupy Bank, this appears to be particularly the case.

While the subgroup focused on the creation of an Occupy Bank may have stalled for the time being, the overall Alternative Banking Working Group appears to still be thriving. As of early 2013, meetings are still held every week or two. Resolutions were made to actively present an alternative model of economics and banking on Wikipedia entries. Speakers were brought in, including a former Senior Vice President of the credit-rating agency Moody's. Educational forums were held discussing a wide range of topical issues from the government's poorly handled HSBC money-laundering scandal, to social entitlement program reform, to the successes of other Occupy initiatives and spin-offs, to the establishment of a public-access television program. In the November 18, 2012, working group meeting, the organization passed a resolution to reach out to the quite successful Rolling Jubilee project, learning from them and offering assistance for their cause, stating, "You have changed the conversation. RJ [Rolling Jubilee] is popular outside of OWS. Debt issue has gotten [the] attention it deserves. We would like to learn from you. We would like to help you."

Yet in a telling post that addresses how to make any community of practice an effective one, one of the deliberative meetings in November 2012 was focused on one singular question, "How can we be more effective at completing projects?" The minutes represent one of the tensions in any community that tries to translate its ideas and ambitions into actionable moment,

"Over the past year, we've said a lot of things are worth doing. Linda created a list. There are a lot of great ideas. It would be good if we can focus attention on a few of them and get them done. . . . Lots of projects sound great. Some come to conclusion. Hard to tell which. Some sit around for a while and then they happen. . . ." It appears that all communities of practice are only as effective as the efforts of their constituent members, and the Alternative Banking Working Group is ever-changing and evolving as new members join and existing ones leave. In the end, it is discourse and community interconnectedness, both online and offline, that creates a vibrant group of practitioners, and, as with the larger Occupy movement, it is still too soon to tell what the long-term outcome will be of the many still working on their respective projects.

CONCLUSION

At its root, every community of practice is a collective that exchanges knowledge through deliberation and discourse. Offline communities are important for this process, and as Wenger, White, and Smith (2009) note, they always have been a part of the history of human cultural interaction. However, the *means* of communication are fundamental to a cultural analysis of any discursive exchange, and the rise of social media and user-generated content through communication technologies has created a new form of exchange that requires a rethinking of the ways in which these communities interact with their members, whether in a protest group or any other community of practice.

The Occupy movement was one that represented a truly new form of protest discourse, drawn from the lessons of successes (and indeed, the lessons of failure) of other groups' tactics of protest, but also innovating on the collective knowledge and experience of its own members. The collective benefits of harnessing the power of the crowd through both offline and online participation contribute to collective narrative, education, knowledge-sharing, and in the end, activist practices.

With a protest community such as Occupy, and, in particular, through the Alternative Banking Working Group, the wealth of established structural knowledge served to develop a common practice that could lead to a means of action that was driven through consensus building, which in turn is derived from the collective agreement of what is (or should be) achievable, as well as what to exclude from the scope of this community's goals and values. Among Occupy's greatest assets were its heavy reliance on the open, online discursive platforms enabled by Web 2.0 principles of social media and user-generated content to both influence, and continue upon, the offline debates and deliberations. As such, it will be interesting to see what comes next from this movement and its spun-off initiatives, especially in their use of these media. In any network-centric, horizontally based organization that takes a hybrid approach to online-offline consensus building and deliberation, it is not just the production of knowledge that allows for a vibrant, active, practice-based community. Rather, it is the sharing of this knowledge and experience that creates community, specifically in a practice-based activist organization such as the global Occupy movement.

For now, the Occupy movement appears to have paused as a singular body, a collective of action and activism tied around the occupation of space, and its future, at least in its 2011 form, remains to be seen. But it is not a valid judgment to assess the movement's success simply on the presence or absence of its physical occupation of space or its presence in the media, as the long-term effects of this collective's establishment of community lives on through a fragmented, but perhaps more effective, series of initiatives. As Milkman, Luce, and Lewis (2013) note, among the Occupy movement's greatest successes was that, "Many of these individuals were deeply radicalized by their participation in Occupy and will likely continue on a life path that includes some type of progressive political activism" (2). The recent advances of a dozen or so of the initiatives that have spurred in the past several months that emerged from connections made through Occupy working groups are quite promising, Strike Debt, The Rolling Jubilee, and Occupy Sandy being noteworthy cases. These efforts' successes have proven that Occupy's approach, like any sound community of practice of motivated individuals, is fluid and moves with time, appropriating new tactics and innovating with current and emerging tools as they become available. Regardless of the outcome of the larger Occupy movement or its spun-off initiatives, the transformative movement continues, and the use of social media and user-generated content in the building of social capital is firmly woven into the fabric of effective twenty-first century protest as an effective strategy of establishing strong communities of practice.

DISCUSSION QUESTIONS

1. In what ways was the Occupy movement different from other social movements, and not only in its social and mobile media use, but organizationally, strategically, and in terms of its practices?
2. What is a community of practice? In what other situations do communities of practice use media technologies to build online-offline identities?
3. Think of other online communities that have used online discourse to build community. In what ways do we see similar types of knowledge-building used within organizations?

4. What drawbacks or problems affect communities of practice that utilize online media technologies, particularly social justice movements?

NOTES

1. My analysis includes two related forums under the umbrella of the New York General Assembly's Working Groups forums: www.nycga.net/groups/alternative-banking/home/ and www.nycga.net/groups/the-occupy-bank-working-group/.
2. The Alternative Banking forum page: alternativebanking.nycga.net/.
3. The Twitter feed for this organization is under the handle @OWSaltbanking.
4. Occupy Bank Blog: theoccupybank.wordpress.com/.
5. The Rolling Jubilee is an initiative started under the Strike Debt organization, a spin-off from the Alternative Banking working group. Available at rollingjubilee.org/.
6. The Statement of Autonomy was passed by the general assembly in November 2011 and revised in March 2012. Available at www.nycga.net/resources/documents/statement-of-autonomy/.
7. Available at www.nycga.net/2012/01/25/groups-policy-implementation/.

References

ACLU (American Civil Liberties Union). 2009. "ACLU Challenges Defense Department Personnel Policy to Regard Lawful Protests as 'Low-Level Terrorism.'" *American Civil Liberties Union*, June 10. www.aclu.org/safefree/general/39822prs20090610.html.

Adams, Sam. 2011. "A Statement from Mayor Sam Adams Regarding Occupy Portland." *KPTV.com*, November 10. www.kptv.com/story/16009714/mayor-sam-adams-statement-on-occupy-portland-camps.

Adbusters. 2011. "#OCCUPYWALLSTREET: A Shift in Revolutionary Tactics." *Adbusters.org*, July 13. www.adbusters.org/blogs/adbusters-blog/occupywallstreet.html.

Adler, Margot. 2012. "Occupy Groups Reimagine the Bank." *NPR News*, March 27. www.npr.org/2012/03/27/149443425/alternative-banking-groups-aid-occupy-movement.

Agamben, Giorgio. 2005. *State of Exception*. Chicago: University of Chicago Press.

Albergotti, Reed, and Elizabeth Rappaport. 2012. "U.S. Not Seeking Goldman Charges." *Wall Street Journal*, August 10: p. C1.

———. 2011a. "The State of Working America's Wealth, 2011: Through Volatility and Turmoil the Gap Widens." Economic Policy Institute Briefing Paper #292. March 23. www.epi.org/page/-/BriefingPaper292.pdf.

———. 2011b. "The Few, the Proud, the Very Rich." *Berkeley Blog*, December 11. blogs.berkeley.edu/2011/12/05/the-few-the-proud-the-very-rich/.

ALEC (American Legislative Exchange Council). 2013. "History." *American Legislative Exchange Council*. www.alec.org/about-alec/history/.

Althusser, Louis. 1971. "Ideology and Ideological State Apparatuses (Notes towards an Investigation)." In *Lenin and Philosophy and Other Essays*, 127–86. New York and London: Monthly Review Press.

Alvesson, Mats, and Dan Kärreman. 2000. "Varieties of Discourse: On the Study of Organizations through Discourse Analysis." *Human Relations* 53 (9): 1125–49.

———. 2011. "Decolonializing Discourse: Critical Reflections on Organizational Discourse Analysis." *Human Relations* 64 (9): 1121–46.

Andersen, Kurt. 2011. "Person of the Year 2011: The Protester." *Time Magazine*, December 14.

Anderson, Benedict. 1983. *Imagined Communities: Reflections on the Origin and Spread of Nationalism*. New York: New Left Books.

Ardener, Edwin. 1975. "Belief and the Problem of Women and the 'Problem' Revisited." In *Perceiving Women*, edited by S. Ardener, 1–27. London: Malaby.

Arizonomics. 2012. "Guest Post: Krugman, Diocletian and Neofeudalism." *ZeroHedge.com*, May 1. www.zerohedge.com/news/guest-post-krugman-diocletian-neofeudalism.

Arpan, Laura M., Kaysee Baker, Lee Youngwon, Jung Taejin, Lori Lorusso, and Jason Smith. 2006. "News Coverage of Social Protests and the Effects of Photographs and Prior Attitudes." *Mass Communication and Society* 9 (1): 1–20.

Ashcraft, Karen Lee. 2006. "Feminist-Bureaucratic Control and Other Adversarial Allies: Extending Organized Dissonance to the Practice of 'New' Forms." *Communication Monographs* 73 (1): 55–86.

Auditedmedia.com. *Alliance for Audited Media: The New Audit Bureau of Circulations.* www.auditedmedia.com/.

Avery-Natale, Edward. 2010. "'We're Here, We're Queer, We're Anarchists': The Nature of Identification and Subjectivity among Black Blocs." *Anarchist Developments in Cultural Studies* 1: 95–115.

Baker, Dean. 2012. "The End of Loser Liberalism: Making Markets Progressive." *Washington, DC: Center for Economics and Policy Research.* www.cepr.net/index.php/publications/books/the-end-of-loser-liberalism

Barakso, Maryann, and Brian F. Schaffner. 2006. "Winning Coverage: News Media Portrayals of the Women's Movement, 1969–2004." *Harvard International Journal of Press/Politics*, 11 (4): 22–44.

Baran, Stanley, and Dennis Davis. 2003. *Mass Communication Theory: Foundations, Ferment, and Future*, 3rd Ed. Belmont, CA: Wadsworth/Thomson Learning.

Barber, Benjamin. 2003. *Strong Democracy: Participatory Politics for a New Age, Twentieth-Anniversary Edition, with a New Preface*, 2nd Ed. Berkeley: University of California Press.

Barron, James, and Colin Moynihan. 2011. "Police Oust Occupy Wall Street Protesters at Zuccotti Park." *New York Times*, November 15.

Becktold, Tom. 2011. "Warren Buffett Remarks on European Debt Crisis, the "Buffett Rule" and the American Worker: Interview by Business Wire CEO Cathy Baron Tamraz." *BusinessWire*, November 15. www.businesswire.com/news/home/20111115006090/en/Warren-Buffett-Remarks-European-Debt-Crisis-%E2%80%9CBuffett.

Berg, Andrew G., and Jonathan D. Ostry. 2011. "Inequality and Unsustainable Growth: Two Sides of the Same Coin?" *IMF Research Department*, April 8. www.imf.org/external/pubs/ft/sdn/2011/sdn1108.pdf.

Berger, Arthur Asa. 2005. *Making Sense of Media: Key Texts in Media and Cultural Studies.* Malden, MA: Blackwell Publishing.

Berger, Peter L., and Thomas Luckmann. 1966. *The Social Construction of Reality: A Treatise in the Sociology of Knowledge.* New York: Anchor Books.

Berkeley Journal of Sociology. 2013. "Understanding the Occupy Movement: Perspectives from the Social Sciences." *Berkely Journal of Sociology,* March 31. bjsonline.org/2011/12/understanding-the-occupy-movement-perspectives-from-the-social-sciences/.

Bey, Hakim. 1985/1991. *T.A.Z.: The Temporary Autonomous Zone, Ontological Anarchy, Poetic Terrorism.* New York: Autonomedia. hermetic.com/bey/taz_cont.html.

Blodget, Henry. 2011. "Here are Four Charts that Explain What the Protesters are Angry About . . . " *Business Insider*, October 14. www.businessinsider.com/here-are-the-four-charts-that-explain-what-the-protesters-are-angry-about-2011-10?utm_source=twbutton&utm_medium=social&utm_campaign=bi#ixzz1b3DqeIBh.

Bowley, Graham. 2009. "Bailout Helps Fuel a New Era of Wall Street Wealth." *New York Times* 17 October. www.nytimes.com/2009/10/17/business/economy/17wall.html?_r=1&th&emc=th.

Boyle, Michael P., and Cory L. Armstrong. 2009. "Measuring Level of Deviance: Considering the Distinct Influence of Goals and Tactics on News Treatment of Abortion Protests." *Atlantic Journal of Communication* 17 (4): 166–83.

Boyle, Michael P., Michael R. McCluskey, Douglas M. McLeod, and Sue E. Stein. 2005. "Newspapers and Protest: An Examination of Protest Coverage from 1960 to 1999." *Journalism and Mass Communication Quarterly* 82 (3): 638–53.

Brown, Jeffrey (host). 2011. "Portland among Cities Grappling with How to Handle 'Occupy' Protesters" (television broadcast episode), November 11. In *PBS NewsHour*, L. Winslow (executive producer). Arlington, VA: MacNeil/Lehrer Productions.

Bryan, D., R. Martin, and M. Rafferty. 2009. "Financialization and Marx: Giving Labor and Capital a Financial Makeover." *Review of Radical Political Economics*, 41: 458–72.

Buffett, Warren. 2003. "Berkshire Hathaway Inc. Annual Report 2002." *Berkshire Hathaway*, February 21. www.berkshirehathaway.com/2002ar/2002ar.pdf.

———. 2011. "Stop Coddling the Super Rich." *New York Times*, August 14: p. A21.

Byrne, Janet, and Robin Wells. 2012. *The Occupy Handbook*. New York: Back Bay Books.

Byron, Ellen, and Karen Talley. 2011. "Luxury Sales at Risk." *Wall Street Journal* August 10: B1.

Campbell, Emahunn Raheem Ali. 2011. "A Critique of the Occupy Movement from a Black Occupier." *The Black Scholar* 41(4): 42–51.

Carey, James. 1989. "A Cultural Approach to Communication." In *Communication as Culture: Essays on Media and Society,* 11–28. Boston: Unwin Hyman.

Castells, Manuel. 1996. *The Rise of the Network Society*. Malden, MA: Blackwell Publishers.

———. 2012. *Networks of Outrage and Hope: Social Movements in the Internet Age*. Malden, MA: Polity.

CBCNews. 2006. "40% of World's Wealth Owned by 1% of Population." 2006. *CBCNews Business,* December 5. www.cbc.ca/news/business/story/2006/12/05/globalwealth.html.

Center for American Progress. 2010. *Center for American Progress*. www.americanprogress.org/.

Chang, Briankle. 2012. "Forum: Editors' Afterwords: Via Palinode." *Communication and Critical/Cultural Studies* 9 (4): 369–70.

Chan-Olmsted, Syliva, and Jiyoung Cha. 2007. "Branding Television News in a Multichannel Environment: An Exploratory Study of Network News Brand Personality." *JMM—The International Journal on Media Management* 9 (4): 135–50.

Charles, Lucas. 2011. "Occupy Portland Survey 2011." *Limitless Channels*. limitlesschannels.com/occupypdx.html.

Chomsky, Noam. 2003. *Hegemony or Survival*. New York: Metropolitan Books.

Christians, Clifford, John Ferre, and P. Mark Fackler. 1993. *Good News: Social Ethics and the Press*. New York: Oxford University Press.

Chung, Juliet. 2013. "Goldman: Insurer Knew Paulson was 'Shorting.'" *Wall Street Journal*, January 14: C3. online.wsj.com/article/SB10001424127887324595704578239801631027268.html

Citigroup. 2005. "Equity Strategy: Plutonomy: Buying Luxury, Explaining Global Imbalances." October 16. www.scribd.com/doc/6674234/Citigroup-Oct-16-2005-Plutonomy-Report-Part-1. Document was removed but is available here: accessed April 7, 2013: pissedoffwoman.wordpress.com/2012/04/12/the-plutonomy-reports-download/.

Clark, Andrew. 2010a. "Lloyd Blankfein Admits Goldman Sachs Failed to Raise the Alarm: Bank's Boss Tells Senate its Derivatives Deals Fuelled Image of Wall Street Out of Control." *Guardian,* April 26. www.guardian.co.uk/business/2010/apr/26/goldman-sachs-sec-senate-hearing.

———. 2010b. "Goldman Sachs Banker Fabrice Tourre Faces the Music: London-Based Banker Says He Has Been the Target of Unfounded Attacks." *Guardian*, April 27. www.guardian.co.uk/business/2010/apr/27/goldman-sachs-fabrice-tourre.

Cohen, Elliot D. ed., 2005. *News Incorporated: Corporate Media Ownership and its Threat to Democracy*. Amherst, NY: Prometheus Books.

Cohen-Marks, Mara, and Christopher Stout. 2011. "Can the American Dream Survive the New Multiethnic America? Evidence from Los Angeles." *Sociological Forum* 26 (4): 824–45.

Collins, Patricia Hill. 2000. *Black Feminist Thought: Knowledge, Consciousness, and the Politics of Empowerment,* 2nd Ed. NY: Routledge.

Colorado Indiemedia. 2012. "Occupy Denver March Against Neofeudalism: Revenge of the Wage Slave." 2012. *Colorado IndieMedia*, June 23. colorado.indymedia.org/node/8679.

Comunello, Francesca, and Giuseppe Anzera. 2012. "Will the Revolution be Tweeted? A Conceptual Framework for Understanding the Social Media and the Arab Spring." *Islam and Christian-Muslim Relations* 23 (4): 453–70.

Congressional Budget Office. 2011. "Trends in the Distribution of Household Income Between 1979 and 2007." *Congressional Budget Office*, October. www.cbo.gov/publication/42729.

Conway, Janet. 2003. "Civil Resistance and the 'Diversity of Tactics' in the Anti-globalization Movement: Problems of Violence, Silence, and Solidarity in Activist Politics." *Osgoode Hall Law Journal* 41 (2 and 3): 505–29.

Cornell, Andy. 2012. "Consensus: What It Is, What It Is Not, Where It Came From and Where It Must Go." In *We Are Many: Reflections on Movement Strategy from Occupation to Liberation*, edited by Kate Khatib, Margaret Killjoy, and Mick McGuire, 163–73. Baltimore, MD: AK Press.

Crenshaw, Kimberlé. 1989. "Demarginalizing the Intersection between Race and Sex: A Black Feminist Critique of Anti-Discrimination Doctrine, Feminist Theory and Anti-Racist Politics." *University of Chicago Legal Forum* 139.

Cresswell, Tim. 2011. "Mobilities I: Catching up." *Progress in Human Geography* 35 (4): 550–58.

Creswell, Julie, and Azam Ahmed. 2012. "Large Hedge Funds Fared Well in 2011." *New York Times*, March 29. dealbook.nytimes.com/2012/03/29/large-hedge-funds-fared-well-in-2011/

Culverwell, Wendy. 2012. "Nonprofits: Oregon's $13B Industry." *Portland Business Journal*, May 2. www.bizjournals.com/portland/news/2012/05/01/nonprofits-are-13b-business-for-oregon.html?page=allcite).

Dahlberg, Lincoln. 2005. "The Corporate Colonization of Online Attention and the Marginalization of Critical Communication?" *Journal of Communication Inquiry* 29 (2): 160-80.

Daniels, Steven E., and Gregg B. Walker. 2001. *Working through Environmental Conflict: The Collaborative Learning Approach*. Westport, CT: Praeger Publishers.

Deetz, Stanley A. 1992. *Democracy in Age of Corporate Colonization: Developments in Communication and the Politics of Everyday Life*. New York: SUNY Press.

———. 2005. "Critical Theory." In *Organizational Communication Theory and Research: Multiple Perspectives*, edited by Steve May and Dennis Mumby, 85–111. Thousand Oaks, CA: Sage.

———. 2007. "Corporate Governance, Corporate Social Responsibility, and Communication." In *The Debate over Corporate Social Responsibility*, edited by Steve May, George Cheney, and Juliet Roper, 267–78. Oxford: Oxford University Press.

della Porta, Donatella. 2005. "Deliberation in Movement: Why and How to Study Deliberative Democracy and Social Movements." *Acta Politica* 40: 336–50. doi:10.1057/palgrave.ap.5500116.

———. 2008. "Consensus in Movements." Paper presented at Accademia di Studi Storici Moro Convegno Internazionale, Rome, Italy, November 17–20.

della Porta, Donatella, Massimiliano Andretta, Lorenzo Mosca, and Herbert Reiter. 2006. *Globalization from Below. Transnational Activists and Protest Networks*. Minneapolis, MN: University of Minnesota Press.

DeLuca, Kevin, Sean Lawson, and Ye Sun. 2012. "Occupy Wall Street on the Public Screens of Social Media: The Many Framings of the Birth of a Protest Movement." *Communication, Culture and Critique* 5: 483–509.

Dempsey, Sarah, E. 2010. "Critiquing Community Engagement," *Management Communication Quarterly* 24 (3): 359–90. doi:10.1177/0893318909352247.

Detenber, Benjamin H., Melissa R. Gotlieb, Douglas M. McLeod, and Olga Malinkina. 2007. "Frame Intensity Effects of Television News Stories about a High-Visibility Protest Issue." *Mass Communication and Society* 10 (4): 439–60.

Di Cicco, Damon T. 2010. "The Public Nuisance Paradigm: Changes in Mass Media Coverage of Political Protest since the 1960s." *Journalism and Mass Communication Quarterly* 87 (1): 135–53.

Diamond, Steven. 2012. "Occupy the Courts: Corporate Personhood Reconsidered." *Truthout*, April 18. truth-out.org/news/item/8597-occupy-the-courts-corporate-personhood-reconsidered.

Dutta, Mohan J. 2011. *Communicating Social Change: Structure, Culture, and Agency*. New York and London: Routledge.

Eavis, Peter, 2012. "With Rates Low, Banks Increase Mortgage Profit." *New York Times*, August 9: A1. dealbook.nytimes.com/2012/08/08/with-rate-twist-banks-increase-mortgage-profit/?nl=todaysheadlines&emc=edit_th_20120809.

Edelman, Marc. 2009. "Peasant-Farmer Movements, Third World Peoples, and the Seattle Protests against the World Trade Organization, 1999." *Dialect Anthropoi* 33: 109–28.
Ehrenreich, Barbara. 2000. "Anarkids and Hypocrites." *The Progressive*, June: 28–29.
emptywheel. 2012. "The Goldman Sachs Department of Justice Would Like to Apologize to Mr. Blankfein for the Inconvenience." *Emptywheel.net*, August 9. www.emptywheel.net/tag/lloyd-blankfein/.
England, Kim V. L. 1994. "Getting Personal: Reflexivity, Positionality, and Feminist Research." *The Professional Geographer* 46 (1): 80–89.
Eschle, Catherine. 2004. "Constructing 'the Anti-globalisation Movement'." *International Journal of Peace Studies*, 9 (1): 61–84.
Fairclough, Norman. 2000. "Discourse, Social Theory, and Social Research: The Discourse of Welfare Reform." *Journal of Sociolinguistics* 4: 163–95.
Fishman, Mark. 1982. "News and Nonevents: Making the Visible Invisible." In *Social Meaning of News: A Text-Reader*, edited by Dan Berkowitz, 210–29. Thousand Oaks, CA: Sage.
Fleming, Andrew. 2011."Adbusters sparks Wall Street protest Vancouver-based activists behind street actions in the U.S." *Vancouver Courier*, September 2011. www.vancourier.com/Adbusters+sparks+Wall+Street+protest/5466332/story.html
Foucault, Michel. 1972. *The Archaeology of Knowledge and the Discourse on Language*. Translated by A. M. Sheridan Smith. New York: Pantheon Books.
———. 1979. *Discipline and Punish: The Birth of the Prison*. Translated by Alan Sheridan. New York: Vintage Books.
Fox Piven, Frances. 2011. "The War against the Poor." *TomDispatch.Com*, November 6. www.tomdispatch.com/post/175463/tomgram%3A_frances_fox_piven%2C_the_war_on_the_home_front/#more.
The Free Dictionary. "Time, Place, and Manner Restrictions." *The Free Online Law Dictionary*. legal-dictionary.thefreedictionary.com/Time,+Place,+and+Manner+Restrictions.
Freeman, Jo. 1972/73. "The Tyranny of Structurelessness." *Berkeley Journal of Sociology* 17: 151–64. www.jstor.org/stable/41035187.
Freire, Paulo. 1970. *Pedagogy of the Oppressed*. Translated by Myra Bergman Ramos. New York and London: Continuum.
Friberg-Fernos, Henrik, and Johan Karlsson Schaffer. 2010. "The Consensus Paradox: Why Deliberative Agreement Impedes Rational Discourse." Paper presented at Oslo-Paris International Workshop on Democracy, Paris, France, October 18–20.
Gadamer, Hans-Georg. 1975. *Truth and Method*. Edited and translated by G. Barden and J. Cumming. New York: Seabury Press.
Gamson, Joshua. 1995. "Messages of Exclusion: Gender, Movements, and Symbolic Boundaries." *Gender and Society* 11 (2): 178–99.
Gamson, William A. 1991. "Commitment and Agency in Social Movements." *Sociological Forum* 6: 27–50.
Ganesh, Shiv, and Heather Zoller. 2012. "Dialogue, Activism, and Democratic Social Change." *Communication Theory* 22: 66–91. doi:10.1111/j.1468-2885.2011.01396.x.
Ganesh, Shiv, Heather Zoller, and George Cheney. 2005. "Transforming Resistance, Broadening Our Boundaries: Critical Organizational Communication Meets Globalization from Below." *Communication Monographs* 72 (2): 169–91. dx.doi.org/10.1080/03637750500111872.
Gelderblom, O., and J. Jonker. 2005. "Amsterdam as the Cradle of Modern Futures Trading and Options Trading." 2005. In *The Origins of Value: The Financial Innovations that Created Modern Capital Markets*, edited by W. N. Goetzmann and G. Rouwenhorst, 189–206. Oxford: Oxford University.
Gillham, Patrick F., and Gary T. Marx. 2000. "Complexity and Irony in Policing and Protesting: The World Trade Organization in Seattle." *Social Justice* 2 (2): 212–36.
Glassman, Jim. 2002. "From Seattle (and Ubon) to Bangkok: The Scales of Resistance to Corporate Globalization." *Environment and Planning D Society and Space* 19 (5): 513–33.
Goldfarb, Z. A., and T. M. Tse. 2010. "SEC Sued Goldman Sachs to Break an Impasse." *Washington Post*, April 20: A1.

Graeber, David. 2002. "The New Anarchists." *New Left Review* 13: 61–73. newleftreview.org/II/13/david-graeber-the-new-anarchists.
———. 2004. *Fragments of an Anarchist Anthropology*. Chicago: Prickly Paradigm Press.
———. 2006. "Beyond Power/Knowledge: An Exploration of the Relation of Power, Ignorance and Stupidity." *Malinowski Memorial Lecture*. The London School of Economics and Political Science, May 25.
———. 2012. "Concerning the Violent Peace-Police: An Open Letter to Chris Hedges." *New Inquiry*, February 9. thenewinquiry.com/features/concerning-the-violent-peace-police-an-open-letter-to-chris-hedges/.
Gramsci, Antonio. 1971. *Selections from the Prison Notebooks of Antonio Gramsci*. Translated by Quintin Hoare and Geoffrey Nowell Smith. International Publishers.
Greeley, Brendan. 2012. "ALEC's Secret's Revealed: Corporations Flee." *Businessweek*, May 3. www.businessweek.com/articles/2012-05-03/alecs-secrets-revealed-corporations-flee.
Greenwald, Glenn. 2013. "The Untouchables: How the Obama Administration Protected Wall Street from Prosecutions." *Guardian*, January 23. m.guardian.co.uk/commentisfree/2013/jan/23/untouchables-wall-street-prosecutions-obama.
Grossberg, Lawrence. 2010. *Cultural Studies in the Future Tense*. Durham, NC: Duke University Press.
Grossberg, Lawrence, and Jennifer Daryl Slack. 1985. "An Introduction to Stuart Hall's essay." *Critical Studies in Mass Communication* 2 (2): 87–90.
Habermas, Jurgen. 1987. *The Theory of Communicative Action Volume 2: Lifeworld and System: A Critique of Functionalist Reason*. Cambridge: Polity Press.
———. 1989. *The Structural Transformation of the Public Sphere: An Inquiry into a Category of Bourgeois Society*. Cambridge: Polity Press.
———. 1990. *Moral Consciousness and Communicative Action*. Cambridge, MA: MIT Press.
———. 1992. "Further Reflections on the Public Sphere." In *Habermas and the Public Sphere*, edited by Craig Calhoun, 421–61. Cambridge: MIT Press.
Hacker, Jacob, and Paul Pierson. 2010. *Winner-Take-All Politics: How Washington Made the Rich Richer—And Turned Its Back on the Middle Class*. New York: Simon and Schuster.
Hadden, Jennifer, and Sidney Tarrow. 2007. "The Global Justice Movement in the United States since Seattle." In *The Global Justice Movement: Cross-national and Transnational Perspectives*, edited by Donatella della Porta, 210–31. Boulder: Paradigm Publishers.
Haigh, Martin J. 1988. "Understanding 'Chipko': The Himalayan People's Movement for Forest Conservation." *International Journal of Environmental Studies* 31: 99–110.
Hall, Chase G. 2012. "Cameron Whitten camps, stages hunger strike at Portland City Hall." *Oregonian*, June 10. www.oregonlive.com/portland/index.ssf/2012/06/cameron_whitten_camps_stages_h.html.
Hall, Stuart. 1985. "Signification, Representation, Ideology: Althusser and the Post-Structuralist Debates." *Critical Studies in Mass Communication* 2 (2): 91–114.
———. 1996. "Introduction: Who Needs Identity?" In *Questions of Cultural Identity*, edited by Stuart Hall and P. du Gray, 1–17. London: Sage.
Hardt, Michael, and Antonio Negri. 2000. *Empire*. Cambridge, MA: Harvard University Press.
———. 2004. *Multitude: War and Democracy in the Age of Empire*. New York: Penguin Press.
———. 2009. *Commonwealth*. Cambridge, MA: Harvard University Press.
———. 2011. "Arabs Are Democracy's New Pioneers." *Guardian*, February 24. www.guardian.co.uk/commentisfree/2011/feb/24/arabs-democracy-latin-america.
Harkinson, Josh. 2012. "Occupy Rallies Against Powerful Right-Wing Group You've Never Heard Of." *Mother Jones*, February 29. www.motherjones.com/mojo/2012/02/alec-occupy-wall-street-protest-f29.
Harvey, David. 2005. *A Brief History of Neoliberalism*. New York: Oxford University Press.
Hauser, Gerard. A. 1998. "Vernacular Dialogue and the Rhetoricality of Public Opinion." *Communication Monographs* 65: 83–107.
———. 1999. *Vernacular Voices: The Rhetoric of Publics and Public Spheres*. Columbia: University of South Carolina Press.

———. 2001. "Prisoners of Conscience and the Counterpublic Sphere: The Stones that Start the Avalanche." In *Counterpublics and the State*, edited by Robert Asen and Daniel C. Brouwer, 35–58. Albany: State University of New York Press.

———. 2006. "Demonstrative Displays of Dissident Rhetoric: The Case of Prisoner 885/63." In *The Rhetoric of Display*, edited by Lawrence Prelli, 229–54. Columbia: University of South Carolina Press.

Hauser, Gerard A., and erin daina mcclellan. 2009. "Vernacular Rhetoric and Social Movements: Performances of Resistance in the Rhetoric of the Everyday." In *Active Voices: Composing a Rhetoric of Social Movements*, edited by Sharon M. Stevens and Patricia Malesh, 23–46. Albany: SUNY Press.

Heath, Renee Guarriello. 2008. "Foregrounding Contestation: Community Collaboration Demonstrates the Challenges of Consensus Decision-making." Paper presented to the Western States Communication Association Annual Convention, Denver/Boulder, CO, February 15–19.

Hedges, Chris. 2010. *Death of the Liberal Class*. New York: Nation Books.

———. 2012a. "The Cancer in Occupy." *Truthdig.com*, February 6. www.truthdig.com/report/item/the_cancer_of_occupy_20120206/.

———. 2012b. "Chris Hedges and Occupy Debate 'Black Bloc' Tactics" (posted by ebecker2000). *YouTube.com*, April 2. www.youtube.com/watch?v=8SoXWuQPrrI.

Herbert, Steve. 2007. "The 'Battle of Seattle' Revisited: Or, Seven Views of a Protest-zoning State." *Political Geography* 26: 601–19.

Hertog, James K., and Douglas Malcom McLeod. 1995. "Anarchists Wreak Havoc in Downtown Minneapolis: A Multi-level Study of Media Coverage of Radical Protest." *Journalism and Mass Communication Monographs* 151: 1–48.

Holland, Dorothy, Gretchen Fox, and Vinci Daro. 2008. "Social Movements and Collective Identity." *Anthropological Quarterly* 81 (1): 95–126.

Holsti, Ole R. 1969. *Content Analysis for the Social Sciences and Humanities*. Reading, MA: Addison-Wesley.

Hudson, Michael. 2011. "Neofeudalism and the Stealing of Assets via Fire Sales—IMF the Hangman." *Zerohedge.com*, July 9. www.zerohedge.com/article/neofeudalism-and-stealing-assets-fire-sales-imf-hangman.

Huesca, Robert. 2001. "Conceptual Contributions of New Social Movements to Development Communication Research." *Communication Theory* 11 (4): 415–33.

Hunt, Scott A., Robert D. Benford, and David A. Snow. 1994. "Identity Fields: Framing Processes and the Social Construction of Movement Identities." In *New Social Movements: From Ideology to Identity*, edited by Enrique Larana, Hank Johnston, and Joseph R. Gusfield, 185–208. Philadelphia: Temple Univ. Press.

Innes, Judith E., and David E. Booher. 1999. "Consensus Building and Complex Adaptive Systems: A Framework for Evaluating Collaborative Planning." *Journal of American Planning Association* 65: 412–27. doi: 10.1080/01944369908976071.

Ivry, Bob, Bradley Keoun, and Phil Kuntz. 2011. "Secret Fed Loans Helped Banks Net $13B." *Bloomberg.com*, November 27. www.bloomberg.com/news/2011-11-28/secret-fed-loans-undisclosed-to-congress-gave-banks-13-billion-in-income.html.

Iyengar, Shanto. 1990. "The accessibility bias in politics: Television news and public opinion." *International Journal of Public Opinion Research* 2: 1–15.

Iyengar, Shanto, and Adam Simon. 1993. "News Coverage of the Gulf Crisis and Public Opinion: A Study of Agenda Setting, Priming and Framing." *Communication Research* 20 (3): 365–83.

Jackson, Pamela Taylor. 2009. "News as a Contested Commodity: A Clash of Capitalist and Journalistic Imperatives." *Journal of Mass Media Ethics* 24: 146–63.

Jacobsen, Thomas, and Won Yong Jang. 2001. "Rights, Culture, and Cosmopolitan Democracy." *Communication Theory* 11 (4): 434–53.

Jacobson, Thomas L., and J. Douglas Storey. 2004. "Development Communication and Participation: Applying Habermas to a Case Study of Population Programs in Nepal." *Communication Theory* 14 (2): 99–121.

Jasper, James. 1997. *The Art of Moral Protest: Culture, Biography, and Creativity in Social Movements*. Chicago: University of Chicago Press.

Johnson, Garrett. 2011. "Slouching Toward Neofeudalism." *Huffington Post*, May 8. www.huffingtonpost.com/garrett-johnson/slouching-towards-neofeud_b_568972.html.

Johnson, Simon. 2009. "Who is Carlos Slim?" *Baseline Scenario*, October 17. baselinescenario.com/2009/10/17/who-is-carlos-slim/.

Jung, Helen. 2012. "Occupy Portland: A Timeline of Key Events in the Past Year." *OregonLive*, October 5. www.oregonlive.com/portland/index.ssf/2012/10/occupy_portland_a_timeline_of.html.

Kapoor, Priya. 2011. "Voicing Dissent: The Digital Divide and the Gradual Unfolding of Post-WSIS Protest in Tunisia." Paper presented at the National Communication Association 97th Annual Convention, New Orleans, LA, November 17–20.

Kaste, Martin. 2011. "Exploring Occupy Wall Street's 'Adbuster' Origins." *National Public Radio*, October 20. www.npr.org/2011/10/20/141526467/exploring-occupy-wall-streets-adbuster-origins.

KATU.com. 2012. "10 Arrested in Occupy Portland March" (television broadcast). *KATU News*, February 6 www.katu.com/news/local/Occupy-Portland-plans-Monday-night-march-in-SE-Portland-138814074.html.

Khasnabish, Alex. 2008. *Zapatismo Beyond Borders: New Imaginations of Political Possibility*. Toronto: University of Toronto Press.

Keck, Margaret, and Kathryn Sikkink. 1998. *Activists Beyond Borders: Transnational Advocacy Networks in International Politics*. Ithaca: Cornell.

Keiser, Max. 2010. "The Keiser Report 45: Goldman Sachs: Undeclared Enemy of the State." *MaxKeiser.Com*, May 25. maxkeiser.com/2010/05/25/kr45-keiser-report-goldman-sachs-undeclared-enemy-of-the-state/?utm_source=feedburner&utm_medium=feed&utm_campaign=Feed%3A+Maxkeisercom+%28maxkeiser.com%29.

———. 2011. "[KR162] Keiser Report – Europe's Neo-Feudalism," *MaxKeiser.Com*, July 7. maxkeiser.com/2011/07/07/kr162-keiser-report-europes-neo-feudalism/.

Kellner, Douglas. 2009. "Toward a Critical Media/Cultural Studies." In *Media/Cultural Studies: Critical Approaches*, edited by Rhonda Hammer and Douglas Kellner. New York: Peter Lang.

———. 2012. *Media Spectacle and Insurrection, 2011: From the Arab Uprisings to Occupy Everywhere*. London: Continuum.

Keoun, Bradley, and Phil Kuntz. 2011. "Wall Street Aristocracy Got $1.2 Trillion from Fed." *Bloomberg*, August 22. www.bloomberg.com/news/2011-08-21/wall-street-aristocracy-got-1-2-trillion-in-fed-s-secret-loans.html.

Keynes, John M. 1936. *The General Theory of Employment, Interest and Money*. Cambridge: Macmillan Cambridge University Press, for Royal Economic Society. www.marxistsfr.org/reference/subject/economics/keynes/general-theory/index.htm.

KGW.com staff. 2012. "7 Arrested in Occupy Portland F29 Protest." *KGW.com News Channel 8*, February 28. www.kgw.com/news/Occupy-Portland-march-downtown-Wednesday-140773533.html.

Khasnabish, Alex. 2008. *Zapatismo Beyond Borders: New Imaginations of Political Possibility*. Toronto: University of Toronto Press.

Klein, Naomi. 2002. "What is this Movement?" In *The Global Activists Manual*, edited by Mike Prokosch and Laura Raymond: 1–10. New York: Thunder's Mouth Press/Nation Books.

———. 2007. *The Shock Doctrine: The Rise of Disaster Capitalism*. New York: Metropolitan Books/Henry Holt.

Korten, David. 2011. "Six Ways to Liberate Main Street from Wall Street." In *This Changes Everything: Occupy Wall Street and the 99% Movement*, edited by S. van Gelder and the staff of Yes Magazine 55–60. San Francisco: Berrett-Koehler Publications.

Kramarae, Cheris. 1981. *Women and Men Speaking: Frameworks for Analysis*. Rowley, MA: Newbury House.

Kristina Smock Consulting. 2011. "Point-In-Time Survey." *Portlandoregon.gov.* efiles.portlandoregon.gov/webdrawer.dll/webdrawer/rec/4319303/view/2011_Point-in-Time_Homelessness_Multnomah-County.PDF.

Kroll, Andy. 2012. "Occupy's Latest Target: Citizens United." *Mother Jones*, January 23. www.motherjones.com/mojo/2012/01/occupy-citizens-united-corporate-personhood-j21.

Krugman, Paul. 2010. "America Goes Dark." *New York Times*, August 8. www.nytimes.com/2010/08/09/opinion/09krugman.html?th&emc=th.

———. 2011. "We are the 99.9%." *New York Times*, November 24. www.nytimes.com/2011/11/25/opinion/we-are-the-99-9.html.

———. 2012. *End This Depression Now!* New York: W.W. Norton and Company.

Lave, Jean, and Etienne Wenger. 1991. *Situated Learning: Legitimate Peripheral Participation.* Cambridge, UK: Cambridge University Press.

Lemke, Thomas. 2011. *Foucault, Governmentality, and Critique.* Boulder, CO: Paradigm Publishers.

Lenzner, Robert. 2011. "Capital Gains: Top 0.1% Earn Half of All Capital Gains." *Forbes*, November 20. www.forbes.com/sites/robertlenzner/2011/11/20/the-top-0-1-of-the-nation-earn-half-of-all-capital-gains/.

Levisohn, B. 2008. "Fannie and Freddie's New Derivative Cliffhanger." *Business Week*, September 9. www.businessweek.com/stories/2008-09-09/fannie-and-freddies-new-derivatives-cliffhangerbusinessweek-business-news-stock-market-and-financial-advice.

Lewis, Michael. 2011. *The Big Short.* New York: Norton.

Lindlof, Thomas R., and Bryan C. Taylor. 2011. *Qualitative Research Methods,* 3rd Ed. Thousand Oaks, CA: Sage.

Litt, A. F. 2011. "Occupy Portland: Wait! This Isn't Cute Anymore! A Statement from Mayor Sam Adams," *Democracy in Distress Blog.* November 10. www.democracyindistress.com/2011/11/statement-from-mayor-sam-adams.html

Logan, David. 2011. "Summary of Latest Federal Income Tax Data." *Tax Foundation*, October 24. taxfoundation.org/article/summary-latest-federal-individual-income-tax-data-0#table6.

Lotan, Gilad. 2011. "#OccupyWallStreet: Origin and Spread Visualization." *Social Flow*, October 18. blog.socialflow.com/post/7120244404/occupywallstreet-origin-and-spread-visualized.

Madison, D. Soyini. 2005. *Critical Ethnography: Method, Ethics, and Performance.* Thousand Oaks, CA: Sage.

Maeckelbergh, Marianne. 2011. "Doing is Believing: Prefiguration as Strategic Practice in the Alterglobalization Movement." *Social Movement Studies: Journal of Social, Cultural and Political Protest* 10 (1): 1–20.

Marcos, Subcommandante Insurgente (pseud.). 2003. "Tomorrow Begins Today: An Invitation to an Insurrection." In *We are Everywhere: The Irresistible Rise of Global Anticapitalism*, edited by Tony Credland, Graeme Chesters, John Jordan, and Katharine Ainger. New York, Verso: 34–37. artactivism.members.gn.apc.org/allpdfs/034-Tomorrow%20Begins%20Today.pdf.

Martinez, Elizabeth Betita. 2000. "The WTO: Where was the Color in Seattle?" *Colorlines* 3 (1): 11–12.

masaccio. 2012. "The Liberal Myth that Morbid Wealth is Just Fine." *My.Firedoglake.com*, October 18. my.firedoglake.com/masaccio/2012/10/18/the-liberal-myth-that-morbid-wealth-is-just-fine/.

Mather, Kate. 2012. "At least 10 arrested in Occupy protest in Southeast Portland." *Oregonlive.com*, February 6. www.oregonlive.com/portland/index.ssf/2012/02/at_least_nine_arrested_in_occu.html.

McCombs, Maxwell, and Donald Shaw. 1972. "The Agenda-Setting Function of Mass Media." *The Public Opinion Quarterly* 36 (2): 176–87.

McCright, Aaron, and Riley Dunlap. 2008. "Social Movement Identity and Belief Systems: An Examination Of Beliefs About Environmental Problems Within The American Public." *Public Opinion Quarterly* 72 (4): 651–76.

McIntire, Mike. 2012. "Conservative Nonprofit Acts as a Stealth Business Lobbyist." *New York Times*, April 22: p. A1.

McKinney, Matthew. J. 2001. "What Do We Mean by Consensus? Some Defining Principles." In *Across the Great Divide: Explorations in Collaborative Conservation and the American West*, edited by Phillip Brick, Donald Snow, and Sarah Van de Wetering, 33–40. Washington DC: Island Press.

McKinnon, J. D. 2010. "Deficit Panel Stresses Spending Cuts." *Wall Street Journal*, July 1: A6.

McLeod, Douglas Malcolm. 1995. "Communicating Deviance: The Effects of Television News Coverage of Social Protest." *Journal of Broadcasting and Electronic Media* 39 (1): 4–19.

McLeod, Douglas Malcolm, and Benjamin H. Detenber. 1999. "Framing Effects of Television News Coverage of Social Protest." *Journal of Communication* 49 (3): 3–23.

McQuail, Denis. 1994. *Mass Communication Theory: An Introduction, 3rd Edition*. Thousand Oaks, CA: Sage.

Meachum, Jennifer. 2012. (2012, October 6). "Occupy Portland Celebrates 1st Year with March, Afghan-war Protest." *KoinLocal6.com*, October 6. www.koinlocal6.com/news/local/story/OccupyPortland-celebrates-1st-year-with-march-Af/3JBGPDcxbEy5Lvy23OKN1A.cspx.

Mesh, Aaron. 2011. "Notes from the Occupation: 48 hours inside Occupy Portland." *Willamette Weekly*, October 26. www.wweek.com/portland/article-18140-notes_from_the_occupation.html.

———. 2012. "Stop the Presses: The Oregonian May Not Be a Daily Paper Much Longer." *Willamette Week*, August 8. www.wweek.com/portland/article-19535-stop_the_presses.html.

Milkman, Ruth, Stephanie Luce, and Penny Lewis. 2012. *Changing the Subject: A Bottom-up Account of Occupy Wall Street in New York City*. New York: The Murphy Institute, City University of New York. www.documentcloud.org/documents/562862-changing-the-subject-2.html.

———. 2013. *Changing the Subject: A Bottom-Up Account of Occupy Wall Street in New York City*. The Russell Sage Foundation. Available: www.russellsage.org/research/reports/occupy-wall-street-movement.

Miller, Rich, and Anthony Feld. 2010. "Economy in U.S. Slows as States Lose Federal Stimulus Funds." *Bloomberg*, June 13. www.bloomberg.com/news/2010-06-13/economy-in-u-s-slows-as-state-governments-lose-federal-stimulus-benefits.html.

Min, Seong Jae. 2012. "Occupy Wall Street in Deliberative Decision-Making: Translating Theory to Practice." Paper presented at the International Communication Association Pre-Conference, Phoenix, AZ, May 23–24.

Mirabello, Mark. 2009. *Handbook for Rebels and Outlaws*. Oxford: Mandrake.

Mishel, Lawrence, and Josh Bivens. 2011. "Occupy Wall Streeters are Right about Skewed Economic Rewards in the United States, EPI Briefing Paper #31." *Economic Policy Institute*, October 26. www.epi.org/publication/bp331-occupy-wall-street/.

Moghadam, Valentine M. 2012. *Globalization and Social Movements: Islamism, Feminism and the Global Justice Movement*. Lanham, MD: Rowman and Littlefield.

Moore, Michele. 2012. "History." *The Occupy Bank: The Occupy Bank Working Group—Occupy Wall Street*. theoccupybank.wordpress.com/history/.

Moore, Niamh. 2011. "Eco/feminism and Rewriting the Ending of Feminism: From the Chipko Movement to Clayoquot Sound." *Feminist Theory* 12 (1): 3–21.

Moyers, Bill (host). 2010. "Simon Johnson and James Kwak" (television broadcast). *Bill Moyers Journal*, April 16. www.pbs.org/moyers/journal/04162010/profile.html.

Moynihan, Denis, and David Solnit. 2002. "From the Salt Marshes to Seattle." In *The Global Activists Manual*, edited by Mike Prokosch and Laura Raymond: 129–33. New York: Thunder's Mouth Press/Nation Books.

Mui, Ylan Q. 2012. "Americans Saw Wealth Plummet 40 Percent from 2007 to 2010, Federal Reserve Says." *Washington Post*, June 11. www.washingtonpost.com/business/economy/fed-americans-wealth-dropped-40-percent/2012/06/11/gJQA-IIsCVV_story.html?wpisrc=nl_headlines_Tue.

Mumby, Dennis K. 1997. "The Problem of Hegemony: Rereading Gramsci for Organizational Communication Studies." *Western Journal of Communication* 61 (4): 343–75.

———. 2005. "Theorizing Resistance in Organization Studies: A Dialectical Approach." *Management Communication Quarterly* 19 (1): 19–44.
Nadesan, Majia Holmer. 2008. *Governmentality, Biopower, and Everyday Life*. New York: Routledge.
———. 2011. "The Biopolitics of Transactional Capitalism." *Media Tropes* 1. www.mediatropes.com/index.php/Mediatropes/article/view/15747.
Naked Capitalism. 2012. "Eurobanks' Latest Scheme to Escape the Pain of Recapitalization," *Naked Capitalism*, October 24. www.nakedcapitalism.com/2011/10/the-eurobanks-latest-scheme-to-escape-the-pain-of-recapitalization-pull-more-financial-firms-into-tbtf-complex.html.
Nanabhay, Mohammed and Roxane Farmanfarmaian. 2011. "From Spectacle to Spectacular: How Physical Space, Social Media and Mainstream Broadcast Amplified the Public Sphere in Egypt's 'Revolution'." *The Journal of North African Studies* 16 (4): 573–603.
New York Times News Service. 2013. "Violence Shows Dissatisfaction 2 Years after Egypt Revolution." *Oregonian*, January 26.
Newcomb, Alyssa. 2011. "Sexual Assaults Reported in 'Occupy' Camps." *ABC News*, November 3. abcnews.go.com/US/sexual-assaults-occupy-wall-street-camps/story?id=14873014.
Nichols, Jason. 2011. "Alternative Banking | Forum | OWS Credit Union | NYC General Assembly # Occupy Wall Street." *New York General Assembly Alternative Banking Working Group*. www.nycga.net/groups/alternative-banking/forum/topic/ows-credit-union/.
Noah, Timothy. 2012a. *The Great Divergence: America's Growing Inequality and What to Do About It*. New York: Bloomsbury Press.
———. 2012b. "The Mobility Myth." *New Republic*. www.newrepublic.com/article/politics/magazine/100516/inequality-mobility-economy-america-recession-divergence.
Norton, Michael, and Dan Ariely. 2011. "Building a Better America: One Wealth Quintile at a Time." *Perspectives on Psychological Science* 6 (1): 9–12.
Norton, Ted, and Travis Paveglio. 2009. "Organizing Step It Up 2007: Social Movement Organizations as Collective Resistance. In *Social Movement to Address Climate Change*, edited by Danielle Endres, Leah Sprain, and Tarla Rai Peterson. Amherst, NY: Cambria Press.
Novarro, Zander. 2007. "Toward a New Democratic Manifesto, Report: In the Name of Democracy," *NACLA (North American Congress on Latin America)*. January–February 2007: 39–45. nacla.org/edition/8482.
Nunberg, Geoff. 2011. "'Occupy': Geoff Nunberg's 2011 Word of the Year" (audio recording). NPR.org, December 7. www.npr.org/2011/12/07/143265669/occupy-geoff-nunbergs-2011-word-of-the-year.
Nycga.net. 2010/12. "Statement of Autonomy." *NYC General Assembly of Occupy Wall Street*. www.nycga.net/resources/documents/statement-of-autonomy/.
———. 2013. *New York City General Assembly*. www.nycga.net/.
Occupy Denver. 2012. "Occupy Denver "Recap of March Against Neofeudalism." *OccupyDenver.org*, July 9. occupydenver.org/recap-of-march-against-neo-fedualism/.
Occupy Wall Street. 2012. "About Us | OccupyWallSt.org." *OccupyWallSt.org*. occupywallst.org/about/.
Occupytheboardroom.org. 2013. "Occupy the Board Room!" *OccupyTheBoardRoom.org*. www.occupytheboardroom.org/#!wallst.
Oregonian. 2011. Occupy Portland: Mayor Sam Adams Orders Camps Cleared at 12:01 a.m. Sunday. *Oregonian Online*, November 10. www.oregonlive.com/portland/index.ssf/2011/11/occupy_portland_portland_mayor.html.
O'Reilly, Tim. 2005. "What Is Web 2.0?" *O'Reilly Media, Inc.*, September 30. oreilly.com/web2/archive/what-is-web-20.html.
Pal, Mahuya, and Mohan J. Dutta. 2008. "Theorizing Resistance in a Global Context: Processes, Strategies, and Tactics in Communication Scholarship." *Communication Yearbook* 32: 41–87.
Palmer-Mehta, Valerie. 2012. "Theorizing the Role of Courage in Resistance: A Feminist Rhetorical Analysis of Aung San Suu Kyi's Freedom from Fear Speech." *Communication, Culture and Critique* 5 (3): 313–32.

Papa, Michael J., Mohammed Auwal, Arvind Singhal. 1997. "Organizing for Social Change within Concertive Control Systems: Member Identification, Empowerment, and the Masking of Discipline." *Communication Monographs* 64: 219–49.

The Partnership for Civil Justice Fund. 2012. "FBI Secret Documents Reveal Nationwide Occupy Monitoring." *Reader Supported News*, December 25. readersupportednews.org/news-section2/440-occupy/15221-fbi-secret-documents-reveal.

Pear, Robert. 2011. "Top Earners Doubled Share of Nation's Income, Study Finds." *New York Times*, October 25. www.nytimes.com/2011/10/26/us/politics/top-earners-doubled-share-of-nations-income-cbo-says.html?nl=todaysheadlines&emc=tha23.

Pederson, David. 2012. "Home of the Bewildered Serf and Land of the Feudal Lords." *The Huffington Post*, May 4. www.huffingtonpost.com/dave-pederson/america-home-of-the-bewil_b_1476594.html.

PEJ News Coverage Index. 2011. "Biggest Week Yet for Occupy Wall Street Coverage." *Pew Research Center's Project for Excellence in Journalism*, November 20. www.journalism.org/index_report/pej_news_coverage_index_november_1420_2011.

Perkins, Harold J. 1999. *The Third Revolution: Professional Elites in the Modern World*. New York: Routledge.

Pew Research Center. 2010. "The Great Recession at 30 Months." *Pew Research Center*, June 30. pewresearch.org/pubs/1643/recession-reactions-at-30-months-extensive-job-loss-new-frugality-lower-expectations.

Phillips, Kevin. 2006. *American Theocracy*. New York: Viking.

Phillips, Matt. 2009. "Goldman Sachs' Blankfein on Banking: 'Doing God's Work.'" *The Wall Street Journal*, November 9. blogs.wsj.com/marketbeat/2009/11/09/goldman-sachs-blankfein-on-banking-doing-gods-work/.

Piketty, Thomas and Emmanual Saez. 2003. "Income Inequality in the United States, 1913–1998." *Quarterly Journal of Economics*, 118 (1): 1–39.

———. 2010. Excel tables and figures with 2008 data updating "Income Inequality in the United States, 1913–1998," *Quarterly Journal of Economics*, 118 (1): 1–39.

Polletta, Francesca. 2002. *Freedom Is an Endless Meeting: Democracy in American Social Movements*. University of Chicago Press.

Polletta, Francesca, and James Jasper. 2001. "Collective Identity and Social Movements." Annual Review of Sociology 27: 283–305.

Portes, Alejandro. 1997. "Globalization from Below: The Rise of Transnational Communities." *ESRC Transnational Communities Programme*, Working Paper No. 1. maxweber.hunter.cuny.edu/pub/eres/SOC217_PIMENTEL/portes.pdf /.

Portlandgeneralassembly.org. 2011. "Occupy Portland Structure Proposal: Submitted by the Facilitation Team and Ad Hoc SpokesCouncil/GA Working Group." *PortlandGeneralAssembly.org*, November 2. www.portlandgeneralassembly.org/wp-content/uploads/2012/01/Occupy-Portland-Spokes-Council-Model.pdf.

———. 2012. *Facilitation Team User Manual and Orientation! Written and Assembled by the Facilitation Team of Occupy Portland*, updated January 4. www.portlandgeneralassembly.org/wp-content/uploads/2012/01/FacilitationTeamUsersManualandOrientationBooklet.pdf.

Portlandonline.com Auditor's Office. 1995. "Chapter 3.74 Oaths of Office." Accessed December 10, 2012. www.portlandonline.com/auditor/index.cfm?c=28447.

Portlandonline.com Office of the Mayor. 2012. "City of Portland, Oregon Office of the Mayor FY 2012–13 Requested Budget." February 2012. www.portlandonline.com/omf/index.cfm?a=383740&c=57785.

Prasad, Pushkala. 2005. *Crafting Qualitative Research: Working in the Postpositivist Traditions*. Armonk, NY: M. E. Sharpe.

Prins, Nomi. 2011. *It Takes a Pillage: An Epic Tale of Power, Deceit and Untold Trillions*. New York: John Wiley and Sons.

Prins, Nomi, and Krisztina Ugrin. 2010. "Bailout Tally Report." May 5. www.nomiprins.com/storage/reports/bailouttally012010.pdf.

Putnam, Robert. 1995. "Tuning In, Tuning Out: The Strange Disappearance of Social Capital in America." *Political Science and Politics* 28 (4): 664–83.

Randerson, James. 2006. "World's Richest 1 Percent Own 40 Percent of All Wealth, UN Report Discovers." *Guardian*, December 6. www.guardian.co.uk/money/2006/dec/06/business.internationalnews.

Ratigan, Dylan. 2009. "Goldman Sachs: Black Magic, Here's How They Did It." *Huffington Post*, October 16. www.huffingtonpost.com/dylan-ratigan/goldman-sachs-black-magic_b_324095.html.

Rauch, Jennifer, Sunita Chitrapu, Susan Tyler Eastman, John Christopher Evans, Christopher Paine, and Peter Mwesige. 2007. "From Seattle 1999 to New York 2004: A Longitudinal Analysis of Journalistic Framing of the Movement for Democratic Globalization." *Social Movement Studies* 6 (2): 131–45.

Rawls, John. 1987. "The Idea of an Overlapping Consensus." *Oxford Journal of Legal Studies*, 7 (1): 1–25.

Raz, Guy (host). 2011. "Portland, Ore., Mayor Orders 'Occupiers' Out" (radio broadcast episode), November 10. In *All Things Considered*, C. Turpin (executive producer). Washington, D.C.: National Public Radio.

Reich, Robert. 2011. "The Limping Middle Class." *New York Times*, September 4: p. SR6.

Rose, Charlie (host). 2006. "A Conversation with Anarchist David Graeber about Anthropology" (television broadcast). April 4. Charlie Rose LLC (producer). www.charlierose.com/view/interview/473.

Ross, Janell. 2011. "Occupy Wall Street Group Looks For Financial System Fixes." *Huffington Post*, November 2. www.huffingtonpost.com/2011/11/01/occupy-wall-street-financial-system_n_1069506.html.

Ryan, Charlotte, Kevin M. Carragee, and William Meinhofer. 2001. "Framing, the News Media, and Collective Action." *Journal of Broadcasting and Electronic Media* 45 (1): 175–82.

Saez, Emmanuel. 2012. "Striking it Richer: The Evolution of Top Incomes in the United States (Updated with 2009 and 2010 estimates)." March 2. elsa.berkeley.edu/~saez/saez-UStopincomes-2010.pdf.

Said, Edward. 1998. *On Orientalism*. DVD. Sut Jhally University of Massachusetts, Amherst: Media Education Foundation.

Sanders, Bernie. 2010. "Full Congressional Record Transcript of Sanders Filibuster." *Bernie Sanders, U.S. Senator for Vermont*, December 10. www.sanders.senate.gov/newsroom/news/?id=e35eddb4-0d83-4c55-92c0-e448c55526ff.

Schneider, Nathan. 2012, Sep. 5. "Occupy, After Occupy." *Nation*, September 5. www.thenation.com/article/169761/occupy-after-occupy.

Schudson, Michael. 1989. "The Sociology of News Production." In *Social Meaning of News: A Text-reader*, edited by Dan Berkowitz, 7–22. Thousand Oaks, CA: Sage.

Schwartz, Mattathias. 2011. "Pre-Occupied." *New Yorker*, November 28. www.newyorker.com/reporting/2011/11/28/111128fa_fact_schwartz?currentPage=all.

Shah, Hemant. 2008. "Communication and Marginal Sites: The Chipko Movement and the Dominant Paradigm of Development Communication." *Asian Journal of Communication* 18 (1): 32–46.

Sheeran, Michael J. 1996. *Beyond Majority Rule: Voteless Decisions in the Religious Society of Friends*. Philadelphia: Philadelphia Yearly Meeting of the Religious Society of Friends.

Sheller, Mimi, and John Urry. 2006. *Mobile Technologies of the City*. New York: Routledge.

Simons, Herbert W. 1970. "Requirements, Problems, and Strategies: A Theory of Persuasion for Social Movements." *The Quarterly Journal of Speech* 56: 1–11.

Singer, Natasha. 2012. "A Rich Game of Thrones: C.E.O. Pay Gains May Have Slowed but the Numbers are Still Numbing." *New York Times*, April 8: p. BU 1.

Sitrin, Marina, ed. 2006. *Horizontalism: Voices of Popular Power in Argentina*. Oakland, CA: AK Press.

———. 2012. "Horizontalidad and Territory in the Occupy Movements." *Tikkun* 27 (2): 32–63.

Smith, Charles Hugh. 2012. "Guest Post: The E.U., Neofeudalism and the Neocolonial-Financialization Model." *ZeroHedge.Com*, May 24. www.zerohedge.com/news/guest-post-eu-neofeudalism-and-neocolonial-financialization-model.

Smith, Jackie, John D. McCarthy, Clark McPhail, and Boguslaw Augustyn. 2001. "From Protest to Agenda Building: Description Bias in Media Coverage of Protest Events in Washington, D.C." *Social Forces* 79 (4): 1397–1423.

Sourcewatch. 2013. "Corporations That Have Cut Ties to ALEC." *The Center for Media and Democracy*, December 15. www.sourcewatch.org/index.php/Corporations_that_Have_Cut_Ties_to_ALEC.

Spradley, James, P. 1980. *Participant Observation*. Fortworth: Harcourt Brace.

Stahler-Sholk, Richard. 2001. "Globalization and Social Movement Resistance: The Zapatista Rebellion in Chiapas, Mexico." *New Political Science* 23 (4): 493–516.

———. 2010. "The Zapatista Social Movement: Innovation and Sustainability." *Alternatives* 35: 269–290.

Starhawk. 2002. "How We Really Shut Down the WTO." In *The Global Activists Manual*, edited by Mike Prokosch and Laura Raymond: 134–39. New York: Thunder's Mouth Press/Nation Books.

Starr, Amory. 2000. *Naming the Enemy: Anti-corporate Movements Confront Globalization*. New York: Zed Books.

Stelter, Brian. 2011. "Protest puts coverage in spotlight." *New York Times*, November 20. www.nytimes.com/2011/11/21/business/media/occupy-wall-street-puts-the-coverage-in-the-spotlight.html?_r=0.

Stiglitz, Joseph. 2011. "Of the 1 Percemt, by the 1 Percent, for the 1 Percent." *Vanity Fair*, May. www.vanityfair.com/society/features/2011/05/top-one-percent-201105.

———. 2012a. "The 1 Percent's Problem." *Vanity Fair*, May. www.vanityfair.com/politics/2012/05/joseph-stiglitz-the-price-of-inequality.

———. 2012b. *The Price of Inequality*. New York: W. W. Norton and Company.

———. 2013. "Equal Opportunity, Our National Myth." *New York Times*, February 17: p. SR 4.

Stone, Arlo. 2012. "Black Bloc: Occupy the Black Bloc!" *Portland Occupier*, February 18. www.portlandoccupier.org/2012/02/18/black-bloc-occupy-the-black-bloc/.

"Strike Debt! Debt is a Tie that Binds the 99%" *Strike Debt*. strikedebt.org/.

Szeman, Imre. 2002. "Introduction: Learning to Learn from Seattle." *The Review of Education, Pedagogy and Cultural Studies* 24: 1–12.

Taibbi, Matt. 2013. "Secrets and Lies of the Wall Street Bailout." *Rolling Stone*, January 8. www.rollingstone.com/politics/blogs/taibblog/secrets-and-lies-of-the-bailout-one-brokers-story-20130108.

Tavakoli, Janet. No date. "Collateraized Debt Obligations." *Tavakoli Structured Finance*. www.tavakolistructuredfinance.com/cdo.pdf.

Tax Policy Center. 2011. "Baseline Distribution of Cash Income and Federal Taxes under Current Law. Table T11-0096." *Urban Institute and Brookings Institute*, May 19. www.taxpolicycenter.org/numbers/displayatab.cfm?Docid=2977&DocTypeID=7.

Taylor, Versa and Nancy E. Whittier. 1992. "Collective Identity in Social Movement Communities: Lesbian Feminist Mobilization." In *Frontiers in Social Movement Theory*, edited by Aldon D. Morris and Carol McClurg Mueller, 104–29. New Haven, CT: Yale University.

Tedmanson, Sophie, and David Byers. 2011. "Protesters in 'Day of Action' Outside London Stock Exchange." *Times of London*, October 15. www.thetimes.co.uk/tto/news/uk/article3195592.ece.

Tewksbury, David, and Dietram Scheufele. 2009. "News Framing Theory and Research." In *Media Effects: Advances in Theory and Research*, edited by Jennings Bryant and Mary Beth Oliver, 17–33. New York: Routledge.

Theriault, Denis C. 2011. "Mayor Tells Occupy Portland: 'The Way Things are Operating Now is Not Sustainable'," *Portland Mercury*, November 7. www.portlandmercury.com/BlogtownPDX/archives/2011/11/07/mayor-tells-occupy-portland-the-way-things-are-operating-now-is-not-sustainable.

———. 2011. "Parks Bureau Announces Occupy Portland Cleanup Tab: $85,850." *Portland Mercury*, November 30. www.portlandmercury.com/BlogtownPDX/archives/2011/11/30/parks-bureau-announces-occupy-portland-cleanup-tab-85850.

References

Troubador. 2010. "'Neofeudalism?' Nice Term, but Inaccurate." *Daily Kos*, May 13. www.dailykos.com/story/2010/05/13/866223/--Neofeudalism-Nice-term-but-inaccurate#.

Trujillo, Nick. 1992. "Interpreting (the Work and Talk of) Baseball: Perspectives on Baseball Culture." *Western Journal of Communication*, 56 (4): 350–71.

Tuchman, Gaye. 1973. "Making News by Doing Work: Routinizing the Unexpected." In *Social Meaning of News: A Text-Reader*, edited by Dan Berkowitz, 173–92. Thousand Oaks, Calif.: Sage.

Tufecki, Zeynep. 2011. "Tunisia Twitter, Aristotle, Social Media and Final and Efficient Causes." *Technosociology*, January 15. technosociology.org/?p=263.

Turkle, Sherry. 2011. *Alone Together: Why We Expect More from Technology and Less from Each Other*. New York: Basic Books.

Turner, Victor. 1974. *Dramas, Fields, and Metaphors: Symbolic Action in Human Society*. Ithaca, NY: Cornell University Press.

Uren, David. 2008. "Sub-Prime Collapse 'Beyond the US Federal Reserve.'" *The Australian: News.com.au*, March 18. www.news.com.au/business/story/0,23636,23393912-462,00.html.

Valtysson, Bjarki. 2012. "Facebook as a Digital Public Sphere: Processes of Colonization and Emancipation." *Journal for a Global Sustainable Information Society* 10 (1): 79–91.

van Dijk, J. J. M. 2006. *The Network Society: Social Aspects of New media*. Thousand Oaks, CA: Sage.

van Dijk, T. A. 1993. "Principles of Critical Discourse Analysis." *Discourse and Society* 4 (2): 249–283.

van Gelder, Sarah. and the staff of Yes Magazine, eds. 2011. *This Changes Everything: Occupy Wall Street and the 99% Movement*. San Francisco: Berrett-Koehler Publications.

van Maanen, John. 1988. *Tales of the Field: On Writing Ethnography*. Chicago: University of Chicago Press.

van Manen, Max. 1990. *Researching Lived Experience: Human Science for an Action Sensitive Pedagogy*. Albany, NY: SUNY Press.

Vandana, Shiva. 2004. "The Suicide Economy of Corporate Globalization." *Countercurrents.org*, April 5. www.countercurrents.org/glo-shiva050404.htm

———. 2009. "From Seeds of Suicide to Seeds of Hope: Why are Indian Farmers Committing Suicide and How Can We Stop this Tragedy?" *Huffington Post*, April 28. www.huffingtonpost.com/vandana-shiva/from-seeds-of-suicide-to_b_192419.html.

Vitali, Stefania, James B. Glattfelder, and Stefano Battiston. 2011. "The Network of Global Corporate Control." *Swiss Federal Institute of Technology*, July 28. www.scribd.com/doc/72201631/Network-of-Global-Corporate-Control-Swiss-Federal-Institute-of-Technology-in-Zurich.

Walia, Harsha. 2012. "Black Bloc: Diversity of Tactics." *PortlandOccupier.Org*, February 17. www.portlandoccupier.org/2012/02/17/diversity-of-tactics-by-harsha-walia/.

Wedel, Janine R. 2009. *Shadow Elite: How the World's New Power Brokers Undermine Democracy, Government, and the Free Market*. New York: Basic Books.

Weick, Karl E. 1995. *Sensemaking in Organizations (Foundations for Organizational Science)*. Thousand Oaks, CA: Sage.

Wenger, Etienne. 1998. *Communities of Practice: Learning, Meaning, and Identity*. New York: Cambridge University Press.

———. 2006. "Communities of Practice: A Brief Introduction." *Wenger-Trayner.com*. wenger-trayner.com/Intro-to-CoPs/.

Wenger, Etienne, Richard A. McDermott, and William Snyder. 2002. *Cultivating Communities of Practice: A Guide to Managing Knowledge*. Boston, MA: Harvard Business School Press.

Wenger, Etienne, Nancy White, and John D. Smith. 2009. *Digital Habitats: Stewarding Technology for Communities*. Portland, OR: CPsquare.

Wikipedia. 2012. "Neo-Feudalism." Accessed November 10. en.wikipedia.org/wiki/Neo-feudalism.

Wittebols, James H. 1996. "News from the Noninstitutional World: U.S. and Canadian Television News Coverage of Social Protest." *Political Communication* 13: 345–61.

Wolf, Naomi. 2011. "The Shocking Truth About the Crackdown on Occupy." *Guardian*, November 25. www.guardian.co.uk/commentisfree/cifamerica/2011/nov/25/shocking-truth-about-crackdown-occupy.

Wolff, Edward N. 2010. "Recent Trends in Household Wealth in the United States: Rising Debt and the Middle-class Squeeze - An Update to 2007, Working Paper No. 589." *Levy Economics Institute*. hdl.handle.net/10419/57025.

World Summit on the Information Society. 2005. "Tunis Commitment. Document WSIS-05/TUNIS/DOC/7-E." *World Summit on the Information Society*, November 18. www.itu.int/wsis/docs2/tunis/off/7.html.

Wweek.com. "Advertising – Willamette Week." *Willamette Week*. www.wweek.com/portland/flex-221-advertise-with-ww.html.

Yack, Bernard. 2012. "Rhetoric and Public Reasoning: An Aristotelian Understanding of Political Deliberation." In *Democratizing Deliberation: A Political Anthology*, edited by Derek W. M. Barker, Noelle McAfee, and David W. McIvor, 21–38. Dayton: Kettering Foundation.

Yin, Robert K. 2009. *Case Study Research: Design and Methods, 4th Ed*. Thousand Oaks: Sage.

Zoller, Heather, and Gail Fairhurst. 2007. "Resistance Leadership: The Overlooked Potential in Critical Organization and Leadership Studies." *Human Relations* 60 (9): 1331–60. doi:10.1177/0018726707082850.

Index

the 99 percent, 18, 20

Abacus, 37, 45, 47
Adams, Sam, xix, 57, 168, 169, 170. *See also* eviction statements and rhetoric by Mayor Sam Adams
Adbusters, xxi, 18, 99, 153
affinity groups and committees, 59, 82, 86, 94, 114
agency as romantic value, 134–136
alliance building strategy, 5
All Things Considered (NPR), 175–177
Alternative Banking Working Group (OWS), 28, 197, 200–206
Althusser, Louis, 130
American Civil Liberties Union (ACLU), 50
American Dream, 26, 33n2, 69, 128, 130
American Insurance General (AIG), 44
American Legislative Exchange Council (ALEC), 30–31, 80
anarchism and anarchists: action and, 106; "anarchist" as pejorative, 81; Bey on, 99, 106; Black Bloc, 66, 73n3, 108; circle-A logo, 73n3; colonization and, 130; consensus processes and, 76; direct action and, 106; media portrayal of, 151, 155; researcher positionality and, 63, 69, 71; romantic perspective and, 63, 93; sensitivities of, 81; structure, distrust of, 59. *See also* violence
Anderson, Benedict, 131
Andretta, Massimiliano, 77
antiglobalization, 100, 102. *See also* Seattle N30 WTO Protests
Anzera, Giuseppe, 11
appropriation vs. distribution of power: defined, 110; horizontal gift economy and, 110–113; spontaneity of action vs. deliberation and, 113–115; violence definitions and authorizations and, 116–118
Arab Spring, 8–10, 11
Argentine Revolt (2001), 105
Ariely, Dan, 20
Armstrong, Cory L., 149
Arpan, Laura M., 152
austerity measures, 42
autonomy, 13, 92, 95

bailouts, 45–46
Baker, Dean, 24–25
banks and banking: Alternative Banking Working Group (OWS), 28, 197, 200–206; Bailouts, 45–46; debt based investment products, 27, 43–45; growth of financial sector, 26–27, 27; Occupy Credit Union (or Bank) proposal, 201, 202–205; Occupy the Banks, 28; reform discussions and working groups, 28

Barber, Benjamin, 76–77, 79, 82, 90, 94, 95
Battiston, Stefano, 41
belonging, 122, 141. *See also* communities of practice
Benford, Robert D., 122
Berkeley Journal of Sociology, 62
Bey, Hakim, 99, 106
bias in media, 152, 157, 163–164
Bivens, Josh, 20, 21, 22
Black Bloc, 66, 73n3, 108, 116
Blankfein, Lloyd, 38
blogs and bloggers, 10, 47
Bouazizi, Mohamed, x, 9, 10
Bové, José, 5
Bowley, Graham, 46
Boyle, Michael P., 149, 150
Brown, Jeffrey, 178–180
Bryan, D., 43
Buffet, Warren, 18

Caleb, Nicholas, 30
capitalism: diversity of tactics and, 108–109; financial crisis and, 51; horizontalism vs., 100; Keynesians and, 37; media and, 130; neofeudalism and monopoly capitalism, 40–47; neofeudalism as signifier and, 38–40; resource scarcity and, 111; romantic vs. critical perspective and, 36, 48; Seattle WTO protests and, 5; system fragility, 19; transnational advocacy networks (TANs) and, 7; violence, relationship with, 14. *See also* banks and banking; globalization; inequality
Carey, James, 192
Carragee, Kevin M., 150
case study approach, 55, 192
Castells, Manuel, 196
censorship, 9
Chang, Briankle, 7
Cheney, George, 100, 101, 109
Chipko Movement (India), 6–7
Chomsky, Noam, 39
Christians, Clifford, 160
Citizens United v. Federal Elections Commission, 29
civil disobedience, 107–109
class, 12–13, 126. *See also* identity

Clayquot Sound peace camp, British Columbia, 7
collateralized debt obligations (CDOs), 37, 44
collective identity, 12, 131–133
colonization and decolonization, 128–131
Colorado Indymedia, 48–49
committees and affinity groups, 59, 82, 86, 94, 114
commodification of news, 162–163
Commodities Futures Modernization Act (2000), 42
Comunello, Francesca, 11
communities of practice: building social capital through, 193–195; common narratives of community values and beliefs, 200–201; community concept in cultural studies, 190–191; critical discourse analysis and, 192; horizontalism and consensus building, 198–199; knowledge-sharing practices, 202–205; social media and community building, 195–196; working group model and, 197–198
confessional tales, 64–72
consensus processes: affinity group model and, 81; consensus agreement vs., 77–78; in critical perspective, 88–90, 92–93, 94–95; DIY culture and, 80; in functional perspective, 85, 94; global social movements' turn toward, 75–76; horizontalism, communities of practice, and, 198–199; ideology of, 76; InterOccupy.net and, 92; leadership structures and, 86, 88; overlapping consensus concept, 199; in romantic perspective, 82–84, 93; spontaneous consensus to action, 113; theory on, 77–78; working-group model and, 201. *See also* participative democracy
Constitution, U.S. *See* First Amendment protections
contestation: consensus processes and, 77; Habermas on decision-making and, 77; horizontalist deliberation and, 118; identity and, 123, 134; participative democracy and, 95–96; Seattle WTO protests and, 14; vernacular voices and, 186. *See also* critical lens

Cornell, Andrew, 77
corporate personhood, 29
corporations, 30, 41. *See also* financial institutions
credit default swaps (CDS), 27, 44–45
Crenshaw, Kimberlé, 124
crime, mayor's rhetoric on, 167, 174, 178, 184
critical discourse analysis (CDA), 192
critical lens: defined, xx, 134, 137, 195; diversity of tactics discourse, 107–109, 119; on identity and marginalization, 137–140; on Mayor Adams narratives, 181–185; on media, 162–164; neofeudalism and, 39; Occupy Wall Street and, 48–49; on participative democracy, 88–93, 94–95; on working groups, 205
cultural studies, 3, 130, 190–191
culture-centered theory, 15

Dahberg, Lincoln, 129
Dalio, Ray, 22
Daro, Vinci, 133
data analysis methods, 62–64
data collection methods, 60–62
debt based investment products, 27, 43–45
decision-making. *See* consensus processes; participative democracy
Deetz, Stanley, 77, 82, 89, 96, 129
deliberation, 78, 95, 112–113, 113–115, 202–204
della Porta, Donatella, 75–76, 77
demand as process, ix, x
democracy, 13, 76–77, 82–84. *See also* participative democracy
deregulation, 42, 102, 161
derivatives, 27, 44–45
Detenber, Benjamin H., 151, 163
dialectical tensions. *See* discourse, power and dialectical tensions in
Di Cicco, Damon T., 148
direct action: deliberation vs. spontaneity of, 113–115; functionalist discourse of, 106–107; gift economy and, 111–113; structural violence critique and, 107
discourse, power and dialectical tensions in: antiglobalization and new activism, 99–100, 104; appropriation vs. distribution of power at Occupy Portland, 110–118; critical discourse of diversity of tactics, 107–109, 119; functionalist discourse of direct action, 106–107; horizontal gift economy, 110–113; ideologies and Foucault's analytics of power, 102–103; process and structure tensions and action vs. deliberation, 113–115; romantic discourse of horizontalism, 104–105, 114; violence, definitions and authorizations of, 116–118
discourse, theory of, 102–103
discursive democracy, 13
distribution. *See* appropriation vs. distribution of power
diversity of tactics, 107–109, 108, 116–118, 119
DIY (do-it-yourself) culture: direct action and, 107, 115; divisions fueled by, 58; participative democracy and, 80; Portland camp and, 57; resource distribution and, 111
dogmatism, 95
domain analysis, 63
drug use, 57–58, 92, 176
Dutta, Mohan, 15

Earth Liberation Front, 7
economy and economics: American Legislative Exchange Council (ALEC) and, 30–31; causes of inequality and upward redistribution, 23–24; corporate personhood and Occupy the Courts, 29; financial sector and, 26–28, 27; government mitigation of, 19, 25; hope for, 31; income and wealth distribution and inequality, 19–23, 21, 22; inequality, critiques of, 18; inequality as restraint on, 25; system fragility, 19. *See also* banks and banking
eco-terrorists, 7
Edelman, Marc, 5
education, political, 80
Edwards, Ethan, 159
Egypt, 11
Ehrenreich, Barbara, 108
empowerment, 134–136
"empty" theme in Adams rhetoric, 184

emptywheel (blogger), 47
eviction statements and rhetoric by Mayor Sam Adams: critical narrative of, 181–185; eviction notice, 173–175; functional vs. romantic narratives of, 180–181; mayor as official voice, 169; moving vs. stopping theme, 183; NPR *All Things Considered* interview, 175–177; Open Letter to the Occupy Portland Encampment, 170–172; *PBS NewsHour* interview, 177–180, 184; rhetorical analysis tradition and, 169–170; safe vs. empty theme, 184; sustainable vs. evolving theme, 185; vernacular rhetoric and, 167; vernacular voices and, 186, 187n5
"evolving" theme in Adams rhetoric, 185
exclusivity, 134
expression, free. *See* First Amendment protections
expressive communication, 88–89

F29 event (February 29, 2012), 30
facilitation: horizontal leadership model and, 84; as leadership, 87–88; proceduralism and, 90; resource distribution and, 112; underdeveloped theory of leadership and, 90–93. *See also* leadership
"Facilitation Team User Manual and Orientation", 83, 90, 114
Fackler, P. Mark, 160
fairness, inequality and, 25
Farmanfarmaian, Roxane, 11
farmers, 5, 6, 16n2
Feather Circle, 114
Federal Bureau of Investigation (FBI), 50
feminist movement, 8, 12, 79, 94, 198
Ferre, John, 160
financial crisis, global (2008): deregulation and, 42; income distribution and inequality since, 23, 46; neofeudalism and, 35, 45–46, 51; wealth consolidation during, 41
financial institutions, 26–27, 27, 45–46. *See also* banks and banking
financial instruments, debt-based, 27, 43–45

First Amendment protections: *Citizens United* and, 29; mayor Adams eviction rhetoric and, 171, 173, 174, 177, 180; money as speech, 29; the press and, 160
Fish, Nick, 159, 170, 173
Fishman, Mark, 162
foreigner positionality, 67
forests, community owned (India), 6
Foucault, Michel, 102–103
Fox, Gretchen, 133
framing effect, 163
freedom of expression. *See* First Amendment protections
Freeman, Jo, 79, 94, 95
free market ideology, 24
functionalist lens: community values and, 200; contradictions in, 119; defined, xx, 134, 195; direct action discourse, 106–107; group affiliation and, 136–137; Mayor Adams narratives and, 180–181; on media, 161–162, 164; on participative democracy, 85–88, 94; on violence, 118

Gadamer, Hans-Georg, 63, 77
Gamson, Joshua, 122
Gandhi, Mahatma, 14
Ganesh, Shiv, 79, 101, 109
gender, 12–13, 139. *See also* identity
general assembly (GA), New York, 204. *See also* consensus processes
general assembly (GA), Portland: as decision-making body, 81–82; "decolonize" vs. "occupy" discussion at, 131; democratic paradigm and, 82–83; expressive communication in, 88–89; proceduralism at, 90; underdeveloped theory of leadership and, 90–93
gift economy, horizontal, 110–113
Glattfelder, James B., 41
global financial crisis. *See* financial crisis, global (2008)
globalization, 4–5, 6, 100, 102
globalization from below, 100
Global Social Movements (GSM), 76, 77–78, 80
Goldman Sachs, 28, 37, 38, 44–45, 46, 47

government action and mitigation, insufficiency of, 19
Graeber, David: on anarchism, 76, 106–107; on counterviolence, 118; on direct democracy, 78–79, 95; on horizontalism, 100; Occupy leadership and, 76, 96n4; on property damage and "Peace Police", 108
Graham-Bleach-Bliley Act (1996), 42
Gramsci, Antonio, 130
Great Recession. *See* financial crisis, global (2008)
Grossberg, Lawrence, 130, 192
group affiliation as functional value identity role, 136–137

Habermas, Jurgen, 13, 77, 80, 128
Hacker, Jacob, 24, 25, 26, 31
Hall, Stuart, 12, 124, 130
hand signals, 96n6
Hardt, Michael, 196
Hauser, Gerard A., 167, 187n5
Hazare, Anna, 8
headnotes, 68, 73n4
Hedges, Chris, 39, 116–117, 118
Herbert, Stacy, 38
hermeneutic phenomenology, 63
Hertog, James K., 151, 158
Holland, Dorothy, 133
horizontal gift economy, 110–113
horizontalism: communities of practice and, 198–199; contradictions in, 119; counterviolence and, 118; direct action and, 107, 114; diversity of tactics and, 109; leadership structures, horizontal, 84; resource tensions and, 113; as romantic discourse, 104–105, 114
houselessness, 57, 96n6, 126, 142n3
Hudson, Michael, 39
hunger strike, 142n3
Hunt, Scott A., 122
Hutchins Commission on Freedom of the Press, 161

identity: collective, 131–133; colonization and decolonization and, 128–131; group affiliation as functional value, 136–137; intersectionality and, 124–127; marginalization as critical value, 137–140; nuanced nature of, 122, 124; outcomes related to, 141–142; research gap on, 122–123; role of, 121–122; social movement studies and theory of, 12–13; solidarity and agency as romantic values, 134–136; value contradictions and, 134
ideology and power. *See* discourse, power and dialectical tensions in; power
ideology of consensus, 76
inclusion, 92, 95, 134. *See also* communities of practice
income, 20–21, 21, 23
India, 6–7, 8
individualism, 95
Industrialized Workers of the World (IWW; "Wobblies"), 107
inequality: critiques of, 18; financial-sector growth and, 43; income and wealth distribution, 19–23, 21, 22; preferred distributions of, 20; as restraint on economy, 25, 46; underestimation of, 19; upward redistribution and causes of, 23–24
International forums and conferences, 7–8
InterOccupy.net, 81, 92
intersectionality, 12–13, 124–127
interviews, 60–62, 175–177
investment products, debt based, 27, 43–45

Jasper, James, 122, 131, 133
Johnson, Garrett, 39
Johnson, Simon, 46
Jones, Alex, 51
JP Morgan Chase, 44

Keck, Margaret, 7
Keiser, Max, 38, 51
Keynesian theory, 25, 36, 37, 48
Khasnabish, Alex, 1
knowledge sharing, 194, 201, 202–205
Kofhage, Matthew, 164
Korten, David, 48
Krugman, Paul, 19, 21, 24, 26

Lave, Jean, 193–194
lawsuit over civil liberties, 49
leaderful movement, 84

leadership: horizontal structures of, 84; leaderlessness, 79; reluctance to accept, 91; theory on structure and, 78–79; training, functional, 87–88; transitional, natural, facilitating, and moral, 79; underdeveloped theory of, 90–93. *See also* facilitation
Lewis, Michael, 44, 61, 196, 207
Lewis, Penny, 12
liberal vs. participative democracy, 76–77
Litt, A. F., 181
Luce, Stephanie, 12, 61, 196, 207

Main Street, 48
Mandela, Nelson, 14
manipulation, 140
marginalization, 138–140, 142n3
market capitalism. *See* capitalism
Martin, R., 43
Marx, Karl, 48
Marxist cultural studies, 130
masaccio (blogger), 47
mcclellan, erin daina, 167, 187n5
McDonald's, 5
McKinney, Matthew J., 78
McLeod, Douglas Malcolm, 151, 158, 163
media: amount of coverage, 148–149; on Arab Spring, 10; bias in, 152, 157, 163–164; campers and protesters, depictions of, 57, 149–152; colonization and media influence, 130; content analysis method, 153–156; critical lens on, 162–164; emphases of, 158, 191, 196; episodic vs. thematic coverage, 157, 158–159; functional lens on, 161–162, 164; landscape of coverage, 156–157; network news branding and political slants, 150; on park damage, 59; reach and influence, 147–148; review of literature on, 149–153; romantic lens on, 160–161; sensationalism in, 58, 148; vernacular rhetoric theory and, 167. *See also* eviction statements and rhetoric by Mayor Sam Adams
Meinhofer, William, 150
Mesh, Aaron, xv, 164
methodology: case study approach, 55, 192; confessional tales and positionality, 64–72; critical discourse analysis, 192; data analysis, 62–64; data collection, 60–62; research team, 59; site of research, 56–59
Meyer, David, 138
mic checking and human microphone, 75, 81, 85
Milkman, Ruth, 12, 61, 196, 207
Mirabello, Mark, 39
Mishel, Lawrence, 20, 21, 22
money as speech, 29
Moore, Michael, 57
Moore, Niamh, 7
mortgage-backed debt, 43–44
Mosca, Lorenzo, 77
"movement" of the city, 183
Mumby, Dennis K., 130

Naked Capitalism site, 47
Nanbhay, Mohammed, 11
Nawaat.org, 10
Negri, Antonio, 196
neofeudalism: definition of, 38; monopoly capitalism and, 40–47; Occupy Wall Street and, 48–51; as signifier for romantics and critics, 35–36, 38–40
neoliberalism, 7, 51, 102. *See also* capitalism; globalization
new activism, 100, 104, 106
New York. *See* Occupy Wall Street (OWS)
NGO Forum (Beijing, 1995), 7–8
nonviolence tactics: definitions of violence and, 116–117; diversity of tactics and, 109, 119; Gandhi, Mandela, and, 16n6; occupation of space, 189; social movement theory and, 14
Norton, Michael, 20

Occupy Bank Working Group, 28
Occupy Credit Union (or Bank) proposal, 201, 202–205
Occupy data, 62
Occupy Denver, 48
Occupy Portland: camp and participants, 56–58; continuing activism, 59; disbandment of the camp, 59; events of, xi; general assembly (GA), 56; participative processes in camp, 80–82. *See also specific topics, such as*

eviction statements and rhetoric by Mayor Sam Adams
Occupy the Banks, 26–28, 192
Occupy the Board Room, 28
Occupy the Corporations, 29
Occupy the Courts, 29
Occupy Wall Street (OWS): Adams (Sam) on founding reason for, 179; Alternative Banking Working Group, 28, 197, 200–206; events leading to, x–xi; events of, x; General Assembly, 204; global spread of, 189; identity theory and, 12; as loose coalition, 48; neofeudalism and, 48–51; post-encampment platforms, 190, 192; self-characterization of, 187n4; social media participatory platforms, 195–196; suppression of dissent and, 50; working-group model, 197, 199, 201, 202
Oliver, James, 167, 170, 177–180, 184
online community building. *See* communities of practice
online-offline communities. *See* social media and online-offline communities
oppression and intersectionality, 125
Oregonian: bias and, 163; description of, 153; episodic news coverage, 157, 159, 160; focus of, 158; landscape of coverage, 156–157; sampling from, 154. *See also* media
O'Reilly, Tim, 194
"other," identification with, 133
overlapping consensus, 199

paranoid state, 51
participative democracy: critical perspective on expression, proceduralism, and underdeveloped theory of leadership, 88–93, 94–95; demand as process and, ix, x; functional perspective on communication practices, tethering, and leadership training, 85–88, 94; Portland camp and, 80–82; romantic perspective on ideal democracy and leaderful movement, 82–84, 93; social movements' turn toward consensus, 75–76; social movement theory and, 13; theory on, 76–79. *See also* consensus processes
Partnership for Civil Justice, 50
Paulson and Co., 45
PBS NewsHour, 177–180, 184
Pederson, David, 49
People's Treasury Global Banking Network, 201
Perkins, Harold J., 39
Pew Project for Excellence in Journalism, 148
phenomenological research, 63
Phillips, Kevin, 43
Pierson, Paul, 24, 25, 26, 31
Piketty, Thomas, 18, 20, 23
plutonomies, 41
police action and tactics: counterviolence and, 117; neofeudalism and, 49–50; nonviolence in face of, 14; OWS lawsuit over, 49; researcher positionality in relation to, 68; social movement theory and, 14; UC David pepper-spraying, 49
political party affiliation, 60
Polletta, Francesca, 131, 133
Portes, Alejandro, 103
Portland, Oregon, 28, 29, 56; Chapman Square and Lownsdale Square, xi, xv, 56, 59, 174, 182. *See also* Occupy Portland
Portland Action Lab, 92
Portland State University Survey Research Lab, 164
positionality and confessional tales, 64–72. *See also* identity
postcolonial theory, 15
power, 11, 95, 102–103. *See also* appropriation vs. distribution of power; critical lens; discourse, power and dialectical tensions in
press coverage. *See* media
privilege, 65, 67, 69, 127
proceduralism, 90
productivity and income trends, 24
Progressives and free market ideology, 24
property damage, 108, 116–117
protestors media portrayal of, 149–152. *See also specific topics*
public autonomy, 13
public space, contestation of, 14

Putnam, Robert, 194

race, 12, 12–13, 126, 139. *See also* identity
Rafferty, M., 43
rape accusation, 138
Rawls, John, 199
Raz, Guy, 175–177
reform, 36, 47, 48. *See also* Alternative Banking Working Group (OWS)
Reich, Robert, 24
Reiter, Herbert, 77
rent seeking, 24, 25, 31, 32
resource distribution, 110–113
rhetoric, vernacular, 167
rhetorical analysis, 170. *See also* eviction statements and rhetoric by Mayor Sam Adams
Rolling Jubilee, 198, 201, 205
romantic lens: agency as romantic value, 134–136; defined, xx, 134, 195; horizontalism discourse under, 104–105; horizontal leadership and, 84; Main Street and, 48; Mayor Adams narratives and, 180–181; on media, 160–161; neofeudalism and, 35–36, 38, 47; nostalgia and, 36; on participative democracy and democratic decision-making, 82–84, 93. *See also* horizontalism
Ryan, Charlotte, 150

Saez, Emmanual, 18, 20, 23
safety theme in Adams rhetoric, 184
Sanders, Bernie, 23
Schneider, Nathan, 190
Schudson, Michael, 163
Seattle N30 WTO Protests, 4–5, 14, 108, 149
securitization of debt, 43–44
sexism. *See* gender; identity
sexual assault, 138
Sikkink, Kathryn, 7
Sitrin, Marina, 107
Slack, Jennifer Daryl, 130
slacktivism, 11, 16n5, 196
slogans: "Lost my job, found an Occupation", 3; "We are the 99 percent", 18, 20; "You cannot evict an idea", 3

Smith, Charles H., 38
Smith, Jackie, 150, 152
Smith, John D., 206
Snow, David A., 122
social capital, 193–195, 196
social media and online-offline communities, 11, 195–196, 200–205
social media studies, 11
social movement studies and communication theory, 11–14, 122, 149–153
social needs, tensions around, 58
social responsibility theory, 161
solidarity, 135
space: as common theme, xxii; occupation of, as populist nonviolent strategy, 189; public space, contestation of, 14
speech and expression, freedom of, in Tunisia, 9. *See also* First Amendment protections
spokescouncils, 82, 86
spontaneity of action vs. deliberation, 113–115
Spradley, James P., 63
Statement of Autonomy, 198
Stiglitz, Joseph, 17, 18, 24, 25–26
Stone, Arlo, 73n3
Strike Debt, 198, 201, 207
structural adjustment programs, 42
structure: anarchist distrust of, 59; camp as, 81; as common theme, xxii; feminist movement and, 94; functional perspective and, 86, 88; Groups Policy Implementation (OWS), 204; inclusion and autonomy vs., 92–93; informal, 79; leadership and, 79; as means, 114; proceduralism, 90; theory on leadership and, 78–79; working group model (OWS), 197, 199. *See also* affinity groups; general assembly (GA), Portland; leadership; participative democracy
student loan debt, 65
Summit on Housing and Homelessness, 142n3
sustainability theme, 185
Szeman, Imre, 5

Taibbi, Matt, 45

tax cuts, extension of, 23
Taylor, Versa, 12
tethering structures, 86, 88
Tewksbury, David, 16n5
textual representation, 63
time, place, and manner (TPM) restrictions, 171, 174, 177, 187n3
time as common theme, xxi
Tourre, Fabrice, 44
transnational advocacy networks (TANs), 7–8
transnational social movements as context for Occupy: international forums and conferences, 7–8; larger pattern of global discontent, 4; Seattle N30 WTO Protests, 4–5; World Summit on Information Societies and Arab Spring, 9–10; Zapatista and Chipko movements, 6–7
Trujillo, Nick, xx
Trujillo interpretive framework (romantic, functionalist, and critical viewpoints): application of, xx; baseball culture analysis, 36, 195; data analysis and, 63; definitions, xx, 101, 134, 195. *See also* critical lens; functionalist lens; romantic lens
truths, xiii, xx
Tuchman, Gaye, 162
Tunis Commitment (2005), 10
Tunisia, 9–10, 11
Turner, Victor, 105
twinkle fingers and twinkling, 96n6, 97n12, 113, 116
tyranny of the minority, 89

unemployment, post-recession, 46

values and beliefs, common narrative of, 200–201
vandalism and property damage, 108, 116–117
Van Maanen, John, 55, 64, 71
Van Manen, Max, 63
vernacular rhetoric theory, 167. *See also* eviction statements and rhetoric by Mayor Sam Adams
vernacular voices, 186, 187n5

violence: Arab Spring and, 10; Black Bloc and, 66; capitalism, relationship with, 14; definitions and authorizations, dialectical tensions over, 116–118; media focus on, 158; structural, 107–108, 109. *See also* nonviolence tactics
Vitali, Stefania, 41

Walia, Harsha, 108
Warren, Elizabeth, 65
wealth: austerity, structural adjustment programs, and, 42; awareness building on, 202; distribution of, 19–20, 22, 23; monopoly capitalism and consolidation of, 41–42
"We are the 99 percent" slogan, 18, 20
web 2.0, 194, 195–196
Wedel, Janine R., 42
Wells Fargo, 30–31
Wenger, Etienne, 193–194, 200, 202, 205, 206
White, Nancy, 206
Whitten, Cameron, 142n3
Whittier, Nancy E., 12
Willamette Week: bias and, 164; description of, 154; embedded reporting by, 161, 164; focus of, 158; landscape of coverage, 156–157; sampling from, 154; thematic news coverage, 157, 158, 160. *See also* media
Wolf, Naomi, 22, 50
Wolff, Edward, 20
working-group model, 197, 199, 201, 202. *See also* Alternative Banking Working Group (OWS)
World Social Forum (WSF), 9
World Summit on Information Societies (WSIS) (Tunis, 2005), 9–10
World Trade Organization (WTO) protests, 1999 Seattle, 4–5, 14, 108, 149

Zapatista movement (Mexico), 6–7, 76, 96n3, 105, 106
Zero-Hedge.com, 38
Zeuss, Hey, 189
Zoller, Heather, 79, 101, 109
Zuccotti Park. *See* Occupy Wall Street (OWS)

About the Editors

Renee Guarriello Heath (PhD, University of Colorado, Boulder), an associate professor of communication studies at the University of Portland, is a scholar of community collaboration and democratic communication practices. Her studies of collaboration and dialogue have been published in *Management Communication Quarterly*, the *Journal of Applied Communication Research*, and *Communication Yearbook*. She is an award winning and nationally recognized teacher who founded the University of Portland's Teaching Our Leaders Civil Discourse and Service (TOLCS) organization—a partnership of faculty, students, and alumni who design and coordinate facilitative dialogues and deliberations for university and community members. She also serves as faculty for the Pamplin School of Business, Environmental MBA program.

C. Vail Fletcher (PhD, University of New Mexico), is assistant professor in the Department of Communication Studies at the University of Portland and currently teaches courses related to interpersonal/conflict communication, environmental communication, international development, gender, and social media and culture. Her research focuses on the intersections of culture, conflict, and identity with an emphasis on romantic relationships and the relationships between humans and the environment. Her most recent research involved the negotiation and resolution of bullying conflict in the workplace and was published in the *Handbook of International and Intercultural Communication*. She loves animals, hiking, and swimming.

Ricardo Munoz (MS Management Communication, University of Portland) is currently a PhD student in communication studies at the University of Colorado, Boulder. Ricardo spent many years in the corporate world, mostly in the brokerage of commodities, sales, and marketing of office equipment, and gained a critical understanding of how corporate power dominates the world. His research agenda centers on how ideology and discourse operate in activist and counter-bureaucratic organizing.

About the Contributors

William Barnes, (PhD, Notre Dame University), is associate professor of economics and environmental studies at the University of Portland. His research interests include barriers and pathways to clean technology and sustainable work systems, performance outcomes associated with corporate social responsibility and sustainability, and comparative economic institutions. His recent work has been published in the Journal of Economic Issues, the Journal of Business and Economics Research, the Case Journal, and the Journal of Business Case Studies. He has an ongoing interest in how sustainability metrics—including metrics measuring social outcomes—can be usefully applied in organizations.

Keeler Brynteson graduated from the University of Portland in 2012 with a master's degree in management communication after receiving his undergraduate degree in psychology and sociology in 2011. His academic interests center around social movements, delinquency, and crime. Originally from Anacortes, Washington, Keeler currently lives in Seattle, Washington, where he works for Amazon.

Priya Kapoor, (PhD, Ohio University), an associate professor of communication at Portland State University, researches grassroots movements, particularly in South Asia, and teaches courses in race, class, and gender in the media, critical and cultural studies, intercultural communication, and Bollywood cinema. Current areas of research include critical media studies, transnational feminism, and qualitative/critical methodology. An ongoing research project is a study of the community radio movement in India. Another research project is a media ethnography examining ethnic Muslim identity, at a time when discourses on wars of terror abound.

Jennette Lovejoy, (PhD, Ohio University), is an assistant professor at University of Portland in the Communication Studies Department. She teaches journalism and media courses. Broadly, Lovejoy's research seeks to understand how media environments and media choices affect the health of individuals and communities. Her research has been published in peer-reviewed journals and presented at national and international conferences. In 2011, she was awarded the Faculty Member of the Year by University of Portland's student body.

erin daina mcclellan, (PhD, University of Colorado, Boulder), is assistant professor in the Department of Communication at Boise State University. mcclellan's work focuses on rhetorical constructions of urban life, identity, and culture in public life. She is most interested in how vernacular and official rhetorics together create particular understandings of, and consequences for, public places and spaces. Her recent work focuses on these aspects in public squares and plazas in four distinct regions of the United States and how vernacular rhetorics inform official studies, projects, and visions of (re)design efforts of urban sustainability.

Majia Holmer Nadesan, PhD, is a professor of communication in the Division of Social and Behavioral Sciences in the New College of Interdisciplinary Arts and Sciences at Arizona State University. She has four books on biopolitics and bioeconomics: *Governing Autism* (2005), *Governmentality, Biopower, and Everyday Life* (2008), *Governing Childhood* (2010), and *Fukushima and the Privatization of Risk* (in press).

David Osborn, (MS, London School of Economics and Political Science), is an instructor at Portland State University and has been involved in a wide variety of social movements. He is a participant in the climate justice movement with Rising Tide North America and was deeply involved in Occupy Portland. This involvement included the collaborative development of the participatory, horizontal processes used by the movement, facilitation and organizing major direct actions. In his academic work David attempts to generate movement-relevant scholarship through active involvement in social movements and participatory methodologies. His work focuses on social movement process and structure as well as agency, hierarchy and narrative.

Doug Tewksbury, (PhD, Penn State University) is assistant professor of communication studies at Niagara University, where he teaches courses on media and social justice. His primary research area is the intersection of technology, culture, and media. His recent work centers on the role of communication technology and new avenues and possibilities of citizenship, democracy, globalization, and the public sphere, particularly in terms of social media uses, as well as the cultural history of communication technologies. Tewksbury was recently awarded a Fulbright Scholarship to look at the social media uses of the Canadian Occupy Movement/Montreal Student Protests, and questions of community/interconnectedness.